NIGGUN

NIGGUN

Stories behind the Chasidic Songs that Inspire Jews

Mordechai Staiman

JASON ARONSON INC.
Northvale, New Jersey
London

This book was set in 11 pt. Galliard by Alpha Graphics of Pittsfield, New Hampshire, and printed by Haddon Craftsmen in Scranton, Pennsylvania.

Library of Congress Cataloging-in-Publication Data

Staiman, Mordechai.
     Niggun : stories behind the Chasidic songs that inspire Jews /
Mordechai Staiman.
        p. cm.
     Includes bibliographical references and index.
     ISBN 1-56821-047-7
     1. Hasidim—Legends. 2. *Niggunim.* I. Title.
BM532.S69 1994
296.7'2—dc 20   93-34028

Manufactured in the United States of America. Jason Aronson Inc. offers books and cassettes. For information and catalog write to Jason Aronson Inc., 230 Livingston Street, Northvale, New Jersey 07647.

Contents

Introduction:
What's a Niggun?

When does a Jew sing? a Hebrew writer once asked. His answer: When he is hungry.

Truth is, a Jew is always hungry, and to most observant Jews the *niggun* (a wordless song, but not necessarily) is the fastest way to feed his hunger. Hungry, a Jew searches because his Jewish soul won't let him rest until he has come to hear what he needs to hear and to say what he needs to say. Hungry, he turns to music when words fail and he looks up to Him and sings his heart out. With the right intent, any Jew who sings a *niggun* always reaches his Creator.

In a sense, a *niggun* is a combination of parent–child sounds that no one else can understand. "Ya—na—na—ya—na—pa—pa—yaya—ya"—a stammering infant language God created for us when our feelings are too delicate or too intimate for others to hear.

"Ya—na—na—ya—na—pa—pa—yaya—ya."

A child speaks this perfect language, but forgets it when he learns his parent's language. Yet nothing is lost to a Jew. One day, when he is at his wit's end, the parent rediscovers suddenly, in singing a *niggun*, the language of the child in him. Then he speaks to his Father, and all becomes right. This is what a *niggun* is for.

As for the person who has not yet a child? He who experiences such inner aspect of a deeply moving emotion through a *niggun* is flooded with light, beauty, and soul, and above all, awareness of details, even those that are related to the emotion.

For, in calling his Father in heaven, is he not also calling for himself? The need for acceptance is forever with us. Hungry, we need our Father to feed us, so we can in turn feed our child—including the child in us or the child not yet born.

What is a *niggun*? Why do I ask the question again? Because a *niggun* means one thing to its singer and another thing to its listener. "Ya—na—na—ya—na—pa—pa—yaya—ya." At this level, when the sounds of the *niggun* reach God, He beholds His beloved, yearning child on earth and there comes an awareness only when the intensity of the joy subsides. God moves toward this lower level of experience; the child becomes closer to the existence of definable experiences and the world of speech. This setting is no more dramatized than in the holiest part of the *Shemoneh Esrei*, in the Jewish prayer service, when both God and the Jew physically move toward each other: Then, nothing better can be exchanged than a simple song in which the highest inner level of experience is expressible.

For me a *niggun* comes down to this: I can't carry a tune across a street, but I can tell a story that reaches up to Him, as long as I keep one typing finger on my computer at such times.

With this in mind I present a collection of stories—stories, did I say? A better word is "prayers"—that have helped me learn more about my ancient Jewish heritage. Guaranteed they'll do that much for you, too. I've been told—and my wife Ada has repeated that over and over to me—that the *niggun* is the quickest way to God's innermost ear.

Countless religious scholars have written much about *niggunim*, and you can look it up—provided you read Yiddish or Hebrew, the languages in which the scholars wrote. This book, *Niggun*, written in English, is not scholarly, although I've kept to the facts and managed to tell the stories behind these unusual songs. And what stories they are!

For centuries, Jews have sung these *niggunim* every chance they had—in synagogue, at *farbrengens* (*chasidishe* get-togethers), around the *Shabbos* dinner table, and surely in the privacy of their own worlds, including the shower. The songs are very special. Some have words, many others don't. But each has a story, expressing an inner state of the soul, that must be told and must be heard.

So now come with me into the ancient and modern worlds of the *niggun*. *Niggun* centers on stories, truth, and poetry, that connect Jews to God through specific *niggunim*. Each chapter generally deals with one *niggun*. Once you take a look at my table of contents you'll see the variety of religious experiences, which I hope will encourage at least one person, besides me, to reclaim his inheritance and share the Jewish legacy. With that in mind I begin my book and with that in mind I end my book.

My "look it up" sections, at the end of the book, include a glossary, a genealogy of outstanding chasidic rebbes, a discography of available chasidic *niggunim* on cassettes, an index, and a final word, "My Swan Song, Kosher, Of Course."

Each person expresses himself on three levels—thought, speech, and deed.

When a *chasid* carries out his rebbe's directives he unites with the rebbe's actions.

When he learns *Chasidus,* he unites with the rebbe's facet of speech.

But when he sings the rebbe's *niggun* he becomes united with the highest of the three levels—the rebbe's thoughts.

Sefer Haniggunim

I

Path One

Have you heard the story about the Chelmite who yearned to see the big city? Once on the road, he laid out his shoes pointing in the right direction, so that when he awoke the next morning he would know which way to go. As things happened, while he slept a tramp came along, saw the shoes, tried them on with a disgusted "Ouch," and threw them back on the ground. Only now they pointed in the direction whence the Chelmite started out. You can easily figure out the rest of the story. He arrived in the "big city" and fell in love with it because it uncannily looked just like his own hometown. With his newfound "wife and children" in an identical house on an identical street, he lived happily ever after.

I am not a Chelmite (although sometimes I wish I were one, for silly reasons), but I yearned to find out why it's been said about Safed (Palestine) that the road through Safed leads everywhere. To *Chasidus*? To chasidic *niggunim*, too? That is what is said.[1]

In writing *Niggun*, I didn't travel to Safed, but my first essay begins there. I was hoping. Who knew? Maybe I'd find the strong connection between the kabbalistic movement of Rabbi Isaac Luria (1534–1572) and chasidic music. I wasn't that lucky, but I found out other things. For one, "The Neo-mystics in Safed, Palestine, . . . made singing their duty and counted it a condition of inspiration and devotion."[2] For another, as Velvel Pasternak notes, "melody stood at the cradle of the *kabbalah* and surrounded it with the mystical yearnings that have touched the hearts of its followers to this day."[3] The third thing I found was an old friend, "*Lechoh Dodi*," and you can read all about it in my essay, appropriately called "The Road through Safed Leads Everywhere."

The only thing that I still can't figure out is how I got myself transported from Safed into chasidic territory. What I do know is that kabbalistic music went over big in Safed but didn't play too well in Peoria (or the Jewish city equivalent to that). In its way, kabbalistic music was very limited, or lost something in translation along the way; it was surely not practical for the secular Jew, and most oppressed Jews elsewhere were not ready for it.

What Eastern European Jews were ready for was music that made sense to their dreary lives. Enter the Baal Shem Tov.[4] For more than 200 years since, countless Jews have been reclaiming their heritage, thanks to this one Jewish man. As it is said, for every mile the Baal

Shem Tov walked through Eastern Europe to rouse the Jewish people to great spiritual heights, there was a *niggun* to accompany him.

I did not bring up the Chelm story for silly reasons. Here, too, it applies. Jews in ever-burgeoning numbers found their old Judaism ever more beautiful, satisfying, and happy. Why? Blame it on the songs, those happy wordless songs (and some not so wordless) sung by rebbes and their followers that, in practical ways, lit up the way and are still lighting up the way of returnees to Judaism like me.

In his charismatic manner, the Baal Shem Tov started out on a path to the "big city," but, unlike the Chelmite, he deliberately "turned his shoes in the direction whence he came," and millions of Jews, loving what they saw and heard, have followed him ever since.

Path One takes you along that path, but don't expect a travelogue. What you'll experience, through a series of essays, is stopping off at many quaint places, many chasidic courts where rebbes and their *chasidim* sang their melodies to God. Here you'll find, for example, why a Gerrer Rebbe counted his blessings that he had great composers/*chasidim* like Rabbi Yankel Talmud around him. Why one rebbe claimed he was a *niggun* from head to toe. Where the music of conductor/music composer Leonard Bernstein can be found—alive and well forever—as never before! Find out why tears unlock gates, but songs tear down walls! Why it's a Jew's privilege to take secular melodies from foreign cultures and incorporate them into the body of chasidic song. Why there were once strong-arm battles and heated words between Jews. How one rebbe surrounded himself with an ostentatious display of wealth to raise the standards of Torah and *Chasidus*. You'll also ask yourself, who or what can explain the healing process of a *niggun*? And, finally (but hardly last), you'll know why, since the days of Moses, every Jew continues to travel in order to come home.

Now, I've "laid out the shoes" and you're on Path One. Need I say more? I think not. So, please turn the page and live happily ever after.

1

The Road through
Safed Leads Everywhere

The road through Safed leads everywhere, but the strangest of all weddings took place near it about 420 years ago. Every Friday, before sunset, many Jewish mystics of the holy town in Palestine dressed in white garments and formed a procession going through the streets. Along the road, other participants —all grooms looking for the same one bride—joined them, and when they reached the end of town, they marched into an open field to the east to welcome the *Shabbos* Bride. According to Jewish mystical tradition, they sang six Psalms,[1] which represent the world of the Six Days of Creation that preceded the holy day, *Shabbos*, day of rest.[2]

From his vantage point next to an olive tree on his land, an Arab farmer stood watching the procession with bitterness in his blood. Why did these Hebrews have to pass him as if they mocked his very existence? Why did they have to sing? Why did they have to dance and trample the grass? Once he raised enough money, the Arab planned to buy that field and put a stop to the Jews' outrages. This road led right near his present land: ancient, holy land that was deeded to him by his own father and by his father and his father. He was there long before these present-day Jews came, and he would be there long after they left. As far as he was concerned there was no such thing as a permanent Jewish neighbor.

Yet the Jews came. For all Jews, *Shabbos* was a holy day in the week, but for these mystics each *Shabbos* was a holy wedding day. Some of the most famous Jewish mystics in history lived in the town of Tz'fat (now city of Safed), such as Rabbi Yehoshua ben Chananya, Rabbi Pinchas ben Yair, Rabbi Shimon ben Yochai, Rabbi Yitzchak ben Shlomo Luria Arizal, Rabbi Moshe ben Yaakov Cordovero, Rabbi Dovid ben Zimra Radbaz, Rabbi Moshe ben Yosef Terani Mabit, Rabbi Yosef ben Ephraim Karo, Rabbi Shlomo Halevi Alkabetz, and Rabbi Avraham Dov of Abritish, among others, and whose remains are buried there. Yet, as our Sages tell us, these holy Jews live on still in their "adobe of the living." "Even after death, the *tzadikim* are called living" (*Berochos* 18a).

Along this road, a veritable "*Shabbos* Road," the mystics sang "*Lechoh Dodi* . . ." "Come, my Beloved, to meet the Bride. Let us welcome the *Shabbos*. . . . Shake the dust off yourself, arise, don your glorious garments—my people . . . Awake, awake, utter a song . . . The Lord is our God, the Lord is one."

"Come in peace, *Shabbos* Queen!" The Jews raised their voices to heaven and the message went forward, heard even by the Arab farmer, who failed to grasp anything about it. In his time Rabbi Akiva was often asked: "What makes you think that your *Shabbos* is more important than the other days of the week?" Once, a Roman officer asked him that, and he boldly answered him with another question, "What makes you think you're more important than anybody else?" Proudly the Roman said, "Because I was chosen to be honored by my emperor." "The same is true about *Shabbos*," said Rabbi Akiva.[3] "*Shabbos* is more important than the rest of the week because the king of kings has chosen to honor it."

"*Lechoh Dodi*, *Shabbos* Queen," the call of exultation ranged through every Jewish home and echoed in the hills. The theme of bride and bridegroom—the Jewish people and God, the *Shabbos* and the Jewish people—has come down to every Jew. It is part of our heritage.

When the tradition of greeting the *Shabbos* Bride began is a story in itself. Every storyteller has his own version, all steeped in the truths of Torah and Talmud. One early source, quoted by Rabbi Shimon ben Yochai (author of the *Zohar*), tells us:

> When God created the world in six days and rested on the seventh day, which He blessed and made holy, *Shabbat* appeared before the Holy One, blessed be He, and complained: "Master of the Universe, each day of the week has a mate, but I am the odd one, without a mate!"[4] Replied God: "The Jewish people will be your mate!" Thus, when God gave his Torah to the Jewish people at Sinai, He began the Fifth Commandment with the words, "Remember the promise I made to the *Shabbat* that the Jewish people will be its mate."[5]

But every Jew bound by the Torah knew, or eventually came to know, of the author of *"Lechoh Dodi."* Renowned for his wisdom and poetry, Rabbi Shlomo Halevi Alkabetz[6] composed the *niggun* around 1571. He lived only a little more than eight more years to enjoy the fruits of his labor.

However, the Arab farmer knew or cared little about such things. Hotheaded and a poor businessman, the farmer witnessed his farmland become fallow. Rarely now did his fig tree bear healthy fruit, even in season. Why was this so? No doubt, he told himself, the Jews were exacting their price for his open belligerence towards them. Jews—Hebrews—or whatever they called themselves!—were his enemies, enemies of all enemies! They were to blame for all his misfortunes, and he was determined to make them pay. But how? Slowly he plotted his revenge. Slowly he picked his victim. Who? Rabbi Shlomo Halevi Alkabetz. Why? Did this Arab need any other reason than that Shlomo Halevi wrote a song called *"Lechoh Dodi"*? "Let's go forth, my beloved." As far as the Arab was concerned, this spiritual, loving *niggun* summed up everything that separated Jew from Arab. It was these Jews, or their ancestors, who had seen the birth of Mohammed (569–632 C.E.), the camel driver who was "imbued with the fervor of Judaism, proclaiming all Arabs descendants of Abraham and calling for all Jews and Christians alike to join him in a true brotherhood of man in the name of Allah"[7]; it was these Jews who walked the road adjoining his land and perhaps in the middle of the night ate up his food, stole his grain, and plotted their evil. Thinking this made the Arab more angry, and one day when he saw a lone Jew—he knew it was the celebrated Rabbi Alkabetz!—walking along the road absorbed in his prayer book, he seized the opportunity. Nobody in the universe could attest to what was in his mind, and clearly no other person was about. Somebody had to pay for the rejection of his prophet Mohammed and his beloved Koran. Somebody had to pay for the loss of his income. With a hostility that Mohammed must also have felt toward Jews, the Arab farmer waylaid the lone Jew along the road and murdered him.[8] The year was about 1580.

The road through Safed leads everywhere, this time to the courtyard of the farmer, directly to the fig tree, where he now buried the Jew. The story is recounted in the book *Safed: The Mystical City*. The following day the tree blossomed and bore fruit—exceptionally large and delicious figs . . . yet it was out of season!

Soon news of the miraculous occurrence reached the ears of the Turkish provincial governor. He summoned the Arab farmer.

"What is your secret of outstanding horticulture?" he asked. "This is the first I've ever heard of a tree bearing fruit before its appointed time."

The farmer remained silent. He was afraid of the consequences should he confess.

The governor asked again, more firmly this time, more demanding of an explanation. The farmer remained mute. Finally, the governor ceased to tolerate the farmer's insolent silence and ordered that he be tortured. The Arab finally confessed to killing Rabbi Alkabetz and admitted that from the day he had buried him the fig tree had begun to bear fruit.

Startled and impressed by this revelation, the governor commanded that the farmer be hung from that very fig tree as punishment for slaying a holy man of Israel![9]

As we're beginning to realize now, the road through Safed leads everywhere, this time beginning with "*Lechoh Dodi*"and ending with immortalizing Rabbi Shlomo Halevi Alkabetz. You can find his name in the first letters of each of the eight verses of the *niggun*, which he composed that way. Beginning with the letter *shin* ("*Shamor vezachor*," and so forth), they spell out his name, Shlomo Halevi. You can also find "*Lechoh Dodi*" as one of the ten *niggunim* of Rabbi Shneur Zalman of Liadi, founder of *Chabad* Chasidism (1745–1812). Rabbi Sholom Dovber Schneersohn (1860–1920), the fifth Lubavitcher Rebbe, used to recite *Shema Yisroel* in his prayers to this tune.

The melody is also a traditional Breslover[10] *Shabbos* table *niggun* that was set to "*Lechoh Dodi*" in recent years and has become very popular in Breslov. There, the song has a total of nine verses.

Finally, on *erev Shabbos*, the road through Safed leads to you, to your lips, to prepare the way for the *Shabbos* Queen.[11]

"Come, my beloved . . . *Lechoh Dodi* . . ."

As *Shabbos* puts her arms around you, there are no words to describe it. That's what a *niggun* is for.

2

The Lullaby

The night before "the morning stars sang together, and all the sons of God shouted for joy,"[1] Rabbi Akiva Greenberg sat by the bedside of his children and lulled them to sleep with a very special *niggun* that few have ever sung or heard of. The *niggun* that Reb Akiva sang could have come only from heaven—like a God-given business card that says, "Call me when you need me." According to a chasidic tradition, however, the *niggun* must have sojourned solely for a time in the heart and soul of one Elimelech of Lizhensk.[2]

For what could be simpler than a *niggun* sung by Reb Elimelech! In his time he was known as the little Baal Shem Tov,[3] who said: "If they had left me alone, if they had left me in peace for two years, I would have made the Messiah come."[4] Brother of Reb Zisha[5] (who was known for his compassion), Reb Elimelech, chief rebbe of Galicia (who was known for his severe authority), was "the practical man who translated abstract concepts into simple language for simple people."[6] But his music to God, like the *niggun* Reb Akiva sang to his children at bedtime, was not only a simple message for simple people, it was also a plea that could readily bring tears to the eyes of God.

"Oy—yoy—yoy yoy yoy—yoy yoy—yoyyyyy." As the song winds along with its precious few notes, in the sing-song sacred to talmudic syllables, Reb Akiva ponders the deep, religious fervor he has found through song—this one in particular. "Oy—yoy—yoy yoy yoy—yoy yoy—yoyyyyy." Reb Akiva recalls the first time he heard that song, and if that were the last song he would ever hear—*chas vesholom!*— but then Orthodox Jews don't deal with "perhaps" and "what ifs"— only in realities, so Reb Akiva perishes the unwanted thought.

Instead he focuses on the reality, and such a reality happened to Reb Akiva, as a young man in search of a *yeshivah* in which to learn and a *niggun* to sing. Leaving the United States, he enrolled in Ponevezer Yeshiva, a *misnaged yeshivah* in Bnei Brak, Israel, in the early 1950s. Quickly attracted to the Vizhnitzer Rebbe who held his court for *chasidim* in Tel Aviv, every *Shabbos* afternoon the young Akiva would sneak out of the *misnaged yeshivah*[7] and walk three-and-a-third hours to Tel Aviv. There he'd spend the rest of *Shabbos* among the Vizhnitzer *chasidim*, deep into the night and early morning partaking of delicious foods, listening to stories of the Baal Shem Tov and, of course, singing *niggunim*. At such times, deep in song and prayer, it seemed to Reb Akiva that he did not belong to this world at all. Reb Akiva found what he was searching for, in a place where lay rich treasures and still fairer hopes. Understandably, each *motzoei Shabbos* it was difficult to leave Tel Aviv and bus back to his *yeshivah*, but Reb Akiva knew he'd be back the following weekend, as it is written, "Man is not taken away before he has heard what he has come to hear and before he has said what he has come to say."

"Oy—yoy—yoy yoy yoy—yoy yoy—yoyyyyy."

Suddenly the scene in Rabbi Greenberg's head shifts. He is back in his *yeshivah*. For some reason he takes a different turn and opens a door. Inside are two *bochurim*, known as the Weisblum brothers, one of them Akiva's classmate. He greets them and they greet him. They do not ask whence he came, and he does not ask them where they spent their *Shabbos*. "*Gut voch*" (good week) allows each to get right to the point.

Akiva speaks first (after he closes the door behind him): "Look, you don't have anything to be afraid of from me, but I would like to know the truth. Are you guys related to or descended from the family of Rebbe Elimelech? Weisblum was his surname, too."

The two looked at each other, smiled, then said yes.

"So what is the relationship?" Akiva asked his classmate.

The classmate's older brother spoke: "We're eighth generation descendants of this Rebbe Elimelech."

Akiva had to take a seat, he couldn't believe his ears and eyes. Then he said, "Tell me, what traditions have been handed down to you about the Rebbe Elimelech in your family?"

The classmate interjected, "I know he was very tall and thin. Red-haired. Held his pants up with a straw belt, I think. Very strict in demeanor. Even in his home."

His brother then told Akiva his ancestor used to preach that the first duty of a *chasid* consists of reverence for the *tzadik*. "In fact, don't quote me, but I was told by my parents that my ancestor opened the era of the *tzadik*. The rebbe-*tzadik* came into his own. Reb Elimelech paved the way for the *tzadik* to be considered a 'middleman between Israel and God,'" he said. "He intercedes with God to bestow upon the faithful all earthly blessings—'life, children, and sustenance.'[8] There's so much to this . . . do you want me to go on?"

"Not for the moment, because the hour's late and I'm very tired, but please tell me," asked Akiva, "do you have any tradition in your family regarding *niggunim* from Rebbe Elimelech?"

Both brothers quickly said yes, and suddenly the yawning Akiva livened up.

"Yes . . . yes . . . ?"

The older brother again answered: "We have one *niggun* that has come down to us that the Rebbe Elimelech made."

"Made? Composed?" Akiva stood up on his feet and ran to the door—the brothers also leapt up, not knowing what to expect. Akiva shut the bolt on the door, then returned to the brothers. "I'm not letting you out of here until you teach me this *niggun*."

So all three sat down again, and they taught Akiva the *niggun*. "Oy—yoy—yoy yoy yoy—yoy yoy—yoyyyyy."

Reb Akiva remembers it well, right from the outset: "I never heard it from anybody else, other descendants of Rebbe Elimelech included. There's a cassette of *niggunim* recently come out that are attributed to Rebbe Elimelech of Lizhensk, but it's not on the tape. The *niggun* has no name; it's bittersweet, beautiful, and short, and it struck me that one day I could use it as a lullaby to rock my children—which," here Reb Akiva chuckled, "I must tell you I had none at the time to rock to sleep at night."

In the stillness of his apartment, with now his children grown up with their own children, Reb Akiva sang the lullaby *niggun* in the same fresh and loving vein we can safely assume he sings to his grandchildren when he is with them.

"Oy—yoy—yoy yoy yoy—yoy yoy—yoyyyyy . . ."

When he finished singing the wordless song, Reb Akiva said: "For me a *niggun* is always very subjective. To the one who listens to a *niggun*, it may be nice or not nice, lovely or not lovely, etc. But it's always full of meaning for the one who sings it because the meaning of the *niggun* is to a great degree dependent on the circumstances under which the person learned the *niggun*.

"That's why a *niggun* my rebbe taught me is very dear to me; a *niggun* that I did not learn from my rebbe can also be very beautiful and very nice, yet it doesn't have the same meaning, the same effect on me. So, it makes sense that a *niggun*—what it means to the person who hears it and to the person who sings it—depends on a lot more than the musical value of the *niggun*.

"This *niggun*, according to these two brothers, was one of the first *niggunim* composed by the Rebbe Elimelech himself. As such, it stands out to me, almost in a class by itself. Learning that particular *niggun*—well, I might say—was like hearing it from Rebbe Elimelech's lips himself."

"Oy—yoy—yoy yoy yoy—yoy yoy—yoyyyyy."

The young Rabbi Akiva Greenberg heard what he came to hear and, profusely thanking the Weisblum brothers for their gift of the *niggun*, said what he had to say. There was no further information from the brothers—under what circumstances Rebbe Elimelech of Lizhensk composed or sang the *niggun*, or anything else about it except that it was his—this song that all sons of Israel needed to hear to brave the dark unknown of sleep and to look forward to the dawn, when their souls returned to their bodies, and "the morning stars sang together, and all the sons of God shouted for joy."

There's another story connected to this *niggun*, which brought a satisfied smile to Reb Akiva's face.

"Talk about a blessing! Talk about a gift!" Reb Akiva went on to explain himself. "In the Talmud,[9] it's said that to get a gift means to return one. What gift? This *niggun*. To return to whom? I didn't know for a long time. Would I ever know? Of course. There used to be in Williamsburg [Brooklyn, New York] up till this year [1992] a descendant of the Rebbe Elimelech, who was the Stashover Rebbe. A very old man, very old, and the story about him was that when he reached a very old age the Rebbe Elimelech of Lizhensk came to him in a dream and said to him, 'Start to give *berochos* (blessings). You've nothing to be afraid of. You're an old man already anyhow. So when the time comes for you to go, you won't have to worry about anything.'

"Immediately the Stashover Rebbe began to give *berochos* in his old age to people, and all kinds of miraculous things happened. Every one of his blessings rang true. Some people had children. Some were cured of harsh diseases. That's the story about him.

"One day I took a couple to see him. And when they were done seeing him, the Stashover Rebbe turned to me and asked me what it was I came for. I said, 'First of all I came to bring this couple to you; second, I came to sing you a *niggun*.' He was very surprised. People don't come to a rebbe to sing him a *niggun*.

"The Rebbe looked surprised. Perhaps he was thinking, everyone comes to ask something from him, and here's a fellow who wants to give him something. A pleasant switch. And it's true, I wanted to give him a gift, a blessing, so I told him the story of under what circumstances I learned this *niggun*, that 'it was my favorite lullaby,' and he settled himself back and listened to the *niggun*, and was very pleased with it, and he gave me a *berochah*. That was the last time I saw him; very shortly after that he passed away."

Reb Akiva sighed, and I sighed, too.

We both sensed the reality of a Jew's life. Every man needs a lullaby, as it is written, "Man is not taken away before he has heard what he has come to hear and before he has said what he has come to say."

3

The Music of Return

There is a Jewish pied piper among us. Often he strolls through Crown Heights and Flatbush, frequently through Greenwich Village. Many times he performs in holy places, invariably in *golus* (exile), yet always the haunting music he plays returns when you need it most.

Wherever he roves, out of his head comes forth the music played on the ancient musical instruments of Yuval, and one of the few things this pied piper of *Chasidus* tells his listeners is, "You don't sing a *niggun*, it sings itself."

"*Niggun, niggun,* though I loved thee, I did not yet know thee. Tell me of my Creator and His creation. You are the reason of the heart that reason cannot understand."

It's in the stillness of rooms made for the heart that this pied piper is surrounded by a mystical circle of ecstatic Jews who follow not him but to the place where it leads: the "ladder to the Throne of God." His songs play like prayers.

But before I tell you why, you should know the *Aggadah* tells

17

us, that one of the musical instruments employed in the Temple service in Jerusalem was a pipe made of ordinary reed, smooth and slender, dating back to the days of Moses.

When the king saw how valuable it was, he ordered the pipe to be encrusted with gold. After that, whenever the pipe was played during the Temple service, its voice was no longer as clear as it was before. So the king had the gold removed from the reed, and the pipe's voice again sounded as sweet as ever.

And so it is with this modern-day pied piper, Chaim Binyomin Burston, whose own musical roots are deep—and unencrusted—in *Yiddishkeit*, except that instead of a reed pipe, he uses the latest digital keyboard to play *niggunim* pure and simple.

As a young *yeshivah* student in Kfar Chabad, Israel, he spent many *Shabbos* afternoons, after the *Minchah* service, joining hundreds of other students in songs that seemed to dance and skip along the darkening walls and ceilings of the *yeshivah*. There, he fully felt the power of the *niggun*.

Others have felt that same power of the *niggun*. For instance, at a different time, across the world, in Crown Heights, a brand-new *yeshivah* student complained how hard it was to comprehend a chasidic text (the *Tanya*). In response, his rabbi asked him to "sing along with us." The new student was about to experience his first *niggun*. The reassuring rabbi said, "Don't worry, Eliyahu, you're in good company. Rabbi Dov Ber,[1] the son and successor of Rabbi Shneur Zalman of Liadi,[2] often used to say, 'My saintly father could penetrate into the innermost recesses of a *chasid*'s soul by either a word of *Chasidus* or a *niggun*.'"

The *yeshivah* rabbi was absolutely right. Eliyahu was never the same again after he sang his first *niggun*. In the words of his chasidic teacher, "Eliyahu's soul had linked, for those brief minutes, in *deveikus* (attaching oneself to divinity). He fully grasped the words of Rabbi Shneur Zalman, himself a young man when he said them, 'Speech is the pen of the heart, while melody is the pen of the soul.'"

In a Jew's heart and mind, there's always room for more tears and more joy, the mix that makes his *neshomah* (his Jewish soul) so well connected to the realms of heaven.

Nobody invents *niggunim*. The *niggun* takes you through a door, to a ladder you climb, whereupon you gaze upon the face of Creation, then you climb down the ladder, whereupon you leave by the door you entered. Where are you then? Not exactly at the same place, but always where you started. For that's the power of the *niggun*: It's a revolving musical door—always returning you to earth so that you can—no, you must!—share the experience with others, your friends, your family, with yourself, the Torah insight, the truth that has never been known to you until that very moment.

To the *chasidim*, the followers of the Baal Shem Tov (1698–1760), founder of Chasidism, and Rabbi Shneur Zalman of Liadi, founder of *Chabad* Chasidism, the eighteenth-century mystical song was an integral part of the prayer experience. Many chasidic rabbis felt that words were an impediment to spiritual expression, a wall standing between the communion of the individual and his God. Consequently, many *niggunim* were sung without words.

There's a legendary story about Rabbi Shneur Zalman of Liadi (the Alter Rebbe). In his time there were anti-chasidic scholars who lived in a town called Shklov. All reasonable intellectuals, they never opposed anything without a rationale. So a group of them confronted the Alter Rebbe with questions concerning *Chabad* philosophy, and he entertained each one's question but did not answer it. Then he took them all in one room and joined them. There, he sang one of his famous wordless *niggunim*.

Everyone heard the same *niggun*, but everyone heard his own answer to his own question. It didn't end there, however. For many years, they continued—as followers—to ask him many more questions.

Who can explain that?

In *Chasidus* there are two kinds of questions. One kind is a purely intellectual question. It could be a simple request, such as, "How do I get to Lincoln Center?" When he receives his answer, with a certain mental understanding about how to go from one place to another, the question is over. There's another question that's called a "heart question." Not a question of the intellect, but a question of the heart. The difference is that when you answer that question, the next day the person will have another question—or even the same question.

"I recall when I first became an Orthodox Jew," said Chaim Binyomin, "one of my closest friends asked me every question on his mind: Why was I doing this? Why was I doing that? And in the beginning I'd answer them and explain and explain. I remember once, as I was preparing to go back to my *yeshivah*, this same friend suddenly raised the same questions again. Why are you doing this? Why are you doing that? That is when I realized that you can explain why for an eternity. The questions are emotional and they aren't satisfied with an intellectual answer."

Wherever he goes, Chaim Binyomin holds classes or musicales to promote his special arrangements of wordless *niggunim*, which he also has produced commercially on audio cassettes. After playing a few *niggunim*, he found that Jews—some who have musical appreciation from Yehudi Menuhin to Heavy Metal—will have more emotional questions than intellectual questions.

"When people bring their emotional resistance to a regular class," Chaim Binyomin said, "then you can intellectualize, you can explain, and after a while you hope they're satisfied and affected. But when people come to a class centered around *niggunim*—in other words, not intellectual by and large but filled with emotionality—where the music is purely Jewish and in a different dimension altogether that reaches straight to the heart, it does something that intellect cannot necessarily do."

A *niggun* plays like a prayer. When a person *davens*, he mouths words. When a person reads a newspaper, he's also mouthing words. Both, of course, are utterances involving the mouth, the lips, and the teeth. What's the difference? The difference is that in the *davening* there is a *koach*—a strength. Every Jew who *davens* uses this *koach* in his words to send them to *Yerusholayim*, where they are picked up by angels and brought to God. With the words of the newspaper, that is as far as they go.

A *niggun* also has its *koach*. Once you hear a *niggun*, you know it's more than music. "The beauty of them is that they're profound and simple at the same time," Chaim Binyomin said. "As *Chasidus* tells us, 'The highest level of Godliness is simplicity.'"

Worth mentioning is another story of the rhapsodic fame and simplicity of *niggunim*, again involving Rabbi Shneur Zalman of Liadi. A man of unconventional ways, he filled his homilies with folk tales and wise sayings of the Jewish people. One day, as he preached in the *shul*, he noticed the bewildered look of an old man who was trying hard to get the drift of his words. After he had finished his sermon and the congregation was departing, he said to the old man:

"I saw by the expression on your face that you did not understand my sermon."

"Yes, you are right, Rebbe," confessed the old man.

The modest Rebbe apologized, saying, "It may have been my fault. Perhaps I was not clear enough. At any rate, I'm going to sing to you now, for melody goes right to the heart and the understanding where words fail."

And so he threw his head back, and closing his eyes, sang with ecstasy a *niggun*, the song of return. As the old man listened, his face lit up.

"I understand your sermon now, Rebbe!" he exclaimed happily.

According to Nathan Ausubel, the author of *A Treasury of Jewish Folklore*, "there are an astonishing number of hasidic songs and dances, representing probably the most distinguished and original element in the musical creation of the Jewish folk. Like their lyrics, hasidic tunes are steeped in mystical rapture. . . . The lively, the ecstatic ones, usually served as vocal obligati to the famed dances of the mystic circle."[3]

Comparatively of slower movement are the cadre of ten *Chabad niggunim*, with a distinctive character and temperament of their own, created by Rabbi Zalman. Although he didn't write the first *niggun* nor did he write the last one, his ten are universally revered as the classics of *Chabad niggunim* the world over.

Chasidic and liturgical music, known as *neginah*, can be traced to the divine service in the Temple of old, where the Levites accompanied it by vocal and instrumental music, which was absolutely essential to the service. Sound and rhythm, beat and movement, meter and tempo—all had their place in the Temple service in those days.

That was way back then. Today, *niggunim* have generally been consigned to proper places in *shuls*, before, during and after *davening*, and *farbrengens* (informal chasidic gatherings). Which means not too many people are exposed to them, unless they happen to be in the right place at the right time.

Many people are not interested in going to a formal class or to a *shul* for a night of *Yiddishkeit* where a rabbi is speaking. But to hear via a friend about a musical experience, a mystical transportation, where there's going to be a live concert atmosphere and food served, they come in ever-increasing numbers to hear Chaim Binyomin perform *niggunim*.

The first person in the Torah who invented musical instruments was Yuval (Jubal). In Genesis, it says he was the father of the flute, the wind instruments, the harp, and the strings. Now what is the etymology of *Yuval*? It means "to transport." The whole idea of music is to transport the person's soul. It's really not only a matter of being transported, however, but also a matter of where you are going—and in what shape you'll return.

Are *niggunim* New Age music?

Admittedly, in the way Chaim Binyomin performs *niggunim* they come off, in a certain sense, very much New Age because people listening to them get the feeling of being transported and raised through meditation to an elevated state.

But *niggunim* listeners quickly learn that these Jewish melodies are hundreds of years old, in a very pure musical form, with melody that is extremely meaningful to them.

Where does a *niggun* come from? It is a pure Jewish song that has its roots in holiness composed by a rebbe, or a *chasid* who's on a high level of attachment to God.

"A *niggun*," Chaim Binyomin said, "is conceived at a time of inspiration in a Jew's *davening* or other Godly experience. Through him, but not from him. He is a vehicle for the *niggun* from a higher source; as it says in *Chasidus* or *Kabbalah*, there are different palaces, there are certain divine realms of influence above; there's the source of *teshuvah* (repentance) above, there's the source of different kinds of *berochos* (blessings) above, and there's the source of a certain spiritual realm of *niggunim* above, where all the *niggunim* exist from the beginning of time, waiting for the right Jewish soul to go up into this realm and bring down a *niggun* like a blessing from the upper world to the lower world."

Niggunim, as recorded in the three tapes by Chaim Binyomin Burston, are truly the music of return. "In Jewish tradition," Chaim Binyomin said, "elevation without return is not valid. The essence of Judaism and Godliness is the combination of opposites.

"Elevation and return are one such combination of opposites. Go up, take your inspiration, come down, and translate it into deeds for everyday life. That is the Jewish point of view."

"After all this, Chaim Binyomin, how does your old school friend feel about your *Yiddishkeit* now?"

Chaim Binyomin grinned.

"Well, you know, he still asks countless questions, but that is the nature of all searching Jews. What pleases me most, however, is that we're closer than ever. He's come to love *niggunim* and through them has involved himself in his own search for answers. Which means he too is well along the path to *Yiddishkeit*."

That is what the haunting music of return—the deep calling unto the deep—is all about.

4

The Singing Tzadik

Whe the eye is ready the vision will appear. When the ear is ready, the song will appear. When the student is ready, the teacher will appear.

Visionary, singer, teacher—such a man, Eizik Taub, was born in Szerencz (Zemplen County, Northeastern Hungary), in 1751. Blessed with a melodious voice, each of his songs rejoices, weeps, sheds light on Torah, and expects the Messiah at any moment. Like King David, Eizik started out life as a shepherd, who, while feeding his flock, would say, "Master of the Universe, I wish to emulate Your attributes and have compassion on every creature." Unusual words for a simple young boy tending sheep, but read on . . .

In Eizik's case, who is the teacher and who is the student? There are at least two schools of thought.

One: Like Jacob who had to come to a place where all the shepherds were gathered before he met Rachael, so too was Rabbi Aryeh Leib Sarah's[1] driven to roam around shepherds who were trying spiritually to control their passions in isolated places.

According to Avraham Yaakov Finkel, "Rabbi Leib Sarah's, the great mystic in faraway Russia, perceived that in Hungary there existed an exalted soul that was waiting to be redeemed."[2] So he set out on a holy calling, as well as to search out other new adherents for *Chasidus.*

On such a walk in Hungary he came upon the young shepherd Eizik Taub. Eizik was singing: "*Shechinah, Shechinah,* how far you are; exile, exile, how long you are. If the exile were not so long, we could be together." After listening for a time, Rabbi Leib Sarah's asked the lad who had taught him the song.

"It's a song every shepherd around here knows," said Eizik.

"With the words you sang?" asked the Rabbi.

"No," explained the lad. "Instead of '*Shechinah,*' they say 'beloved.'"

And here Eizik sang the song again, as it once was:

> Forest, O forest, how vast are you!
> Rose, O rose, how distant you are!
> Were the forest not so vast,
> My rose wouldn't be so far.
> Who will guide me out of the forest,
> And unite me with my rose?[3]

Then he sang it as Rabbi Leib Sarah's heard it.

> Exile, O exile, how vast are you!
> *Shechinah, Shechinah,* how distant you are!
> Were the exile not so vast,
> The *Shechinah* wouldn't be so far.
> Who will guide me out of the exile,
> And unite me with the *Shechinah?*

Deeply impressed, Rabbi Aryeh Leib Sarah's couldn't help wonder whence came this boy's Torah knowledge. In reply, Eizik told the Rabbi that until then he had studied under a tutor, Rabbi Yitzchak of Przeworsk. Returning home with Eizik, Rabbi Aryeh Leib Sarah's asked Eizik's mother (his father was deceased) for permission to take the boy to study under Rabbi Shmuel Shmelke Horowitz of Nikolsburg (1726–1778); the mother readily agreed;

and the little shepherd's melody quickly became popular with many *tzadikim*.

As for Eizik, under the tutelage of Rabbi Shmelke, he became an outstanding Torah and *Chasidus* scholar. His knowledge of both *niglah* and *nistar*, the revealed and mystical aspects of Torah, was legendary. Returning home to Hungary, he became the teacher of the children of Yaakov Fisch, the head of the Jewish community of Nagy Kallo. He married Feigi, the daughter of Ansil Kohn of Tarezak. Within a short time, he was named the Rabbi of Kalev, serving forty years and gaining thousands of new followers for the chasidic movement.

A second school of thought: The Kalever Rabbi learned from the *Maggid* of Mezeritch[4] a melody for the hymn of the *haggadah*, "The Mighty in His Kingdom," and was greatly pleased with it. The *Maggid* said he had learned it from a shepherd.

From then on, the Kalever made it a habit to walk in pastures to listen to the melodies sung by the shepherds. Like his discoverer, Rabbi Aryeh Leib Sarah's, the Kalever chanced upon a shepherd surrounded by his flock and singing a Hungarian love song. Different words, but the melody could never be forgotten. Moved to tears by the song, the Kalever insisted on buying the song from the shepherd. Readily the shepherd agreed. At the request of the Kalever who wished to memorize the song, the shepherd sang the song once, then twice, but on his third attempt he could not recall the song at all. Forever after the *niggun* belonged *again* to the Jews. The Kalever said many times about the song, "that it was once chanted by the Levites in the Holy Temple and was in exile among the unlearned common people."

Perhaps it was the Kalever's ability to be both shepherd and sheep that endeared him to all Jews. His vision and *niggunim* earned him the nickname of "the Singing *Tzadik*." So many times did he appear in the cloak of a shepherd and did he mix with simple Jews that it seemed to many that he came to learn from them. He did. He listened to their concerns, helped them to solve their problems, and thanked them for helping him draw closer to God. He also told stories of the great *tzadikim*. His point: "All are equal in prayer before the Lord."[5] He also helped heal many people's illnesses. And he taught, in his own way, that "prayer is greater than sacrifices."[6]

The Kalever also sang:[7]

The rooster crows,
Dawn brightens the sky
In the green forest, in the verdant meadow
A little bird skips around.
Who are you, little bird?
Who are you, little bird?
Of golden beak and golden feet
That waits for me.
Just wait, dear little bird,
Just wait, dear little bird!
If God destined you for me,
I will be one with you.
The rooster sings his morning song,
The sun is slowly rising—
Yiboneh hamikdosh, ir Tzion temolei
(May the Temple be rebuilt, the City of Zion
      replenished)—
When, O when will it be?
Veshom noshir shir chodosh uvirnonah naaleh,
(There shall we sing a new song, with joyous singing
      ascend),
It's time, O let it be!

In another version,[8] the Kalever sings: "The cock is already crowing. It will soon be dawn. In the green forest, in the open field, a bird is walking. But what a bird. With yellow legs and wings of blue. It is waiting for me there. Wait, my rose, wait, always wait. If God willed me for you, I shall be yours. But when will this come to pass? *Yiboneh hamikdosh ir Tzion temolei* . . . (May the Temple be rebuilt and Zion be populated)."

The Messiah is never far from the thoughts and songs of the Kalever Rebbe.

Another *niggun*, another shepherd. It is almost dusk. The shepherd's flock have finished grazing and lie around waiting for the shepherd to take them home. For some reason he's delayed the departure. And as every Jew, hearing the *niggun*, now grasps why, it's perfectly clear: He has been watching something in the distance. What? Someone on a donkey is approaching him on a seemingly endless trek. By the looks of it, the shepherd is transfixed and excited; he can't help wonder who the rider is. Can it be? . . . Is it truly the long-awaited Messiah? The donkey and its rider draw nearer and nearer—and as you hear, for instance, this Hungarian *niggun* of the Kalever Rebbe sung at a Friday night chasidic get-together of the Sanzer Rav or Vizhnitzer Rebbe, every *chasid* there also wants it to be the Messiah riding the donkey. And when the shepherd leaps up, waving his staff to welcome the long-awaited one, so too do the *chasidim*, ready to march off to greet the Messiah.

But it's not the Messiah. The shepherd—and the *chasidim*—take it in stride. The man on the donkey is a fellow Jew. Baring his plaint, the shepherd tells the man on the donkey,

> The sheep are weeping,
> The herders are moaning,
> Go, tell the master
> The hay needs the flock.

And the man on the donkey, realizing that he had been mistaken for the Messiah, weeps too, for the plight of his fellow Jews. In comfort, he says,

> Greetings, dear shepherd,
> How are my sheep?

And the shepherd replies,

> Your flock will be well tended
> So long as I am their shepherd.

The Kalever Rebbe's "melodies express the grief of the *Shechinah* in exile and the yearnings of the House of Israel for redemption."[9] Rest assured always through this *niggun* about the coming of the Messiah that there's hope. The shepherd asks the donkey rider the question on the lips of every longing Jew. "When will the Messiah come?" The answer—and it has to suffice until he arrives: "He's ready to come."

In 1821, the Singing *Tzadik* passed on. No longer in exile. United once more with the *Shechinah*.

5

Song on Fire

L egend has it that the most inspiring and exalted *niggun* that Rabbi Hershele Eichenstein of Ziditchov (died 1837) left behind was one he heard the angels singing in honor of God. When? How? Where? Until now, not too many people outside the Ziditchov, Rozdol, and Komarno Rebbe dynasties knew for certain. Now, at last, the current Komarno Rebbe, *shlita*, Rabbi Alter Yitzchak E. Safrin, has pinpointed the time and place.

Notes the Komarno Rebbe: "I heard it from my father, who heard it from his father, who heard it from his father, who heard it from his father, who heard it from the lips of Rabbi Hershele himself. This is what he told him:

"'In disgrace I was driven out of the village of Brody [in Galicia], on the day before *Shabbos*. It was not easy for me to walk home and tell my family and friends that I felt I was at a low point of my life. But just before *Shabbos*, I reached a small town [Putkamin, Galicia] and went directly to the *shul* in my weekday clothes. There I was recognized by some of my *chasidim*, who, shortly before *Minchah*, brought me my *Shabbos* garments. In my prayers during *Minchah* I spoke to Hashem, saying: 'Lord of the world, you see the humiliation of those who have been humiliated, and you see my crushed heart. Give me light so that I can pray to you.' Then suddenly, my prayers, my heart, my soul, my body—all caught fire. My prayer was an eternal flame. Never before had I experienced such holiness in *Minchah*, never before had sublime, holy ecstasy happened to me, and it may never happen again. "

Out of that experience came Reb Hershele's *niggun*, "In Ziditchov burns a fire that is never extinguished."

About the fire that is never extinguished, the *niggun* of flowing flame, Reb Hershele of Ziditchov passed it down through three dynasties—Ziditchov, Rozdol, and Komarno—made up of brothers and nephews, forming a close-knit family that was at the same time a school whose patriarch/teacher he was.

Reb Hershele himself demonstrated that fiery power. In his time there was a deadly epidemic that was cutting down many Jews' lives. In a moment of great self-sacrifice, Reb Hershele said he "is sacrificing his own life to save the Jews." Upon his passing away, the epidemic stopped.

"I recall another story," said the Komarno Rebbe. "When my great-great-grandfather, Rabbi Eisikel Komarno, was about ten years old, his father Alexander passed away. Homeless, he went to live with Reb Hershele, who saw the genius in his nephew; by six, it is said, Eisikel already knew *Kabbalah*, *Gemara*, and much of the Torah. But the nephew was also very sensitive. Quickly he came to share Reb Hershele's holy ecstasies. He saw that the Ziditchover Rebbe, whenever he was carried away with *kedushah* and could not find anything else to do or say, would break into song. Thus, 'In Ziditchov there burns a fire . . .' became the nephew's theme song, too.

"On the night before Shavuos, the nephew was awakened by the walls vibrating with sounds. Where were they coming from? Perhaps next door from his uncle's room? At moments he could discern an angelic voice singing, humming, lamenting, warbling; he could hear the prayers and meditations of a man so close to his God, he could hear the *niggun* 'In Ziditchov there burns a fire . . .' What was going on? he wondered. Was Reb Hershele alone? To the nephew's ear, it sounded like a congregation of angels—or . . . ?

"The nephew was truly scared. He had no fear for his uncle's safety, but what did he really know? Perhaps they were not angels, but the Evil One himself and his disciples who were tormenting his uncle. Perhaps his uncle was in serious trouble. He had to do something. In a burst of energy the nephew entered his uncle's room. 'Uncle, dear uncle,' the nephew cried out, 'why are you crying?'

"Suddenly the Ziditchover Rebbe caught himself and turned to his young ward. He saw tears of fear and wonder streaming down his nephew's face, genuine concern in his voice. At this sight, the Ziditchover Rebbe was deeply moved.

"But what could he say to a ten-year-old boy? What could the boy say to him? Yet the two—generations apart—always seemed to understand each other. So he decided to explain his night of pain to his nephew.

"'Child, I cry because this year more people are coming to pray with me than last year, and how can I really give personal attention to every person? I cry also because I am afraid the unholy one, Satan, is sending many of these people to me to test me, trying to make me prideful. And I don't want that.'"

It is said that Reb Hershele Eichenstein, from the village of Ziditchov, never raised a glass of water to his lips without going through a special mystical concentration (*kavonah*). One handed-down story to the Komarno Rebbe tells us that one night, Reb Yitzchak Eisik from the village of Safrin (died 1800), who generally would pace the floor in the early morning hours because he couldn't sleep, began weeping aloud. His weeping was so bad it roused his wife, Hinda. "What is the matter?" she wanted to know out of concern for him. He bemoaned to her that he feared he had little time to live, and who knew if he merited getting into the Garden of Eden, where all holy Jewish people go after they pass away. For him, this was no idle thought; she could see he was genuinely tormented.

"Do not worry," she said to him. "We have five children. They will help us with their holiness, their righteousness, to gain entrance to *Gan Eiden*." Hearing this, her husband started to calm down. Then she reminded him how Moses and the Jewish people, on the way to *Eretz Yisroel* (then *Eretz Kenaan*), wanted to go through the land of Edom. "So he petitioned the king. 'We are in Kadesh, a city on the border of your territory. Please let us pass through your land; we will not pass through fields or through vineyards; we will not drink water from the wells; we will go by the king's highway; we will not turn aside to the right or to the left until we have passed through your territory.'

"Then Edom sent word to Moses: 'You shall not pass through, or else I will come out to meet you with the sword.' The sons of Yisroel sent word to him in return: '*Bamesilah Naaleh*—We will go up by the side road and if we should drink from your waters, I or my livestock, then I will pay their purchase price—[I will do] nothing else whatsoever; only let me pass through with my feet.'[1] Edom still refused the Jewish people to pass through their land."

Rebbetzin Hinda paused so that the words could take effect on her husband's troubled mind. Then at the right moment she went on. "Yes, '*Bamesilah*,' which is an acronym for our five sons: Berish, Moshe, Sender [Alexander], Lipa, and Hirsh. *Bamesilah*—this is the path we will take to *Gan Eiden*, my dear husband, and we are going on our pathway to Heaven by honor of them."

As for the dynasties of Ziditchov, Rozdol, and Komarno (all five generations), they were not generally known for their *niggunim*; rather, they had the same *nusach*[2] as Reb Hershele, the same understanding of Torah and *Kabbalah*, and *avodah* (service to God) as he. Yet every Rebbe descended from Reb Hershele, to this day, *davens* with that same angelic approach and carries that song of the eternal flame in his heart and soul. And why not? As it is said, "As the fuel, so is the fire."[3]

6

Song of the Dead:
A Happy Story

Where can we buy a little joy?" the *Imrei Chaim*[1] often asked his followers. "Can we go to the drugstore and buy it? Where can we find a little *simchah*?" And when a *chasid* said to him that he found *simchah* by the side of his Rebbe, the *Imrei Chaim* smiled, pinched the cheek of his follower, and said, "You are a true *chasid*."

Then, added the *Imrei Chaim*: "*Simchah* is not a *mitzvah*, and sadness is not a sin. But what *simchah* can accomplish, the greatest *mitzvah* cannot. And what sadness can destroy, the worst sin cannot destroy. Therefore a person must seek constantly to be in joy."

These words are also attributed to another Rebbe (Rabbi Nachman of Bratzlav, 1772–1810), whose *chasidim* to this day base their joy, their *gadlus hamochin* (exuberant frenzy), on being part and parcel of his followers. To them he is as much alive today as when he really lived. "Do not despair. Always be happy." The Bratzlaver *chasidim* took him at his word. They continue to be united with him through song and story and laughter.

The life of Rabbi Nachman is replete with reasons for him to be sad. Each step, painful as it was, he took toward reaching *Eretz Yisroel* he learned the meaning of joy. In poor health and almost penniless, with death dogging his every step (he died at the age of thirty-eight), he reached Haifa, Israel, the land of his dreams, on *erev* Rosh Hashanah, September 10, 1799. Rabbi Nachman was clearly now happy and alive. His pain eased, he proclaimed that "through song, calamities can be removed. Music has a tremendous power to draw you to God. Get into the habit of always singing a tune," he enjoined his followers. "It will give you new life and send joy into your soul. Then you will be able to bind yourself to God."

In his *Likutei Moharan*, he wrote:

"Every field of knowledge in the world has a *niggun*, a melody all its own. It is from its *niggun* that it draws its strength. Yes, even atheism and heresy have their own special songs. The higher the level of a particular science, the more exalted is its *niggun*, reaching its climax in the wisdom of *Ein Sof*—infinity, the knowledge of God Himself. We cannot perceive Him intellectually [Rabbi Nachman forbade his disciples to study philosophical texts, prohibiting even the philosophical writings of the Rambam. He advocated simple, innocent belief in God.]—we must simply have *emunah* (faith) and believe that His Infinite Light surrounds all existence.

"This faith also has a *niggun* uniquely its own. We note that each religion, even the erroneous idolatrous religions, have their own liturgical music; but the song pertaining to the faith in the Most High is more glorious than the song of any science or [any other] religion.

"It is, in fact, the source of all other melodies. And in the end of days, when all nations will come to recognize God as the Creator, they will all sing this *niggun* of *emunah*, this song of perfect faith. . . . By virtue of this *niggun* all souls that have fallen into the clutches of atheism will be raised. This melody will put an end to all disbelief, and all other melodies will vanish, being absorbed in this sublime *niggun*."

Preceding grace after meals on *Shabbos* and festivals, it was a custom in Bratzlav to learn the *Sipurei Maasi'ois* (collected stories) of Rebbe Nachman during the Second Meal. After this learning, a joyful song was sung and sometimes spontaneously a dance erupted. This particular *niggun*—"*Shir Hamaalois*" ("Song of Ascents") was often a favorite at such times during the past forty years. It was brought to *Eretz Yisroel* from Uman by the previous Bratzlaver *rosh yeshivah*, Reb Eliyahu Chaim Rosen, who would offer it as his first choice whenever a joyous *niggun* was required.

Almost 200 years later, this story is told: Every day a *Yerusholayim chasid* of the Bratzlaver Rebbe visited the *kotel* (Western Wall of the Temple) where he *davened*. In his depressed state, he was watched over by everyone.

One day the *chasid* appeared at the *kotel* in an ecstatic mood, happy, joyful, and singing a *niggun*: "*Shir Hamaalois*." The words come from Psalm 126:

> When the Lord will turn once more to the return of
>   Zion, we will have been like those who dream.
> Then our mouth will fill with laughter and our
>   tongue with exultation; then they will say among the
>   nations: "The Lord has done great things with these."
> The Lord has done great things with us at all times;
>   we have remained glad.
> Though he who bears the measure of seed goes on his
>   way weeping, he will surely come home with exultation,
>   bearing his sheaves.

Seeing the *chasid* reach moments of ecstasy, the onlookers waited till he finished his song to speak to him:

"You of all people should be so elated, to be singing a *niggun*. We know that your wife has been very ill for the past twenty years and has left your house since then. We know that you have a daughter who is mentally unbalanced. We know that your grandchildren are plagued with all kinds of illnesses. You yourself live in poverty, with no chance at making a good living. What has changed to make you so happy?"

The Bratzlaver *chasid* smiled and said:

"I want you to know that when I am confronted with all these adversities I say to myself, 'Where will I find a little bit of *simchah*, a little bit of happiness, of joy?' And then I remind myself: *Yom Tov*! Then, it's a *mitzvah* to be happy. Yes, I'll borrow a little *simchah* from *Yom Tov* for my weekdays, to liven up each day, to give me sustenance; thus, I'll be able to meet all these problems and adversities. The moment I sang the holiday *niggun*, I felt like my Rebbe when he first alighted on *Eretz Yisroel*: alive and well! I no longer feel pain or sorrow. I have something to live for." And then the *chasid* took the hands of the onlookers and they all started to do a little dance.

Rabbi Nachman once wrote: "When you're filled with joy all day you can easily find an hour in which to pour out your heart before the Holy One blessed is He. When you are depressed it is very difficult to seclude yourself and speak to God. Therefore, do your best, even force yourself to be always happy, especially when you are praying. It is impossible to reach a true state of happiness except by doing [what may be seen as] foolish things [that is, by removing every trace of self-importance, and not caring what others think of you]." (From *Mekor Hasimchah*—"Always Be Happy.")

He also wrote:

"How do you pray to the Lord? Is it possible to pray to the Lord with words alone? Come, I will show you a new way to the Lord, not through words or sayings alone but through song. We shall sing and the Lord on high will understand us."

Probably, if Rabbi Nachman were asked why such emphasis on *simchah*, he might lay out the whole map of *Eretz Yisroel* in words and song, saying that it represents simplicity and joy. Then he'd tell his tale about a peasant shoemaker who found even eating simple and joyful. His midday meal consisted of dry bread. First he used it as a spicy soup, then as a juicy roast, finally enjoying it as a delightful cake. He lacked nothing.

Today, the many thousands of Bratzlaver *chasidim* still don't have a living rebbe. Yet their movement continues to flourish in the United States, Israel, and in many other countries. They continually attract many new adherents. Every year thousands of his followers travel to Uman to visit the tomb of Rabbi Nachman, who remains their Rebbe. "After my death," he told his followers, "any man may come to my grave and recite ten chapters of Psalms and contribute to charity on my behalf. Then, even if his sins are many, I will do my utmost to intercede for him."

There is little doubt that Rabbi Nachman died with part of a song on his lips, or as Rabbi Nathan, his closest disciple and biographer turned hagiographer, noted, "with a kind of smile on his face." After him, there has never been another Bratzlaver Rebbe. His *chasidim* have become known affectionately as the *toite chasidim* (dead followers). Always they have remained faithful to the living memory of their departed Rebbe. Even today they speak of him in the present tense.

And their Rebbe continues to be faithful to them. Three years before his death he moved to a house in Uman, with all his heart and soul bent on dying in *Eretz Yisroel*. So sick was he that he dared not make the perilous trip to Israel, terrified that he might die along the way and nobody would tend his grave in some out-of-the-way cemetery.

In *Yerusholayim* today, his followers have erected a magnificent *yeshivah* and synagogue where they study the works of their Rebbe. After each service they dance. *Chasidim* join hands in a circle and sing verses from the Psalms. In the center of the circle is Rabbi Nachman's armchair, the one he left in Bratzlav. Ask any *chasid* and he'll tell you about this armchair. It was smuggled out of the former Soviet Union, dismantled piece by piece, crossing many frontiers. The *chasidim* will proudly point out that not one piece is missing, and not one *chasid* of the Bratzlaver brotherhood who carried a piece of the armchair died along the way. And as you watch the *chasidim* dance with *simchah* around the armchair, it takes no vivid imagination to feel the eyes of the Bratzlaver Rebbe on you. Yes, he's there, sitting in his armchair, listening to his *chasidim* singing the song of the dead, perhaps even singing along with them.

"By strengthening their hearts and clinging to my advice," said Rabbi Nachman, "my followers will ultimately cause others to recognize the truth of my teachings. The fire which I have kindled will burn until the coming of the Messiah."

What better reason, then, to continue dancing around the armchair and singing the song of the dead![2]

7

Bringing the Glad Song Home

To Shimon Spira[1] there was nothing worse than "to be hidden among the baggage."[2] So one day, shortly after World War II began in early September 1939, Shimon Spira left his baggage and escaped with his life.

Other Galician *chasidim* from Spira's hometown of Bardiov, Czechoslovakia, had the same idea and began to run every which way; many of them, rumors abounded, were caught and shot on the spot by the invading Germans.

With a newly devised escape plan, Shimon Spira took a page out of his departed parents' life: He would travel across the safe part of Poland, near the border of Russia, to the town of Belz, where he would seek the counsel of Grand Rabbi Aharon Rokeach, the fourth Belzer Rebbe (1880–1957).

This was no superficial decision. It had been in place for generations. Spira's father was a Belzer *chasid*, and so were his uncle and grandfather. He had heard so many stories about the first Belzer Rebbe, Rabbi Shalom Rokeach (1783–1855), who turned a small town in eastern Galicia into the birthplace of a chasidic dynasty.

Belz—a movement that for over 150 years propelled European Jewry toward greater Torah observance, fighting off the threat of assimilation from within and anti-Semitism and poverty from without. Belz—where after his marriage, this same Reb Shalom, also known as *Sar Shalom* (Prince of Peace), devoted 1,000 days and nights to the uninterrupted study of both the revealed and the kabbalistic Torah. Belz—where Eliyahu Hanovi appeared to the Belzer Rebbe and taught him the secrets of erecting a *shul,* according to the *Kabbalah.* Belz—whose synagogue, the life work of the first four Belzer Rebbes, stood as "a storehouse for Torah and *yiras shomayim* (fear of heaven) until the redemption." The copper balls that adorned its roof, shining brightly in the morning sun, beckoned the faithful from all across Galicia. Belz—where, when a *chasid* pleaded to the second Belzer Rebbe, Rabbi Yehoshua Rokeach (1825–1894), "Help me die as a Jew," the Rebbe pointedly replied, "You are making the request that Bilaam made. Bilaam the wicked prayed, 'Let me die the death of the righteous and let my end be like his' (*BaMidbar* 23:10). This is understandable, for Bilaam was a Gentile but wished to die like a Jew. Try to live the life of a Jew first. The rest will come naturally."[3] Belz—the home of the glad song.

Belz beckoned and Shimon Spira came. In his twenties, he sought out the *tzadik,* Rabbi Aharon Rokeach, the fourth Belzer Rebbe. Reaching Belz shortly before Rosh Hashanah, in the middle of the day, Shimon Spira wasted no time meeting with the Rebbe's *gabbai* to explain his mission. One thing struck the traveler. The Germans were breathing down the necks of every Jew all over Poland, but here in Belz life seemed normal, with the household *chasidim* of the Belzer Rebbe showing no sense of urgency. Was there a war going on? In 1914, with the outbreak of World War I, the third Belzer Rebbe, Rabbi Yissachar Dov Rokeach (1854–1927), was driven out of Belz, which was destroyed during the war. But in 1922, the Grand Rabbi, returning to a decimated Galicia, raised hopes of local residents that the area could be returned to its former glory; within two years it was.

But now it was 1939; World War II had started. Yet, in Belz, Jews prayed, Jews sang, Jews kept the Sabbath. Would the holy city of Belz this time remain unscathed? Or was it a case of "crying peace, peace, where this is none!"[4]

Clearly, Shimon Spira was happy he was in Belz.

Many years later, when he made good his escape to America, he could easily grasp why this Rebbe's court had been a haven for European Jews during the Holocaust. Here was a Rebbe who offered blessings and hope to a shattered people who were desperate for both. Here was a Rebbe who now offered him the best possible escape plan: If he wanted to escape eventually to America, as he had planned, he should go directly to the Russian border and cross it at once. That the Rebbe gave Shimon Spira advice at all was in itself a highly unusual move, for during the war the Belzer Rebbe rarely offered advice.

The Rebbe, in fact, was known for his blessings and *shmirah* (safety) coins. Occasionally, during the war, the Belzer Rebbe dispensed *shmirah* coins to Jews along his own escape path to permanent safety. Even today, of all those people who received such coins from the Rebbe, not one claims he or she still has it. Amazingly, many of the *shmirah* coins disappeared once the safety of each person was assured. Numerous coin holders have confirmed this. As one Jew noted, "Out of danger, out of sight—but then what else was a safety coin for?"

Immediately, Shimon Spira left with the Belzer Rebbe's advice and blessing. Their paths would not cross again, but Spira and his children stayed strongly linked to Belz over the years.

In the meantime Belzer *chasidim* took their cue from their Rebbe and went about their daily routines. The High Holy Days were about to begin, and the Rebbe exhorted everyone to prepare themselves through repentance, prayer, and charity. In the tradition of his ancestors, the Rebbe blessed the Jewish Nation with *bonei, chayei, umezonei* (children, life, and sustenance).

Although the roads were virtually impassable, *chasidim* made the trip to Belz for Rosh Hashanah, war or not. There were, of course, obvious signs right in Belz that a great war storm was brewing. To protect them from the destructive hands of the Germans, well-packed and well-concealed Torah scrolls were removed from the Great Synagogue and *beis hamidrosh* in Belz and taken for safekeeping to towns like Sokol. Jews booked passage on trains going into Russia. Others left for parts unknown or known and were never heard from again.

Still, Belz's glad song was sung. The synagogue stood in its full glory. Now it is no more, but there is a scale model of it in Jerusalem. Inside the synagogue there were nine copper inverted cups—

inverted domes on the inside. Called "the Heavens," they were painted in various shades of blue sky, with stars, and represented the heavens at various times of the day. Every little detail of the *Shulchan Aruch* in the *shul* was observed. There were thirteen windows—twelve for each tribe and one, which is mentioned in the *Shulchan Aruch*, called the All-Inclusive Gate. In this way, no prayer can ever get lost; in this way, the gates of prayer are always open; that's how it was in the old days of Belz.

But this was a time for war. One old Belzer *chasid* who was there in those days, for that last Rosh Hashanah, tells[5] of the mood of the Jews. War was imminent. Slowly their lives were changing for the worse. People were seen weeping in the streets. He said that people who had been coming to the *shul* for many years saw a different *shul*. There were columns in the *shul*, against which numerous Jews leaned and prayed and cried out to Hashem. Once, he himself saw an old *chasid* who stood by a column, crying, "*Shul, shul*, holy *shul*, when will I get to see you again? When will I get to *daven* in you again?"

By now even the household people of the Great Synagogue were worrying. They asked the Rebbe, "When are we leaving? What shall we do? It's getting dangerous to stay here."

The Rebbe gave them no answer. Rosh Hashanah passed. Yom Kippur passed. The Belzer Rebbe showed no sign of worry and he made no comment about leaving.

Came Sukkos and something interesting happened.[6] There was an *esrog* (a citron, used during Sukkos for the *mitzvah* of the Four Species) dealer from Israel, who earlier in the summer had sent a box of *esrogim* from Israel to the Rebbe. As they were meant to be used strictly for decorating the tops of *sukkahs*, they were of inferior quality, not meant to say blessings over. The dealer had intended to send the Belzer Rebbe a box of excellent *esrogim* for Sukkos, but the raging war blocked the possibility of that. In the end, all the Rebbe had was the box of inferior *esrogim*. Before Rosh Hashanah, the Rebbe, thinking he might find one *esrog* fit to make a blessing over, had the box opened and lo and behold all the *esrogim* inside were beautiful and perfect. A miracle! At that time there were no *esrogim* in all of Galicia, so the Rebbe sent out a number of the *esrogim* to neighboring Jewish city communities and kept some for himself and his *chasidim*. War or not, Sukkos was a happy time, as well it should be. "The Holy Spirit rests only in a heart that rejoices."[7]

What was the secret of these *esrogim*? The answer was also part of the glad song of Belz. Eventually, five years later, the Belzer Rebbe and his brother, Rabbi Mordechai Rokeach (1900–1950), having survived the war, emigrated to Israel. There, they were met by, among others, the *esrog* dealer. The Rebbe said, "Thank you for the beautiful *esrogim* you sent me for Sukkos that year." The dealer was surprised. Suddenly a knowing smile dominated his face. It was then that the dealer understood and revealed the singular happenstance.

It turned out that, at the time, the dealer had entrusted to his assistant a special box of perfect *esrogim*, which he intended to sell to some wealthy people. He instructed his assistant to put them aside on a shelf for the customer. The assistant followed out the order. When the time came to present the box to the waiting customer, the assistant brought it out and opened it. Customer and dealer were aghast. All they found were *sukkah esrogim*—an inferior lot. The owner started accusing the worker. "I gave you the *esrogim*—where are they? All I find in the box are these!" Even when the assistant protested his innocence, the owner refused to believe him. For the next five years he had suspected the worker. Now he realized what happened. There had to be a big switch—made through Divine Providence. And, agreed the Rebbe and the dealer, because of that switch many, many Jews in Galicia were able to have an *esrog*.

Sukkos of 1939 passed. No change was discerned in the Rebbe's attitude. Everything was as it should be, as far as he was concerned. That in itself was a tremendous source of inspiration to all the *chasidim*, because everyone knew that the Germans were rapidly approaching, the war was in full swing, and their Rebbe did not show any fear. Nothing could stop their glad song.

Finally came *Shemini Atzeres*. The first night is *hakofos* (circlings), when the *chasidim* circle around the *bimah* (a platform in a *shul*) seven times, singing and dancing with the Torah scrolls in their arms. Earlier that day, the local government announced that there would be one last train out of Belz at midnight going to the Russian border, and after that there would be no more trains. The Belzer Rebbe and his followers also took that in stride.

During *Shemini Atzeres*, every chasidic custom (*minhag*) was observed. Nothing was hurried. Everyone was encouraged to sing and dance along with the Rebbe at *hakofos*, as if the biggest peace in the world were happening. During *hakofos*, the seven *niggunim* were sung, one for each circuit. Part of the Belzer *minhagim*, during *hakofos*, involves singing the prayer of "*Kel Mistater*" ("God Conceals Himself"), which is traditionally sung by *chasidim* during *Shalosh Se'udos*, the Third Meal of *Shabbos*. In Belz, they utilize the prayer, sung as a *niggun*, only at *hakofos*, divided into seven parts. And it seemed so appropriate as they sang their last glad song at their last Sukkos in Belz.

The prayer[8] begins with: "God conceals Himself in the beauty of secrecy, the wisdom hidden from all conception," and ends with: "Those emanations hewn from sapphire, may they illuminate together—bringing my glad song near You, *Hashem*!"

So the *chasidim* and their Rebbe danced and sang with Torah scrolls in their arms. "God conceals Himself," they shouted out, but there was no question they were not abandoned; as they circled the first time, Avroham appeared; on the second turn, Yitzchak danced with them; on the third, Yaakov sang out with the most ecstatic *chasidim* in the *shul*; it was the same in the fourth, when Moshe joined them. During the fifth turn, everyone was in such a triumphant state that they fully expected Dovid Hamelech to show up and personally announce the long-awaited Messiah; instead Aaron pranced into the *shul* and marched proudly with a Torah; during the sixth circle, Yusef strutted forth in song; and, finally, in the seventh circuit King David appeared, waving his arms in unison with everyone else. *Chasidim* laughed, *chasidim* cried. This was a night to remember. The pitch of the dancing and singing carried everyone up to the gates of heaven as they watched another parade of sorts: a parade of prayers. The first Belzer Rebbe, Reb Shalom Rokeach, once told his son Reb Yehoshua: "I cannot explain to you how high and how important *hakofos* on Simchas Torah is, but the one thing I can reveal to you about *hakofos* is that all the prayers, all the *davening* of the entire year, which did not enter heaven, because all the *davening* was not as it should have been, for whatever defect the *davening* may have had, during *hakofos*, at that time all prayers enter heaven." Man's prayer should exceed his grasp—or what's a *hakofos* for! And it was so, beheld by every Belzer *chasid* in that *shul*. Everyone was in tears, having poured out their hearts. They wanted to believe that their glad song had brought about peace and joy; perhaps, they dared to hope, the Messiah would come down to them right then and there and destroy all the Nazi oppressors. They wanted to believe.

After *hakofos*, the *chasidim* put back the few remaining Torah scrolls in the *aron hakodesh* (the Ark). And it is here where the *chasidim* heard the last glad song in Belz: one of the *Tehillim* (Psalms).

This also has its story: Once, there was a very important *chasid* who was called Reb Mordechai Peltz. In his own right he was considered a great man, but he preferred to be a *chasid* of the second and third Belzer Rebbes. On various missions he represented the Belzer Rebbes; once, he was sent to Franz Josef, Emperor of the Austrian-Hungarian Empire. And just as we have in America, when the president of the United States enters the room, the song "Hail to the Chief" is played, there was a melody that was played for Franz Josef when he entered the room. When Mordechai Peltz heard this melody he felt it was not worthy of a flesh-and-blood human king. It was worthy only of *Hashem*—the true king. Memorizing it, he returned to Belz and introduced it to the Rebbe. Since then, this melody became the *niggun*, with proper words from the Psalms— "May the God of Glory Enter the Gates." The Belzer *chasidim* sing this *niggun* as they return the Torahs to the Ark after *hakofos* and on other very special occasions.

Finally, the Rebbe made *Kiddush* just as he did every year at that moment, after which he asked for a second cup of wine and drank it. Although this may seem odd to some Jews, there is a halachic opinion that if a Jew has no meal to follow *Kiddush*, he should drink a second cup of wine, which is enough to give that *Kiddush* validity; the second cup of wine thus serves as a meal.

After *Kiddush*, he told his *gabbai*, "Bring me the clothing of *golus*."

The *gabbai* handed him the clothes. The Rebbe took off his *Yom Tov* clothing, put on his weekday clothes, and told everybody to take a few belongings. "Let us all get on the train," he added.

This *hakofos* had to be the saddest in Belz; nobody, however, would have ever known that, gazing at the faces of the beaming Rebbe and his band of followers.

That night, the Belzers boarded the last train to Russia, to safe areas.

What happened to Belz after they left? In the early 1940s the Nazi persecutions all but wiped out the splendor that was Belz. To destroy the Great Belz Synagogue, the Nazis first bombed it; that failed. Then they tried to burn it down, which was partly successful.[9] Finally, years later, the synagogue was torn down brick by brick. Was this the end of the synagogue? It depended on whom you asked.

Said the first Belzer Rebbe: "When the Messiah will come my *shul* will be transplanted to Jerusalem. And my *shul* will be among the most beautiful *shuls* in Jerusalem. Before the *Kohen Gadol* [High Priest] enters the *beis hamikdosh*, he will stop at twelve *shuls* to meditate and prepare for *davening*, and my *shul* will be one of the *shuls* in which the Messiah and *Kohen Gadol* enter into *Yerusholayim*."

After the destruction of the Belzer *shul*, people asked the Belzer Rebbe Aharon, "What about your grandfather's promise? The *shul* is no longer standing." Said the Rebbe: "Whatever my grandfather says, that's the way it will be. I'm confident that my grandfather's words will be fulfilled."

Again it depended on whom you asked. There was a legend among the Gentiles of Belz, after the Belzer *shul* was destroyed: In the twilight hour, the Gentiles claim they saw an old man with a white beard walking on the grounds of the old synagogue, crying, "Oh my synagogue, O my city, what will be with my synagogue?"

Some *chasidim* maintain that this was the first Belzer Rebbe who built it, mourning over the loss of his *shul*, and that he would stay there on that hallowed ground until his glad song returned.

For years it looked as if that might never happen. During the war years, the Russians overran the Germans and occupied Belz. That saved many Jewish lives. By the hundreds they were deported from Belz to Siberia. At the time they thought this was a great tragedy, but in reality this was exactly what saved their lives. There, they were not persecuted or put to death. They just had to endure the hardships of weather and living conditions. In the end, they came out of Siberia alive and well.

When we last left Shimon Spira he trained out to Russia, to the city of Lemburg. Staying in Russia, he returned briefly to Poland, then to Hungary. Then he fled to Czechoslovakia. There, with the help of Rabbi Meir Gruenberg, Chief Rabbi of Kezmark, Czechoslovakia, he hid in an attic and helped hundreds of other persons flee to safety; later, he lived in the woods. Several times Shimon Spira was caught (on three occasions, thinking his end was at hand, he said a final "*Shema Yisroel*"), but was rescued miraculously. Once, near Budapest, Hungary, he was incarcerated in a detention camp called Tolenzhaz, where many Polish nationals of Jewish faith were put. In fact, today's Belzer Rebbe's father, Rabbi Mordechai Rokeach, was also jailed there,[10] although not necessarily at the same time Spira was detained there. Somehow, Shimon Spira managed to escape from there, and the story goes that there was an underground safe house at number 7 on Kiraly Utca (King Street) in Pest, so Spira took a buggy to number 9 on the same street, to throw off the driver. As soon as the driver disappeared, he knocked on number 7 and told the owner, Reb Moishe Mordechai Glick, that his life was in danger. Within a few minutes, the Gestapo came and knocked on number 9 but couldn't find him. After five and a half years on the lam, Shimon Spira was liberated on the last day of Pesach 1945.

On Simchas Torah 1939, the Belzer Rebbe traveled from Belz to Sokol in Eastern Galicia, where he offered advice and counsel to a distraught and confused European Jewry. Finally he was forced to leave Sokol; he reached Przemysl, Hungary;[11] there he was told that thirty-three members of his family were murdered. When told of the murder of his firstborn son, the Rebbe's only reaction was: "Thank God that I also contributed a sacrifice among the Jewish nation."

In 1942, the Grand Rabbi Aharon Rokeach and his brother Rabbi Mordechai of Bilgorai, Galicia, who joined him in Przemysl, were rescued by Belzer *chasidim* and moved to Budapest. There, they worked tirelessly to warn community leaders of what the Nazis were doing in Poland and to urge them to help Jewish refugees. And finally, in 1944, Grand Rabbi Aharon Rokeach and his brother were rescued miraculously from the killing fields of Europe and delivered to *Eretz Yisroel*. After the war, the Rebbe sent his brother Mordechai on a mission to inspire and cheer the Jewish war survivors. He said to tell them that "whoever survived had two angels protecting him throughout the war."

As long as communism was alive and kicking, no Jew was able to enter Belz. Supposedly there was a secret army base in Belz, which allowed the Russians to deny access to Belz to anyone. It looked as if the wandering Jew would continue to haunt the site of the old *shul* forever.

Meantime, today's Belzer Rebbe, Rabbi Yissachar Dov Rokeach, installed in 1966 as the fifth Belzer Rebbe, proposed that the Belzer *chasidim* build a worldwide Belzer Great Synagogue/*beis hamidrosh* in Kiryat Belz, *Yerusholayim*. In 1984, on the tenth day of *Sivan*, the Belzer Rebbe laid the cornerstone, with a chunk of stone smuggled from the old Belzer *shul*. This magnificent structure, based on the original Great Synagogue in Belz, will have, when completed, 5,000 seats and plenty of standing room. Its ten stories, with 30,000 square yards of floor space, will house the movement's main synagogue and its *beis hamidrosh*, as well as lecture halls, classrooms, archives of European Jewry, a Memorial Hall for Holocaust victims in which *kaddish* will be recited and *mishnayos* (passages from the *Mishnah*) learned in their memories, four *mikvahs*, a Torah library, a *matzoh* factory, and a kitchen and dining hall that can accommodate thousands.

When the Belzer Rebbe started it in 1984, he said, "We are not building something new. We're transferring the *kedushah* [holiness], which was in the old *shul* in Belz, and we're replanting it here." In fact, on the day they started to build the *shul*, the Belzer Rebbe got a telegram from somebody he had sent to pray at the graves of the old Belzer Rebbes for the success and holiness of this *Yerusholayim shul*. It read: "I visited your parents, and all is well." It was signed: *The Bochur*. Truly, *Hashem* had seen to it that the cry of the old man with a white beard, wailing on the old Belzer *shul* site, was heard across the land.

One person did manage to visit Belz: the current Ziditchover Rebbe of Borough Park. He told how he went to Europe and realized how impossible it was to get a visa to Belz. Yet he was determined. At the time he was in Lvov. There he requested a visa to Belz.

"What do you want it for?" "Are you a spy?" "Why didn't you request such a visa before you arrived in Lvov?" The questions were flung in his face like an iron glove.

The Ziditchover would not be put off. He answered logically and kindly. "I didn't ask for a visa before I came here because I knew you would say no. I want to pray at Belz. No, I am not a spy. I'm a descendant of the Belzer dynasty."

"Come," they offered, "let us introduce you to Jewish people here."

"I didn't come here to meet people."

Finally they said, "Let us show you a *shul* here; it'll be of interest to you."

He smiled and said, "There are enough *shuls* in Borough Park where I live. I didn't come to see synagogues in Russia."

The Ziditchover had all the right answers. Finally, he had to promise the Russian officials to write nice things in the Jewish newspapers back home about how helpful the border guards were. He said he would do so—and he kept his word. After a long interrogation, he was issued a visa and the border guards allowed him to visit the grave sites of the Belzer Rebbes. He brought back the first photographs taken of the area since 1939.

Three nights before they started to build the Grand Synagogue in Kiryat Belz, at a *Se'udas Mitzvah*, the Rebbe gathered his *chasidim* and spoke about the new project, so dear to him and all his ancestors. He said, "If all the Jews who perished in the war could speak to us, what would they tell us? They would say: 'Take revenge for our holy blood!' Yet how can we do that? We're not worthy of avenging their blood. Hitler meant not only to decimate the bodies of the Jews, he also meant to eradicate the Jewish religion at all costs. The best way to take revenge is to rebuild the *shul*. We can *and will* fulfill their wish. By rebuilding the *shul* and by building more *yeshivahs*. That is our revenge."

So the Great Synagogue/*beis hamidrosh* in Kiryat Belz was begun. An interesting item: In *Chumash Devorim*, Rashi (Rabbi Shlomo Yitzchoki, 1040–1105, greatest commentator of the Torah and Talmud) quotes the Gemara (*Perek* 33, *Posuk* 12), that when Dovid Hamelech was looking for a site to build the First Temple he picked the highest mountain in Jerusalem. *Hashem* told him no. He should pick the second highest mountain. Why? Because the *posuk* says that the best part of the ox is not the shoulder, but the in-between section, slightly below the shoulders. Thus advised, King David then planned to build the *Beis Hamikdosh* on the second highest mountain.

Today, the Belzer *shul* is being built on the highest mountain of Jerusalem—the very site Dovid Hamelech proposed for the First Temple.

Another very important incident happened on the 7th of *Cheshvan*, in 5749 (1988). The Belzer Rebbe's son Aaron Mordechai Rokeach celebrated his *bar mitzvah*. Appropriately it was held in the raw shell of the new synagogue. In a tremendous *simchah* (celebration of joy), thousands of Jews from all over the world arrived in Kiryat Belz to celebrate the great event. Perhaps it was another case of Divine Providence that, shortly after the *bar mitzvah*, the Rebbe and some of his *chasidim* obtained visas to Belz. The situation in Russia was rapidly changing. On the *yahrzeit* of the Rebbe's grandfather, after whom he was named, on the 22nd of *Cheshvan* 1988, the Rebbe visited the old city of Belz.

Not even a shell of the old Belz synagogue was standing when he arrived there, but it mattered little to the Rebbe. With *tefillin* and *tallis* wrapped around him, he took his place and led the *davening* for *Shacharit* (morning services). For the occasion, there were exactly ten men—a *minyan*.

After that, the Rebbe and his followers went to the graves of the Belzer Rebbes. There, they prayed long as the Rebbe blessed the entire Jewish nation in every manner.

Near twilight, after a long day, they returned to the site of the *shul*. In merit of his ancestors, the Rebbe suddenly started to sing and dance *hakofos*. Forming a circle around him, the *chasidim* also began to dance. No one knew for certain whether the old man of twilight legend danced with them and sang "*Kel Mistater*," but every Jew there, with tears in his eyes and joy in his heart, joined in the singing and dancing. No one knew for certain in the ecstasy of the moment whether they were celebrating the *bar mitzvah* of Aaron Mordechai in Belz or in *Yerusholayim*. Nobody knew for certain whether Avroham, Yitzchak, Yaakov, Moshe, Aaron, Yosef, and Dovid, arm in arm, also toed the dance line, forming a protective outer circle around the Belzer Rebbe and his *chasidim*. But it was as if everybody danced at two weddings!

In the end, we can safely assume that no one was more happy than the Prince of Peace himself, Rabbi Shalom Rokeach. His *shul* lives! His *shul* stands! The glad song was finally brought home!

8

How a Niggun
Came Marching Home

T

he Sanzer Rav[1] couldn't carry a tune, but he was the father
to some of the greatest musical and nonmusical chasidic
dynasties the Jewish people have ever known. Among so
many other things, he was a celebrated halachist (an expert on Jewish law) whose rulings were regarded as law by contem-
porary scholars.

Yet, when he had to, he went to learn from others. Through his
relationship with the Ropshitzer Rebbe,[2] the Sanzer Rebbe acquired
an appreciation of song and melody. Rapidly and wisely he learned
from the Ropshitzer that "through song, the gates of heaven can be
opened. Sadness closes them. The origin of all songs is holy, for
impurity has no song. It is the root of all sadness."

And from this point on, our story[3] about the Sanzer Rebbe
begins.

A profound lover of holy music, Reb Chaim's *Shabbos* services
and *tischen* (chasidic get-togethers) were punctuated and defined by
glorious songs. One man, the Rebbe's *baal-tefillah,* a sort of choir-

51

master and leader of prayer who stands at the pulpit in the synagogue, was responsible for such compositions. It was amazing, considering all the work he had to do during the week, that he came up time and again with a new *niggun* for the part of the Friday night service called "*Kabbolas Shabbos.*"

Ever appreciative of his *baal-tefillah*'s compositions, at the end of the service the Sanzer Rebbe always profusely thanked him.

One time, the *baal-tefillah* was extremely busy and forgot to compose a *niggun*. By Friday morning, he was in a panic. What to do, what to do? Then an idea came to him.

Near Sanz was a military camp, and each day an Austrian brigade's band practiced in marching form and music. Determined, the *baal-tefillah* went as near to the military fence as he could, put his ear to the wall and listened; he was not disappointed. He heard a melody he'd never heard before. Aha, this would do perfectly! he told himself as he ran off with the melody in the pocket of his head.

By *Shabbos* night he had turned the military march into a rousing *niggun*. And after "*Lechoh Dodi*," he opened wide his mouth and out came the new *niggun*. Naturally, everyone, including Reb Chaim, was enthralled. The *baal-tefillah* had every reason to be pleased, but he was not. In fact, he was terrified that his Rebbe might discover where he got the *niggun*. He might be criticized severely, perhaps even let go from his job. No, he mustn't let his Rebbe know the truth. He must exit the *shul* as soon as possible and let the whole incident die down.

But Sanz wasn't a big city where he might disappear for a few days. Sanz was relatively small, and where could he hide, when almost half the population was Jewish (in 1880, 5,163 Jews lived in Sanz)? Then, too, he was obligated to show up at his Rebbe's *tisch* that night. So, expecting the worst, he went to tell the Sanzer Rebbe the truth.

As soon as the Sanzer Rebbe saw his composer, he effusively praised his new work.

"But Rebbe, I am not worthy of your praise. That song was taken from the *goyim*. Yesterday I overheard an Austrian military band practicing this tune and I adapted it into a *niggun*. It was that or nothing. I knew how much you love new *niggunim*. Forgive me, Rebbe."

"Forgive you?" laughed the Sanzer Rebbe. "Do you know what you sang, what you thought you stole from the *goyim*?"

"No," the *baal-tefillah* said hesitatingly.

"In the Temple, the Levites used to sing beautiful songs in conjunction with the sacrificial practices of the *kohanim* [priests]. Do you know why they sang such beautiful songs?" the Rebbe asked rhetorically. "What was their purpose? Let me tell you. Once a Jew—a big sinner—came to the Temple and wanted to repent of all his sins. To do that, he had been told by the *kohanim* to make a *korban* [sacrifice]. So the big sinner arrived at the designated time with his sacrifice.

"The *kohanim* accepted his *korban*. Seeing this, the Levites, as part of the divine ritual, began to sing very sad music, the kind of music that would break any Jew's heart. The big sinner wept; he couldn't stop crying, his tears falling unabashedly from his face. The Levites sang—no, they themselves were weeping, for this Jew, for all Jews who stray from *Hashem*.

"The sinner well knew how deeply and how long he had sinned; yet he was repentant. Would it be enough to make one sacrifice? the sinner wondered. The Levites, with their sad songs, were helping— surely he had to believe that. With each tear that flowed, he felt a little piece of evil leave him. More tears, more cleansing. As it is written," said the Rebbe, "'O that my head were waters, mine eyes a fountain of tears!'

"And there came that moment when the big sinner was no more sinner; all his tears had dried up. Seeing this, the Levites sang a beautiful march. A beautiful march," repeated the Rebbe to his *baal-tefillah*.

"Excited, the *baal-tefillah* said, 'Rebbe, was it the one I just sang? Are you trying to tell me that the *niggun* I sang tonight is a Levite song?'

"Dear friend, singer of such beautiful songs. Hear these words well: '*Makdish zain a niggun*' ('Making a song holy'). This very night you have done this. It is a Jew's privilege to take secular melodies from foreign cultures and incorporate them into the body of chasidic song. Why? Because this *niggun* you sang never belonged to the *goyim*. It's ours; it always has been ours. For when the Temple was destroyed, when we Jews went into Exile, so did our *niggunim*. Thanks to you, we have reclaimed one of our very own."

And that is how a *niggun* came marching home.

9

Bam, Bam, Bam

For most armchair Jewish generals today, the strong-arm battles and heated words between the eighteenth- and nineteenth-century *misnagdim*[1] (opponents of the then upstart *chasidim*) and *chasidim* (the upstarts) make for colorful Jewish history and a conviction that they were—and are—on the winning side. But that was not the case in those days.

Imagine for a moment that you're living in September 1796, in the month of *Elul*, and you receive the following epistle—a Jewish New Year's message?—from none other than the greatest Torah scholar of his—and your—generation, Rabbi Elijah Gaon, the Vilna Gaon:

> Ye mountains of Israel—cried the great zealot—ye spiritual shepherds, and ye lay leaders of every government, also ye, the heads of the Kahals of Moghilev, Polotzk, Zhitomir, Vinnitza, and Kamenetz-Podolsk, you hold in your hands a hammer wherewith you may shatter the plotters of evil, the enemies of light, the foes

of the [Jewish] people. Woe unto this generation! They [the *chasidim*] violate the Law, distort our teachings, and set up a new covenant; they lay snares in the house of the Lord and give a perverted exposition of the tenets of our faith. It behooves us to avenge the Law of the Lord, it behooves us to punish these madmen before the whole world, for their own improvement. Let none have pity on them and grant them shelter! . . . Gird yourselves with zeal in the name of the Lord![2]

Strong fighting words!

If you were a Jewish "soldier" from Lithuania, White Russia, Volhynia, or Podolia, you were waiting for just this kind of letter to join in the fray with other *misnagdim* against the late Baal Shem Tov's followers. In Jews the call to arms brought out the best and the worst of times.

As time went on, as any chasidic armchair general knows today, most *misnagdim* laid down their arms, realizing the *chasidim* had become one of the greatest forces for spreading *Yiddishkeit*, furtherance of Jewish education, and for hastening the arrival of the Messiah.

Along the way all this happened also, over 100 years ago, to a former *misnaged* known as the Sanzer Rav (Rabbi Chaim Halberstam,[3] a Galiciana rabbi of note, deeply involved in the *mitzvah* of *tzedakah*, giving with an open hand from his own funds and soliciting from others as well) who saw the chasidic light. His wife, among other great *mitzvos*, bore the eventual Rebbe of Shinov,[4] the father of the first Rebbe of Stropkova, and as the story goes, he begat the second Stropkover Rebbe, who in turn begat grandchildren who lived in the 1940s and 1950s in Williamsburg, Brooklyn, NY. By then, fortunately, there were no *misnagdim* living in the family, so the family communication was an exchange of handed-down Jewish traditions, culture, and *Chasidus*.

One such handed-down story was given to Rabbi Akiva Greenberg, a *chasid* of the Vizhnitzer Rebbe[5] who had spent time in Williamsburg in the late forties and personally knew two of the grandsons of the Stropkover Rebbe.

Rabbi Akiva: "One day the Shinover Rebbe was sitting and humming to himself when the Sanzer Rav happened to walk by. Suddenly, he stopped to listen. After his son finished the tune, the Sanzer Rav asked him, 'Where did you learn that *niggun*?' The Shinover said, 'Father, I don't know. It came to me like that.' Excitedly, the father said, 'My son, my son, this *niggun* is the very *niggun* sung by the angels, and it is going to be sung by the Jews when they go out to meet the Messiah.'

"And from then on," Reb Akiva added, "that *niggun* became known among the sons of *chasidim* as 'The Stropkover Rebbe's *Moshiach Niggun.*' It's been sung in many ways, some fast, some slow, and before I say another word I'll sing it for you the way I learned it."

Out of Reb Akiva's mouth came exactly 280 "bams," the only syllable used in the slow, stately processional march.

"Always a rebbe's *niggun* is highly subjective," said the rabbi, after he himself sang the wordless melody. "A *niggun* is a song of the soul. Everybody's soul is different, has a different experience, a different reason for being, and is affected in a different way. For me the significance of this *niggun*—I can see in my mind's eye right now—are the hordes of Jews—*Tzivos Hashem*, if you will—marching out to greet the Messiah and saying, 'We're awfully glad you came, but why oh why did it take you so long to get here?' Bam, bam, bam—to greet *Moshiach*—with a little bit of complaint: That's the Jewish way!"

Bam, bam, bam, he's right.

10

The Rizhiner Connection

Before you enter the palace, outside you notice the owner's splendid horse-drawn coach with silver buckles on the four horses. Once you alight from your own simple, one-horse-drawn carriage, the staff of servants greets you as if you are a royal personage. Inside the palace you can hear an orchestra warming up. Your eyes take in everything, yet there's not a bone of envy in your body. After all, the rabbis of Rizhin are virtually the exilarchs of Chasidism, and this is the "home" of the Rizhiner Rebbe, Rabbi Yisrael Friedman of Rizhin (1797–1850), who dresses with elegance and lives in the style that befits descendants of the House of David. One of the most beloved rebbes of all time, and one of the humblest, his door is always open to all Jews.

When the Rizhiner finally greets you, he downplays his royal trappings. "What can I do?" asks the Rebbe. "It's not my choice. I am forced from above to take the road of honor and glory, and it is impossible for me to deviate from it."

There's no doubt in your mind that what he said to you is true.

The Rebbe's motive for the ostentatious display of wealth, as you well know, is to raise the standards of Torah and *Chasidus*. He derives no personal enjoyment from it. It's been said he often fasts, walks on hard peas that he placed inside his elegant leather shoes, and sleeps only a few hours each night.

In private, you learn more about this dedicated holy man. The Rizhiner tells you: "Coarse trades are held in contempt. A tinsmith is little esteemed, and a bricklayer less, for they handle lowly substances. How do matters stand with me? What is coarser than a clod averse to spiritual elevation? And yet do I not work with this material, for the greater glory of God?"[1]

A very definite man, the Rizhiner Rebbe began drawing lines in the sand as a youngster. Once, he dug himself a small garden in which to play. Seeing him busy at work, his elder brother Reb Avroham reminded him: "*Shabbos* will be starting soon." The child looked upward and said: "You're right." "And how do you know that?" asked his brother. "Why," said the youngster, "can't you see how the heavens are changing?"[2]

Another time, the youngster was walking up and down in the yard on a Friday toward sundown; by then, most of the *chasidim* were in *shul*. A *chasid* approached him to say: "Why don't you go in? *Shabbos* has already begun."

"It has not," he replied.

"How do you know that?" asked the *chasid*.

"Because on *Shabbos*," he answered, "there always appears a new Heaven, and I can't see any sign of it yet."

The Rizhiner's ability to draw *chasidim* to him was legendary, and there were times, taking a lesson from his early life, when he had to draw a line when confronted with phony kinds of characters. In your travels from Buchacz, you must have heard about the time a young man came to the Rizhiner and asked to be ordained as a rav. The Rizhiner inquired regarding his daily conduct, and the candidate replied: "I always dress in white; I drink only water; I place tacks in my shoes for self-mortification; I roll naked in the snow; and I order the synagogue caretaker to give me forty stripes daily on my bare back."

Just then a white horse entered the courtyard, drank water, and began rolling in the snow.

"Observe," said the Rizhiner. "This creature is white; it drinks only water; it has nails in its shoes; it rolls in the snow, and it receives more than forty stripes a day. Still it is nothing but a horse."[3]

And surely you heard the story about the *chasid* who complained to the Rizhiner Rebbe that his son-in-law didn't *daven* or learn, nor did he go to the *mikvah* (ritual bath for purification) as all the other *chasidim* did. The Rizhiner asked him, "What does he do during that time?" The *chasid* said, "He walks around and sings to himself one of your *niggunim.*" "If that's the case," the Rebbe then said, "you should know that my *niggunim* purifies him just like a *mikvah.*"

But you the visitor are not seeking that kind of meeting. You come in earnest. On a business trip from your hometown of Buchacz to Russia, you arrived in Rizhin just as the High Holy Days approach. So you decide to visit the Rizhiner Rebbe. In response, he offers you to stay in his palace. That night you hear many things from the lips of this rebbe, things that you will bring back to your rebbe and your fellow *chasidim.*

For one thing, the Rizhiner declares that *Chasidus* demands not only nobility of spirit, but also nobility of dress and manners. He wishes to emphasize not only the duties of man to God, but also the duties of man to man. He cites the following parable: A man walked on a country road one moonless night. From time to time flashes of lightning illumined the path. Once when he looked toward the sky to observe how the flash split the heavens, he fell into a pit. He climbed out with difficulty and henceforth resolved to avail himself of the light from the flashes in order to see the road clearly.

"Chasidism," adds the Rizhiner, "is a flash of lightning in a dark universe. Avail yourself of it in order to walk through this world without disaster."[4]

Then something unexpected happens. On Yom Kippur, as the Rebbe is sitting in his place in *shul* and concentrating on *teshuvah* (repentance), he breaks out into a *niggun*, which you immediately recognize. Yet you're struck by his singing of it. How does the Rizhiner knows this *niggun* that your rebbe, the Buchaczer, sings in the company of his *chasidim*? And how is that the Rizhiner should suddenly sing this *niggun* on the holy day of Yom Kippur, with such *deveikus* (ecstatic state of cleaving to the Creator) and with such sweetness of *kedushah* (sanctity)?

Hearing it from the Rizhiner's lips, it's as if your own rebbe is singing. Immediately you are transported back to Buchacz, during *Shabbos Se'udos* (the third meal of the Sabbath). In front of you, Rabbi Avraham Dovid of Buchacz (the *Baal Daas Kedoshim*, 1771–1841) is preparing to discourse on the Torah. As is his custom, before he begins to recite a *divrei Torah* (a formal or informal discussion of

Torah subjects) the Buchaczer Rebbe sings a song—"*Shabbos Hayom lahashem*" ("Today is the Sabbath for *Hashem*"), whose special melody has been known only to the members of his family. In a *niggun* filled with *deveikus* and *hispashtus hagashmiyus* (the state of losing all sense of physical being and reaching an elevated spiritual state), he alternates this unforgettable melody between discourses. To prolong the sweetness of *Shabbos*, your rebbe and his *chasidim* stay up very late into the night. During that time, he is afraid of losing one minute of the prolonged *Shabbos*, so, well aware of the shortness of summer nights, he has his *chasidim* shutter all the windows of the *shul*, to bar any early morning bright light from disturbing the *Shabbos*. The song goes on, the Sabbath goes on, and . . . and here in Rizhin the Rizhiner is singing his rebbe's song. How is that possible?

The next day you cannot contain your curiosity any longer and you ask the Rizhiner how he knows this particular *niggun*. The Rizhiner opens his eyes wide and says, "Are you surprised? This is the song that Yaakov Avinu sang as he was herding his sheep."

That answers suffices for you now. But when you return to your own rebbe and tell him exactly what the Rizhiner told you, the Buchaczer nods, his face aglow with insight.

Says the Buchaczer Rebbe: "Well, what do you expect? The Rizhiner's name is Yisroel; Yisroel is also the *neshomah* [the Jewish soul] of Yaakov Avinu. It makes all the sense in the world that, being he too is the *neshomah* of Yisroel, the Rizhiner Rebbe perforce has to know what this *niggun* is."

Many other things are said of the Rizhiner Rebbe. *Chasidim* believe that the soul of the Baal Shem Tov, who once said, "My soul will return to earth after forty years," found a second home in Rizhin. Besides being the great-grandson of the *Maggid* of Mezeritch (who succeeded the Besht after he passed away in 1760), he was the father of the chasidic dynasties of Sadagora, Chortkov, Boyan, and others, all of which are keeping alive the Rizhiner tradition today with large *yeshivahs* and chasidic centers in *Eretz Yisroel* and the United States.

So, every *Shabbos*, as you continue to sing "*Shabbos Hayom lahashem*" along with your rebbe and the other *chasidim*, you close the *shul*'s shutters and open your heart and mind. *Shabbos* connects all Jews. You have a long history. You have a long soul. You have a long memory. One thing you'll never forget is the time the Rizhiner sang that *niggun* in your presence.

Why? Because the Rizhiner also said: "Return, O *Yisroel*, to the Lord your God!" (Hosea 14:2). Was he admonishing *kelal Yisroel*? No, he was addressing himself; now you know. "You, *Yisroel*," the Rizhiner repeated the phrase, "You, *Yisroel*, return; return to the Lord your God."[5]

Living in royalty or imprisoned for a time, the Rizhiner had his own humble way of drawing another line in the sand. What more can we ask of a rebbe who gave so much to us in prayer and song!

11

David without the Slingshot

Young David[1] stood there—no slingshot in hand—ready to stand up or die for his Jewish faith; in those last sweet moments that ran the course of his young life, he sang—in the face of the Nazi commandant of Plaszow concentration camp, who was about to have him shot!

Once, there was another David who stood toe to toe with his Goliath, and death was no less proud then. Now it was this David's turn, although there was no certainty he'd live beyond the end of his song. Yet he began. His quivering lips opened, a bird of song flew out, and David was placed safely on the wings of the Divine Presence: "*Keil Molei Rachamim . . .*" It begins . . . "O God, full of mercy, Who dwells on high, grant proper rest on the wings of the Divine Presence. . . ."

It is here that the mind pauses and takes it all in, leaving behind for those stunned moments a terrifying Nazi captain whose gun at his side had the power to separate young David from life, but who now hesitated because of the song.

And so David's young soul was carried aloft, to the world of Yechiel Michel of Zlotchov, whom the Baal Shem Tov described as having "access to the treasure-houses of heaven, where he acquires the most beautiful tunes"; to the world of Shneur Zalman of Liadi, who once said: "Three things I have learnt at Mezeritch: what God is, what Jews are, and what a *niggun* is"; and, finally, to the world of David's own father's rabbi, the Gerrer Rebbe, Rabbi Avroham Mordechai, whose words floated before David: In response to a young man who said, "The *Gemara* says 'He who sees no dream in the course of seven days' sleep is called a wicked man.' Now I haven't had a dream for months!" the Gerrer Rebbe replied, "So who says you have to serve your Creator in your dreams? Serve Him while you're awake!"[2]

Ever since he could remember, David had been serving *Hashem* every waking hour. Right from the start, he had been born into a family of singers named Werdyger of Lodz, Poland, in the year 1924, welcomed by all his Jewish neighbors in Cracow, where his parents had moved to be closer to several of David's older brothers and sisters who had recently married and settled there.

Not far from Warsaw and Cracow was the small town of Ger. Young David had heard all about it from his father. Ger was the seat of one of the greatest chasidic rabbinic dynasties in recent Jewish history. Whenever he and his father could, they repaired for *Shabbos* to Ger, host to literally thousands of Orthodox *chasidim* from all parts of Europe. Even at the ages of four, five, six, and seven, he appreciated the seemingly endless *niggunim*, mostly wordless songs, sung by the famous choir in the Gerrer beis hamidrosh, led by Rabbi Yankel Talmud. David may not have known, or appreciated, it at the time, but Rabbi Talmud, like David, had been a child prodigy; he sang under the direction of the well-known Yisroel Moshe Eckstein and Kalman Yoneh. In time, David would come to know a great deal about this man. One of the things he learned was that while he was still a young man, Rabbi Talmud became independently famous as a choir leader and composer. Thousands of *chasidim*, upon leaving Ger, took along with them to all parts of the world many of the new melodies composed by Rabbi Talmud[3]—an impressive total of more than 1,500. David, too, flew away from Ger like a very young songbird.

Who could have known that, in 1931, seven years after David's birth, Rabbi Talmud would pay a visit to Cracow. The first time he saw and heard David was when he was praying at the local Gerrer *shtibel* (house of worship and study). At that very moment the wings of the Divine Presence lit upon him, and he was so taken with David's voice that all he could do was praise him profusely to the beaming father, who took it all in, but who, perhaps, anticipated something else not yet said from the famous choirmaster. Whatever it was, it was left unsaid. Nor could it be divulged after *Shabbos* dinner, when David sang at *zemiros* (songs sung after *benching*).

"In those days," said Cantor David Werdyger, "I had a beautiful soprano [alto] voice, and I eagerly looked forward every *Shabbos* to sing at *shul* and at *zemiros*. No doubt nothing's lost or overlooked in Heaven: Rabbi Talmud and I, a mere boy of seven, wound up at the same *Shabbos* dinner table together, among the other guests, including my father. Singing along with the other guests, I could see that this man, who had spoken earlier to my father and me at *shul*, was no ordinary listener to my voice; not content to follow every note or intonation, nor concerned with conventional beauty of sound, Rabbi Talmud seemed, as I look back at him now, to reflect a tension of feelings, a desire for an innermost experience. Who knew what was in this great music man—a joyful heart, a devoted soul yearning for our Father in Heaven, a breath of the heart in ecstasy! Probably all of them!"

But David and his father soon found out. On *motzoei Shabbos* Rabbi Talmud arrived at the Werdygers' house and persuaded the father to let his son sing in the Gerrer choir for the High Holidays. In a choir of thirty magnificent voices, David Werdyger became a boy soloist, and an instant hit. It was the beginning of a career that took him for further voice studies to Poland, Italy, Austria, and Paris, where, in developing a unique blending of musical virtuosity with the heart, the *krechtz* of chasidic warmth and feeling, he achieved great recognition as an outstanding *helden* (dramatic) tenor.

Then came 1939. The Germans invaded Poland, in the month of *Elul*. From the start of that first day of war, Cracow was almost a ghost town, Werdyger said. People were too afraid to go out, terrified that the German planes would bomb the *shuls* that they would pray in, and too terrified to stay in their homes lest they die there by bombs. David, impressionable and alert, saw people on *erev Shabbos* running here and there. "If they weren't on their way to *shul* where were they heading? my father asked some of them. Nobody gave straight answers because nobody knew where they were going."

Four days after starting the war, the Germans entered Cracow. "Germans came in," Werdyger remembers, "and shot at anything, living and dead, sacred or not. Chaos and despair were everywhere. No Jew stood a chance of living." This was the same city of Cracow where, centuries ago, nonobservant Jews once held a wedding in a house across the street from the ReMo Synagogue, at the beginning of *Shabbos*, making merry and dancing to unholy music. Seeing this desecration right outside his synagogue, the ReMo Rav, Rabbi Moshe Isserles (1520–1572), warned the wedding party three times not to desecrate the *Shabbos*; they ignored his warnings. Suddenly the house they were in collapsed totally and crushed most of the wedding party to death. Would *Hashem*, David Werdyger wondered, and hoped, now destroy these Nazis who dared to desecrate this *Shabbos?* Any moment his young mind expected that to happen. It happened, but not then. For then, the Germans installed a mayor named Frank, who quickly exiled all Jews from Cracow proper.

Out of fear Jews began to hide. The Werdygers found sanctuary in surrounding towns, first moving thirty miles away hidden by a family in the town of Proszowicz. But soon the order came and, from 1939 to 1942, Polish Jewish families in the countryside were rounded up and put in ghettos. After that, until the war finally ended in 1945, David Werdyger survived eight concentration camps. Along the way he lost track of the fate of his family.

It was in 1943 that David Werdyger sang to save his life. Around Cracow there were several ghettos of Jews, one of them being Plaszow, where the nineteen-year-old David lived. One day a Nazi order was issued: 280 ghetto residents were headed for parts unknown—read "being shot." Not one Jew in Plaszow doubted that.

Herded together early one morning, the 280 Jews, including David Werdyger, awaited their end, kept silent by the armed German soldiers sticking their rifles almost in their faces; yet, who knows, perhaps like millions of Jews who went to their deaths in the black age of Nazi Europe, these Jews, too, marched to a different sound in their hearts and souls—the sounds of "I believe with a perfect faith in the coming of the Messiah; and although he may tarry, I daily wait for his coming."

David Werdyger strongly felt the Messiah was coming at any moment. Suddenly another decree was issued: Forty of the Jews would be held back for labor details, men who had trades: mechanics, electricians, carpenters, blacksmiths, and so forth. The rest of the

240 Jews were doomed: In short shrift they'd be lined up in front of a firing squad and be done with. David, knowing this, had to act fast. Not more than twenty feet from him stood the feared, hard-as-nails commandant of the ghetto, Captain Gett, who was in the process of selecting the forty. At his side was his usual blunt instrument, a thick stick, often used to whip, at other times to bludgeon a person to death.

When David's turn came to face the captain, he blurted out, "I'm a singer, and I have a very trained voice. Maybe you want to hear something?" At first, Gett pushed David along the line with his stick to get to the next victim, but David persisted. Finally, seeing that this scrawny kid wouldn't go away, the captain shouted at him, in German, "Sing what you Jews sing when you prepare fresh Jewish graves."

"*Keil Molei Rachamim,*" that's what the Nazi commandant was asking for. And David had to sing it, and sing he did—"O God, full of mercy, Who dwells on high, grant proper rest . . . in remembrance of their souls . . . may the Master of mercy shelter them in the shelter of His wings for eternity"—and his words gained "access to the treasure-houses of heaven" where Yechiel Michel of Zlotchov, and Rabbis Shneur Zalman and Yankel Talmud acquired "the most beautiful tunes" to bring back to the Jewish people. Long before David Werdyger found them in his heart and soul to burst out, the words have been recorded for all time. You can look them up in most *siddurim*, in the section reserved for death and bereavement. But you can never hear again the *niggun* as sung then by David Werdyger, using those words like a kiss of endless love. Like a Jewish soul in human body destined to carry out a lone *mitzvah* on earth and then to return to Heaven, the *niggun* flew back to where it was found. It had done its deed. It is said that when the words "on the wings of the Divine Presence" are used to mean heavenly protection from danger, we say "*tachus,*" meaning "under" the wings. In analogy, a bird spreads its protective wings over its young. In this prayer, where we speak of spiritual elevation, we reverse the analogy, comparing God's presence to a soaring eagle putting its young on top of its wings to carry them aloft.[4] This is how the *niggun* was returned, *on the wing,* and this is how David Werdyger, *under the wing,* was spared. It is also said that the German captain was so stirred by David's moving rendition of "*Keil Molei Rachamim*"—one moment bent on death, another moment yielding life—that he used his stick to let David off with a whack and sent him back to the ghetto. Until we know otherwise, when the Messiah arrives, the rendition of the *niggun*—that was his slingshot—saved the life of young David Werdyger.

After the war, David Werdyger found a brother and sister, both living and newly remarried to Jews of Budapest. In 1946, he himself married a woman from Makow, near Budapest; when she died, he remarried and is living in Brooklyn, New York. In America, he won further acclaim, along with getting a different kind of prod from the late Rabbi J. J. Hecht, who told him, "Cantor Werdyger, if you don't make records, nobody will know about you. You have a wonderful talent. Record your voice!"

In his time, Cantor Werdyger has composed several hundred *niggunim* and has issued about thirty records and cassettes. But the *niggun* that saved his frail young life was the sweetest music he ever sang—even if he cannot recall the melody—for now.

Ah, but when the Messiah comes . . .

12

I Am a Niggun

Somewhere out there is a *niggun* made of flesh and bones, having a Jewish soul, probably joined together at a Friday night *Shabbos* chasidic get-together with other *chasidim* of a rebbe—or perhaps it is the rebbe himself, whose own *niggunim* have the power to open the gates of heaven. If ever a *niggun*—truly one of God's gifts to man—resided in a rebbe, was his divine essence, that person had to be the Vizhnitzer Rebbe, Rabbi Chaim Meir Hager (1888–1972), who was not exaggerating when he once said, "I am a *niggun*."

"I am a *niggun*." Lalalala—lala . . . and his song, once started, went on all night. Once, a holy man was asked why he took so long to pray. He said he took a lot of time to pray to pray. Unlike that *tzadik*, the Vizhnitzer was already in prayer the moment he opened his mouth. "*Shabbos* knows no night," the Vizhnitzer would often say, quoting Rashi in *Masechto Shabbos*—"Friday is considered the night of *Shabbos*. *Shabbos* is completely day, made up entirely of light, life, and purity." Lalalala—lala.

Rabbi Lipa Brenner, a Vizhnitzer *chasid* who attended many such chasidic get-togethers, sets the tone for such a Vizhnitzer *tisch*:

"Suddenly all was quiet. The Rebbe silently made his way through a hastily formed lane, the throng held back by broad-shouldered *chasidim*. He took his place at the head of the table and, with outstretched arms welcoming the *Shabbos*, he began '*Gut Shabbos, gut Shabbos, gut Shabbos, heiliger Shabbos, taiyere Shabbos, shreit shet, Yiddalech, gut Shabbos.*'"

If anything, the *niggun* of the Vizhnitzer was like a symphony. And it had its consummate musicians to perform. One of them was from Galicia of old Poland: the Djikover Rebbe, Rebbe Eliezer Horowitz,[1] well known for his marches. He and his family used to summer in Marienbad and Carlsbad, Czechoslovakia, barely today the same places as they were in the middle of the nineteenth century. Then, it was the custom, nearly up to the First World War, for military bands to march through the streets. They rarely needed a holiday or even a "media event" of any kind to entertain with military marches.

Nearly everyone, no matter what he or she was doing at these twin spas, welcomed the music, for a variety of reasons. The Djikover Rebbe and his court composers and *chasidim* were always on the "hear-out" to cull the melodies of some of these marches and incorporate them into *niggunim*. The idea was to turn the secular into the sacred. Right from the very beginning of *Chasidus*, the Baal Shem Tov[2] preached that we must elevate the mundane to the level of the sacred. As he put it, "Whatever God created has a spark of sanctity in it." Everything thereafter flowed from that.

Rabbi Eliezer Horowitz was the son of Rabbi Naphtali Tzvi Horowitz of Ropshitz,[3] whom many considered one of the wisest of the rebbes. It's said that his demeanor, his sermons, and his witticisms—"I would rather sit next to a wise man in purgatory than next to a fool in paradise"[4]—concealed a depth of thought that could be grasped only by his closest students, foremost among whom was Rabbi Chaim Halberstam of Sanz, the Sanzer Rebbe.[5]

Ropshitz *Chasidus* distinguished itself for the captivating *niggunim* it created, all soul-stirring melodies of ecstasy and yearning for nearness to God. Lipa Brenner tells one story that must not be forgotten, nor must its punch line be lost. A *niggun* for the future, the words of the song concern themselves with a *spodek*, which was a hat that chasidic rebbes of Ropshitz wore during weekdays. Composing the *niggun* in Yiddish, the Ropshitzer sang the praises of the *spodek*, which, he said, "we should hide in a closet, so that we will be able to show our grandchildren that at one time a good Jew wore that many years ago." Why was that important? Clothing styles were changing dramatically, along with many other things. The *spodek* may have been a thing of the past, but the Ropshitzer, using it to make a Jewish connection, wanted to stress that we should try to remember what the previous Jewish generations did and how they lived.

Another "I am a *niggun*" story: Reb Eliezer of Djikov was very sick at one time. He was visited by his grandson's father-in-law, the Sanzer Rebbe, who said to him that he wanted to say farewell because he was told that Reb Eliezer was dying. Reb Eliezer didn't want to hear that. He hoped that the Sanzer Rebbe would bless him for a long life. "I'm not ready to die; in fact," he insisted, "I must live. I want to *daven* Rosh Hashanah and sing the prayer '*Ein Kitzvah*' one more time."

What Reb Eliezer was so adamant on singing was the tune he had composed in the form of a marching *niggun*, set to the prayer "*Ein Kitzvah*," which follows the *kedushah* of *Musaf* of Rosh Hashanah and is understood as heralding the coronation of *Hashem* as King of the Universe.

"There is no limit to Your years and no end to the length of Your days; it is not possible to estimate [the countless angelic hosts of] your glorious Chariot, nor can one explain Your inscrutable Name. Your name befits You and You befit Your name, and You have called our name by Your name."

No, Reb Eliezer told the Sanzer, he wouldn't give up life yet until he sang "*Ein Kitzvah*" at least once more. His mission, he said, was to hear that *niggun* until he became himself the *niggun* in this world. In fact, he lived a number of years after this meeting with the Sanzer Rav and kept on singing that melody until he too became a *niggun*.

Today that prayer "*Ein Kitzvah*" and its applied melodies are central to the Vizhnitzer and Djikover liturgies as part of their Rosh Hashanah and Yom Kippur services.

Reb Eliezer had a son named Meir (1819–1877), and it is he who connected the Djikover Rebbe with the old Vizhnitzer Rebbe, Rabbi Yisroel, who was Meir's son-in-law. When Reb Yisroel was prepared to marry the Djikover's daughter, he asked his father-in-law (the Djikover Rebbe) for one thing as a dowry. Not money. Not books. No, he wanted the Djikover Rebbe's composer, Reb Nisson

Chazzan, to take him from the Djikover court to his own Vizhnitzer court. This composer constantly produced outstanding Vizhnitzer *niggunim*, which were sung at Friday night *tischen.*

So now we come back to the Vizhnitzer Rebbe, Rabbi Chaim Meir Hager, who loved to describe himself as a *niggun* from the tips of his toes to the top of his head. Like the Djikover Rebbe, he too had a passion for marches. During his visit from his home in Bnei Brak, Israel, to Brooklyn, New York, in 1948, his *chasidim* took him one particularly sweltering day to Prospect Park in Brooklyn, NY, for fresh air. And in the park, there was a concert, the Goldman Band conducting—you guessed it—military marches. Carlsbad and Marienbad all over. Who knows how many Sousa melodies were turned into Vizhnitzer *niggunim* after that night!

And now the symphony: Hear the music streaming through Lipa Brenner's words: "Following the soup [at the *tisch*] the Rebbe pauses and then begins the '*Menuchah Vesimchah.*' This is no ordinary tune. It is a symphony. Its composer was the great Reb Nisson Chazzan, who had sung in the court of the Rebbe's father (known as the '*ahavas Yisroel*' after his *sefer*), Reb Yisroel, of blessed memory. The Rebbe sang the first movement. It was repeated by the entire group. He then carefully taught the group the refrain and was gratified by the quick response and some able voices. His pleasure was obvious, for his face shone. But pity the one who went off key! No matter how many people were assembled, his sensitive ear would rebel at a false note and he would pound on the table with his fingers, interrupt the singing, and have the congregation repeat the melody perfectly.

"'*Menuchah Vesimchah*' sometimes took close to twenty minutes by the clock. But who was looking at the clock? We had lost all sense of time, as if transposed into *Gan Eiden*—some *olom habo* [the world to come] beyond space and time. Our joy knew no bounds as we sang and opened our ears to the voice of his singing, for he pierced many ears that were tone deaf and many hearts that were laden with grief and adversity. He taught us how to *daven*, how to chant, how to sing, and we felt closer to him with every note. He blended everyone into one symphony of prayer and song. From hundreds of individuals, drawn from dissimilar backgrounds and temperaments, he welded together one solid group of *chasidim* bent on one purpose: tasting the joys of the *Shabbos.*

"The song completed, we took our leave of him with the same '*Gut Shabbos*' with which he had begun the *tisch.*

"He was now alone, in his own room, and almost everyone had left. Only a few of us lingered, and we listened. Alone, the Rebbe was dancing a *Shabbos* song by himself; he was dancing around his own *tisch* laden with *seferim*, singing aloud to himself. No weariness and no exhaustion marred his *Shabbos*. He sang and danced until the rays of the sun entered his room."

Somewhere out there is a *niggun*, made of flesh and bones, having a Jewish soul, and that *niggun*, which burns with a spark from Reb Chaim Meir Hager, will forever be on the lips of every *chasid* wherever and whenever Vizhnitzers or Djikovers or Sanzers meet. Lalalala—lala!

13

The Story of the Boxes

The boxes couldn't have arrived on a hotter day, a more miserable moment, when it was difficult enough to concentrate on running a big *yeshivah* in Bobov. But the Bobover Rebbe, Rabbi Bentzion Halberstam,[1] took them in stride. It seemed like any other shipment to the *yeshivah*—until he opened one of the boxes and saw its contents. He was shocked. The boxes, filled with anti-Torah literature, had been sent by missionaries from London bent on confusing the minds of Jewish students.

The Rebbe knew what he must do. Immediately he called in his *rosh yeshivah*, Rabbi Mendel Rottenberg, showed him the contents, and said, "Rabbi Mendel, we must begin our task." He asked the *rosh yeshivah* to take the boxes and follow him. Together they left the office, went down a stairway, through several corridors, then outside to a house. Neither man said anything until they reached a fireplace in the house.

Then, without waiting another moment, the Rebbe prepared to

start a big fire in the fireplace, with Rabbi Rottenberg vigorously chopping wood. When the fire was roaring, the Rebbe began throwing one book at a time into the fire. When he finished with one box's contents, he tossed the box, then the wrapping paper, then the string that bound the box—every thing of each box went directly into the fire.

Soon his oldest son, Shlomoh,[2] entered the room and was shocked at the sight he saw. Yet, he did not question his father or the *rosh yeshivah*, then or later. He just took it all in silently.

Finally, his father and the *rosh yeshivah* burned everything to a crisp. For this is what the Torah dictates. Nothing impure must be left—or be allowed to stick to anything holy. Even strands of the wrapping string were gathered together and burned. By the time they finished eliminating the idolatries of a madman's mind, the room was aglow and stifling.

Whatever evil powers were in those boxes were no more. As the Rebbe and his *rosh yeshivah* sang *niggunim*, it was as if they were putting the final nails in the evil, fiery coffin.

Rabbi Bentzion Halberstam was no ordinary Torah scholar and teacher. He was born in 1874 in Bikovsk, a town in western Galicia, where his father Rabbi Shlomoh (1847–1906) was rabbi. Rabbi Shlomoh lived first in Vizhnitz, near Cracow, and then in 1893 he settled in Bobov, where he became the founder of the great Bobover dynasty. When he passed away on 1 *Tammuz*, 1906, his son, Rabbi Bentzion Halberstam, succeeded him as the Bobover Rebbe. Establishing a *yeshivah* there, the Rebbe based his lifestyle on Torah, *avodah*, and the practice of charity. To counteract the secular spirit of the interwar years (World War I and World War II), the Rebbe established and maintained *yeshivahs* in which he forbade the reading of secular or heretical literature. Yet he urged his students not to be ascetic, for, as he put it, "asceticism weakens the body and enables the evil powers to dominate."

An extraordinary singer, it's been said[3] that when Rabbi Bentzion Halberstam sang "By the Rivers of Babylon," Cantor Yossele Rosenblatt (1882–1935) exclaimed, "Without *ruach hakodesh* [prophecy] it is impossible to compose such a melody." Even Rabbi Bentzion Halberstam's own father, Rabbi Shlomoh, was moved to say, "If a Jew can pray like this before his Maker, we cannot stop him. He literally pours out his soul before his Creator."

It seemed inevitable, then, that Rabbi Bentzion Halberstam introduced on the following *Shabbos* a *niggun* based on the entire *"Shemoneh Esrei."* A long song, *"Yismach Moshe"* ("Moses Rejoiced") recounts how "Moses rejoiced in the gift of his portion that You called him a faithful servant. A crown of splendor You placed on his head when he stood before You on Mount Sinai. He brought down two tablets in his hand, on which is inscribed the observance of the Sabbath. So it is written in the Torah."

Later, the Rebbe explained to his *chasidim* why he made such a *niggun*. Telling them the story of the boxes, he cautioned his students to be on guard against *goyishe* souls who have tried for thousands of years to taint the *neshomahs* (Jewish souls) of the Jews in any way they could. "We have to strengthen our holy side, counterbalancing the *yeitzer hora* [evil inclination]."

In composing this song, the Rebbe wanted not only to protect his students, but also to guarantee to keep them forever in holy ways. For, truth to tell, this Rebbe knew something the *yeitzer hora* didn't know.

He was keenly aware of how often the *yeitzer hora* came to him and other Jews to distract them from praying. But for some reason, songs tricked the *yeitzer hora*. When he saw a Jew pray, he'd say "Aha!" and then proceed to distract the Jew from his *siddur* (prayer book). But when the evil inclination saw a Jew singing, he'd say to himself, "Why waste my time! Let me go bother someone else who's praying."

This is what Rabbi Bentzion Halberstam knew: Never once does the *yeitzer hora* realize that a *niggun* reaches a higher plane of praying.[4]

So Rabbi Bentzion Halberstam of Bobov composed a *niggun* on the words of *"Shemoneh Esrei"* to fool the *yeitzer hora*—no matter how many impure boxes he sends.

On the 4th day of *Av*, July 25, 1941—"Black Friday"—the Nazis murdered Rabbi Bentzion Halberstam and most of his family, along with 2,000 other Jews rounded up to die. Dressed in his silk *Shabbos kapote* (long coat) and his *shtraimel* (fur hat), the Rebbe, disregarding those who tried to get him to escape, marched to his death in a dignified manner. "One does not run away from the sounds of the Messiah's footsteps," he said. The Jews were taken to the outskirts of Lvov, compelled to dig their own graves, and brutally murdered by the Nazis and their Ukrainian collaborators.

Yet, during the Holocaust, there was a Bobover who survived, a man destined to restore Bobov to heights far beyond anything yet achieved. He was Rabbi Shlomoh, named after his grandfather, the third generation of Halberstams to be raised to the position of Bobover Rebbe. And it was he who watched his father way back then burn the boxes of sacrilegious books, and he remembered how strongly his father had forbidden the reading of secular or heretical literature in his *yeshivah*. In reviving the spirit of Bobov in New York, and in 1958 laying the foundation of Kiryat Bobov in Bat-Yam, Israel, he learned the lessons of the boxes well.

Several years after World War II, Rabbi Shlomoh, the Grand Rabbi of Bobov, was asked to visit a school in Williamsburg, Brooklyn, by a prominent *rosh yeshivah* of the area. This was no ordinary request, the Rebbe found out. The students, all Holocaust survivors with no or little family, were diligent students, but they had the *yeitzer hora* on their back, too. Movies were the big thing in those days, and often the cinemas were crowded with *yeshivah bochurim* after school. The *rosh yeshivah* was beside himself. "Help, please, Rabbi Halberstam! Maybe you can say a few words to the boys to get them back on the right track," pleaded the principal. Of course, the Rebbe, who remembered his father and the boxes, readily agreed to do something.

On the day of the visit, the *yeshivah* students were agog that the Bobover Rebbe himself was going to visit them. They had heard so much about this man of words and song. How, throughout the Holocaust, Rabbi Shlomoh Halberstam, though forbidden by penalty of death, gave spiritual comfort to his Jewish brethren. How he lived a double life, using forged papers to secure a position as an overseer in a concentration camp to rescue hundreds of doomed Jews from the jaws of the Gestapo. How he was arrested, sentenced to death, and saved only because his compatriots were able to bribe the Nazi officials. How, disregarding personal safety, he immediately returned to his perilous efforts to save the lives of Jewish children. How he planned and helped design undetectable bunkers that saved the lives of hundreds. And how, through the years, as he fled across war-torn Poland until at the end of the war he wound up in Bucharest, like a Daniel in the lion's den, Rabbi Shlomoh Halberstam emerged from the Holocaust with his faith in God and His Torah stronger, and his determination to rebuild unshakable.

So this was the rebbe who now faced an audience who knew much about him. He was a holy man they wanted to listen to. And when he came out on the stage and took a seat, he brought out a Bobover *chasid* named Yiddle Turner. Perhaps not too many *bochurim* of that *yeshivah* had heard of him and his violin as yet, but they would, surely they would, from the moment he played for them.

Everybody loves a story, and these boys were no different. The Rebbe began. One story after another, about simple Jews, about *tzadikim*. And when he finished telling stories, the Rebbe said he wanted to teach them a song.

"A song that my father composed," he announced. "My father, Rabbi Bentzion Halberstam, of blessed memory, had a beautiful voice. He composed hundreds of songs. And he composed a song from the Book of Proverbs."

And as the Bobover Rebbe sang the words in Hebrew, Yiddle Turner played his violin. In English the words are: "My son, do not walk in their ways; restrain your foot from their path; for their feet run to evil. . . ."

Over and over the Rebbe sang these words and sobs could be heard all over the auditorium. It was a song that fit the life of every student in that room, and they knew it, and were deeply affected. "My son, do not walk in their ways; restrain your foot from their path."

After ten minutes, the Rebbe stopped singing. In parting, he told the audience of boys and teachers, "I hope the strength from this song will help you."

From then on, this song became that school's anthem. Years later, there were *bochurim* from that *yeshivah* who met the Bobover Rebbe in Israel and told him how much they were inspired from this song, how it changed the entire school, how it dissuaded every *bochur* from going to the movies or watching TV. As one *bochur* put it, "That song became embedded in my soul. As the years went by, its words kept ringing louder and louder in my ears. 'My son, do not walk in their ways; restrain your foot from their path; for their feet run to evil.'"

About the other *yeshivah* students: They grew up in holy ways, married and had children, and, who knows, at this very moment they may be teaching their own students this song. That's what a *niggun* is for.

Once there were two smart-alecky brothers, Jewish, of course, and young, breezing through their lives and studies at a local *yeshivah* in Vienna. They got wind of the visit by the Bobover Rebbe, Rabbi Bentzion Halberstam, to their city, in the mid-1920s. Perhaps out of curiosity or perhaps they couldn't understand why a rabbi spent so much time singing instead of praying, they decided as a lark to get on the visiting line to greet him.

Dressed in modern fashion, the brothers waited their turn. When finally they came face-to-face with the Bobover Rebbe, he asked one of them, "Do you know how to sing?" The lad laughingly said yes, he knew how to sing. This seemed to please the Rebbe, who asked them to step aside, near him, as he wished to speak to them further.

After he greeted everyone, he called over his *gabbai* (secretary), Rabbi Heshkel Rottenberg, and he told him to teach the lad and his friend his *niggun*, "*Kah Ribon.*"

> O Creator, Master of this world and all worlds,
> You are the King who reigns over kings
> Your powerful and wondrous deeds
> It is beautiful to declare before You. . . .

In instructing his *gabbai*, the Rebbe added: "Teach the *niggun* well, as I'm going to ask them to sing it tomorrow night, in front of all my *chasidim*, at my *tisch.*"

Hearing this, the two smart alecks were stunned, yet happy the Rebbe had chosen them for the honor. Not the least bit disturbed were they that the Rebbe had turned the tables on them, had made them into singers. Young and raring to go, they learned the *niggun* well and sang it without inhibition at the *tisch Shabbos* night. Of course, no one's perfect; so when they finished singing, the Rebbe himself corrected them until he felt they had it down pat.

Then the two lads, in modern dress, left and nobody heard anymore about them for many years.

On a rainy day, somewhere in Tel Aviv, about 1976, a Bobover *chasid* by the name of Naphtali Benyomin Eckstein went out to pray in a *shul* of his choice, but never got there. The driving rain drove him into a nearby modern temple.

As things happen to newcomers in a synagogue, he was asked to make an *aliyah*. Approaching the *bimah*, from where the open

Torah is read, he said the ritual prayers. Then he made a *berochah* for the Bobover Rebbe.

Hearing this, a long-white-bearded man, the *gabbai* of the *shul*, approached him and asked him if he were a Bobover *chasid*. The *chasid* replied yes. Happy to hear this, the *gabbai* invited him to stay for *Kiddush*.

After *Kiddush*, two men with long white beards, one obviously the *gabbai*, sang the *niggun*, "*Kah Ribon*"—"O Creator, Master of this world and all worlds . . ."

Completely taken aback, the *chasid* rushed up to them and asked how they knew that song. "It is one of my Rebbe's [the current Bobover Rebbe, Rabbi Shlomoh Halberstam, *shlita*] favorites," the *chasid* said.

One of the men, stroking his long beard, said, "We once met your Rebbe's father, of blessed memory. Of course we were young then; happy-go-lucky brothers; and we came to poke fun at your singing Rebbe. Instead he won us over with a song, that song." Here, both of them laughed, thinking back at those days in Vienna when they thought they knew it all. "He," said one of the brothers, "he turned us into singers. But he did a lot more for us than that. About 1931, we came to Israel, and it wasn't easy being Jewish here. We couldn't find food. We could hardly find jobs. Yet we never worked on *Shabbos*, and there were jobs then. We stayed true to Judaism. Every time we faltered, we reminded ourselves from the song that the Bobover Rebbe, blessed be his memory, taught us that we couldn't work on the *Shabbos*."

In their way, too, the two former smart alecks burned a lot of unholy boxes in their days.

It is said that Rabbi Bentzion Halberstam of Bobov has no tombstone. Nor is his grave site known. But his *niggunim* always seem to reside in the right places: in the souls and hearts of millions of Jews serving the Lord with joy.

14

For the Love of a Niggun

I am at a loss for words!"

"I think, Mr. ————, the confusion will clear up once you hear what I have to say," the Israeli bureaucrat said.

Saying nothing, Mr. ————, seated at the bureaucrat's office desk, gestured to him to go on with what he wanted to say.

"You say you were confronted recently outside Moscow by an old Jew and he gave you a *Megillas Esther* to give to a rabbi?"

"Yes . . . ?"

"There's always a story behind a story[1] and . . ." And with that opening began a tale that was yearning for an ending, one that happened once upon a time, around 1910, in the then Polish town of Modzitz. In those days, Modzitz—also called Demblin (the Polish name) or Ivanogrod (as the Russians called it)—was a thriving Jewish community that attracted Jews from many miles away. Home to the then Rebbe of Modzitz, the first Modzitzer Rebbe, Yisroel Taub (1848–1920), who was known throughout Poland and Russia as one of the most prolific composers of chasidic *niggunim*, it also was home to a Russian-occupied military fortress in Poland, which controlled the strategic waterway of the Vistula, which runs lengthwise north and south through Poland. In its way, the combination of Jewish community and Russian soldiers occupying that little part of Poland worked well, at least for the safety and steadfastness of the Jews and their Rebbe.

Thousands of Jews would come from distant parts to be with their Rebbe on *Shabbos*, and their accommodations would not be found wanting. For a period of twenty-four years, the Rebbe lived in an impressive villa with a *shul* and an open courtyard. In the late spring and summer Modzitzer townsfolk could hear the beautiful, heartfelt voices and songs of the Rebbe and his *chasidim* flowing from the courtyard as they celebrated the Third Meal of *Shabbos*. Often *goyim* would take walks not far from the villa just to catch an earful of the music, and it was not uncommon to hear one of them humming part of a *niggun* in a store or on the street during the week. Was there a particular *niggun* that caught the ear of outsiders? It would be hard to say explicitly because the Modzitzer *rebbeim* had a rich treasury of their own melodies. From one *Shabbos* to another they would sing a variety of different melodies. Of course they had certain *niggunim* that they repeated more often than others; such was the *niggun* "*Benei Heicholo.*"

Could it have been this very *niggun*, dignified and regal as a king and mover of heaven and earth, which was composed around 1887 by Reb Yisroel Taub of Modzitz, that attracted a certain high-ranking Russian officer from the citadel on the Vistula? Of all the men in the Russian army stationed there he was the most likely to be attracted to the Rebbe's music. Why? Because he was the Russian grand orchestra conductor of the fortress, a person always interested in fine music.

Who knows how many weeks or months he mulled it over in his mind before he made his move. Suddenly, one day he decided to hear this music close at hand and began to stroll near the villa on *Shabbos*, coming to a halt near one of its windows just to catch the strains that were by now a common sound on *Shabbos*. Dressed in civilian clothes, to disguise his real identity, he became a fixture for many weeks standing outside the villa on *Shabbos*. If anyone exiting or entering the villa knew his real identity, he didn't let on. To the *chasidim*, he was just another *goy* who couldn't help be attracted to and impressed by the glorious *niggunim* of the Rebbe.

In fact, the Russian officer was not a *goy*, but a Jew. For many years that was his well-guarded secret. Like many other Jewish orphans of that era, he was kidnapped one evening and conscripted into the Russian army for twenty-five years, and now, many years later, had risen to a high rank, which had allowed him a career in music, his only love in life. As a musical conductor, he loved the march, strident, boisterous, proud, defiant—but why did he feel the need to perform it with a certain bitter abrogation? Bitter of what? He had everything he ever needed as a Russian officer. There was nothing he lacked. Already his name was getting known beyond the fortress in polite Russian musical circles, and in his own way he had a number of admirers of his music. Definitely, he had a bright future in Russian music, and in the army. So why was he attired now in civilian clothes, drawn to chasidic music—strange music—haunting music—that spanned the entire gamut of grief and deep concern to extreme joy? Standing outside the Rebbe's villa, he found himself moved as he'd never before been moved, from a meditative mood to ecstatic exaltation, from purposeful melodic construction to words that were songs unto themselves. Was he now in his life having a real desire for an innermost experience? What was it about these songs he was hearing? At times he heard a *chasid* singing, if it could be called that, returning to a stammering childlike language in order to express before God feelings too delicate or too intimate for a conventional verbal statement. Never in his life had he heard anything like it, and he found himself at moments in tears, at a loss for words, without knowing why.

But he knew he had to do something more than stand outside a window forever; he knew he had to go inside the villa, come what may. Perhaps somebody in there could help him in his dilemma. Dilemma? What dilemma! He had no idea what it was. But he knew he had to find out something about himself and that music that reflects the mythical struggle of the entangled "divine spark" in the soul to disengage itself.

Finally he went in. Through a dark passageway he made his way until he reached the courtyard where, he was certain, he would be able to mill about with the crowd of *chasidim* without being noticed. The *chasidim* were in the process of making *havdalah* and at first took no notice of him. But once the courtyard was lit up, the Russian officer could no longer remain in the dark, and several *chasidim* immediately recognized him. One of them alerted the Rebbe, who said he wished to see the Russian officer.

Brought in to the Rebbe's private quarters, the officer revealed his true, military identity. At first, he told the Rebbe that he was highly impressed with some of the music he heard there, but deep into the conversation he finally revealed for the first time that he was a Jew, and his anguish, laying out in harsh detail how he was forced as a child to join the Russian army and how he lost all memories of his Jewish past. "Except," he added, "I have some memory of *alef beis*, I guess, because at an early age I was put in *cheder*."

Reb Yisroel told the officer that one thing he had not lost was his *pintele Yid*, the spark that makes him a Jew.

Pouring out his heart, the officer said, "I know that I am nothing, but I know that I am a Jew. And I know your music has been opening a lot of doors to me. I've been coming to your gates for the past eight weeks, each Sabbath day, and every time I come—until now only outside your gates—it brings me back to my Jewish roots. I don't know how I can face it. I'm supposed to be a Russian. Nobody in the fortress is supposed to know I am a Jew. Rebbe, I really want to know what to do. I truly now want to accept *Yiddishkeit*. I want to return to my ancient religion, my God, my heritage."

Reb Yisroel, who was very taken by his story, told him in effect that he had come to the right place for help. "The gate of song is not only adjacent to the gate of repentance, but is rather one and the same." For starts, the Rebbe suggested that the Russian officer begin his journey back into *Yiddishkeit* by leading a *kosher* life, as best as he could on *Shabbos* in the fortress, becoming *Shomer Shabbos*, and not eating *traif* food. Reb Yisroel said that he would help him as much as he could.

In a short time, the Russian officer, like other Jews earnestly seeking God, realized that the gates of prayer are always open. He successfully managed, without letting on his true self. Slowly his Jewish spark lit up more of his life.

But when it came to Pesach he felt he had an insurmountable problem. Again he consulted Reb Yisroel. This time, the Rebbe told the Russian officer it was time for him to disclose to his superiors in the fortress that he was a Jew, that he had to clean his house according to Jewish laws. This was no easy matter, confessed the officer, but he was prepared to carry out the wishes of the Rebbe. For his part, the Rebbe reassured him that his military superiors would do nothing about it, that they would not interfere in this matter, nor indeed would he be held back in rank.

And that's what happened. As time went on, this Russian officer transformed himself into an observant Jew in the Russian army. It was never easy, but it satisfied the Russian bandleader, as nothing had satisfied him before. Forever he was indebted to this Rebbe who had helped give him back his old life. So it was quite understandable that when the time came for the Rebbe to marry off one of his daughters, the Russian military officer brought the entire military band to the wedding to play for the occasion, for the *mitzvah* and to express his deep gratitude.

"That is more or less the culmination of the story, as I knew it until now," said the bureaucrat.

"This story interests me very much," said Mr. ————.

"Do you know why?" asked the other.

"I'm not sure exactly."

"Then let me explain," the bureaucrat said. "You happened to be walking down a street outside Moscow, you say. Suddenly you're approached by a very old Jew—by your account, at least ninety-five years old. You exchange pleasantries. He tells you he is a Jew. You tell him you're an Israeli delegate on business there. He's happy to meet you, he says, and begins to tell you a story that must have happened a very long time ago because his details are sketchy: something about his growing up Jewish, being conscripted into the Russian army as a young boy, that about seventy-five years ago he lived in Poland, stationed at a Russian fortress near a river. That's about as much as he can remember about the setting. Yet, he tells you, he will never forget the rabbi who was also a very wonderful singer. He used to accompany the conductor of his Russian military band, a good friend of his, to the *Se'udah Shelishis* at the rabbi's villa. Of course, after listening to this story about a man who could offer you very little more, but insisted that you find the rabbi's descendants and give him the *Megillas Esther* he's been carrying all those years, what else could you do but take the scroll and promise you'll do your best to carry out his request? What do you know, Mr. ————? This much: that as an Israeli delegate to the Soviet Union you finish your mission only to be handed another, indeed farfetched, mission by an old man you've never seen before and may never see again. This old man hands you a *Megillah*. He says he has no more use for it, because he expects to die within the year. He hints at this whole story about the rebbe and the Russian officer. Was he the Russian officer? No. He reveals to you that his friend helped him eventually reveal his own *Yiddishkeit* with impunity. 'Now I don't remember the name of the rebbe,' he tells you, 'but I have a *Megillas Esther* I purchased in Poland and if possible since you're going back to Israel, please try to find a descendant of this rebbe and give it to him. It was from this holy man I derived all the pleasures of *Yiddishkeit*. His descendants should have this holy scroll. It's the only thing I have of value to give.'

"Yes, yes," agreed Mr. —————. "So I took the *Megillah*, no more questions asked because the old man was hardly in a position to answer them. And here I am, the scroll in my briefcase. And if what you just told me—your story, my story, they add up to—what?"

"Don't you see, Mr. —————," the bureaucrat said excitedly, "it is my rebbe—the Modzitzer Rebbe. The old man was talking about him. No one else fits that description in all of Poland. The town was Modzitz. It's the only place on the Vistula that had a Russian fortress and a well-known rebbe living in the town at the same time. Mr. —————, you're speaking about my rebbe. I am a *chasid* of his."

So the delegate gave the *Megillas Esther* to the *chasid* and asked him to present it to the present Modzitzer Rebbe, Admur Reb Yisroel Don Taub.

On Purim 5751, two events happened, perhaps not related, perhaps related, but then who really knows! The day before Purim the enemy forces of Iraq were defeated, thereby sparing Israel any significant damage in the Persian Gulf War, and on Purim day, the Modzitzer Rebbe received the old man's *Megillas Esther* in Tel Aviv.

All for the love of a *niggun*.

15

The Mysteries of a Niggun

What mysteries are left?
Let me tell you of one—no, several. Let me tell you what I know.[1] No more, no less. After that I cannot say.

Many Jews have heard some wondrous stories about the first Modzitzer Rebbe, Reb Yisroel Taub (1848–1920), who wrote the classic *sefer, Divrei Yisroel,* and always emphasized the value of music in Chasidism. To this day, some of us still wonder how he underwent a major operation without anesthesia. Such a mystery needs to be cleared up. But first:

"What does *neginah* accomplish?" he used to ask. And he would answer this way: "*Neginah* causes people to do *teshuvah* and brings them closer to *Hashem.* Let me explain this with a *moshol* [parable]:

"A miller once went to the city to buy an alarm clock. While wrapping the alarm clock for the miller, the clock maker ridiculed him: 'How can you use an alarm clock? Your mill makes so much noise and yet you sleep through it all. You'll never hear the ring of the alarm!'

"The miller answered, 'You may be a clock maker, but you don't know human nature. I'm so accustomed to the mill that I can sleep through all the noise it makes. But I'm not used to the alarm clock, so its sound will awaken me.'

"The same applies to *neginah*. Everyone has his regular lifestyle with its sounds and rhythms, but a *niggun* will break him out of his reverie, and can bring him to *teshuvah*."[2]

So beloved was this Reb Yisroel that many of his *chasidim* would probably not have hesitated to lay down their own lives for him. He was at that time suffering with heart trouble and advanced diabetes, so terrifying because there was talk that his leg would have to be amputated. Who knew! No mystery there, said his doctors. It was his leg or his life. But of course he must seek a second opinion, said his doctors. Where? In Berlin. Who? A foremost surgeon, Dr. Israels, said his doctors in Warsaw. When? Now!

So he had to go to Berlin. He had to save his life. There was so much work to continue, Jerusalem had to be rebuilt, the Messiah had to come, the Jews had to prepare the way . . .

And the words came forth from Reb Yisroel—"*Ezkerah Elohim Ve'ehemoyah*"[3] ("God, I remember and I moan when I see every city built on its high pedestal, while . . .").

The year was 1914. Before the Great War. Berlin was still a grand city—it knew how to live, it knew how to paint, it knew how to strut—filled with pomp and circumstances, its boulevards and cafes alive with plenty, a city "built on a high pedestal." When finally he would see Berlin firsthand, on his way to Dr. Israels, he would observe the city's disparity and the barrenness, he would hear the wail of millions of Jews for the City of God, and its *neginah*, the ways of song that went together with the age-old mystical exercises of concentration, fast, contemplation of *kavonah*, and rhythmical movement of the body. To look up to the sky over Berlin was to be reminded of the parable told by the Baal Shem Tov:[4]

> A migratory bird of rare beauty flew past the royal palace and perched itself on the top of a high palm tree. The king desired to own this exquisite creature and instructed his servants to form a human ladder, one to stand on the shoulders of the other until the highest could throw a net upon the bird. Only men of strength were chosen, but one weakened, and the entire human structure

collapsed. Because of one man's fault, the king's desire could not be fulfilled.

"So it is with us," the Baal Shem Tov said. "The holy *tzadik* depends upon the support of the lesser man, and the latter depends on those of lowlier quality in order to attain the summit of holiness and to elicit God's love. But when one person weakens, the whole structure totters and the *tzadik* must begin anew."

Berlin, Berlin, as it stood then, what Godly music could be played there—and was not! So Reb Yisroel had to pass through this city on his way to the City of God, occupying his time with prayer and the connection between music and ecstasy.

Who can explain the healing process of a *niggun*?

"God, I remember and I moan when I see every city built on its high pedestal, while the city of God is cast down to the depth of the abyss. . . ."

And when he finally reached the beautiful city of Berlin and he saw its rich and high pedestal, with its wide boulevards and well-stocked stores, he moaned even more, as he looked up to Him.

Within an hour, he was in the inner offices of Professor Israels, who greeted him warmly and told him how honored and respected the Rebbe was by many Jews even this far from Warsaw. Reb Yisroel asked Professor Israels if he could save his leg. One look at it and the surgeon knew it was a lost cause. As he prepared to physically examine it, he said, "Rabbi, this is going to hurt a lot, but I must touch it and examine it." Reb Yisroel did everything he could to calm the surgeon down, whose anguished face looked as if he wouldn't want to hurt a fly.

"Go on, Herr Professor, examine me, I assure you I'll be all right."

In itself, the examination was a painful matter, and any mortal with gangrene in him would probably be in a great deal of pain no matter how gently he was touched. Reb Yisroel merely closed his eyes and worked on his *niggun*.

"God, I remember and I moan when I see every city built on its high pedestal."

As he watched the Rebbe with closed eyes transported to a safe distance from pain, Professor Israels was amazed. Not a sound came out of the rabbi's mouth, not even a wince. What kind of man was this rabbi? Here the doctor had princes and consorts in his waiting room who would cry at his mere touch, and this rabbi was not making a sound! Who could explain that mystery to him!

Finally, it came down to this—said the surgeon. Based on his experience, he would have to amputate the leg or the Rebbe would die.

"When?" asked Reb Yisroel.

"In two days."

"That soon?" he said stoically.

"We cannot wait any longer," said Professor Israels.

On the day of the surgery, Professor Israels was confronted with another mystery.

"How, Rabbi, can you ask me to do this? How can you force me to operate on you without anesthesia? Do you realize what you're asking of me? What pain you'll inflict on yourself? I'm a doctor, not a butcher. Your life is at stake, Rabbi. You cannot have this operation without anesthesia. No one can."

"Doctor Israels, was there life before anesthesia?"

"Yes, and many people endured untold suffering long after the operation—if they lived."

"Will I live with a gangrenous leg?"

"No, simply no."

"Will I live with my leg removed?"

"Simply, possibly. But Rabbi, you told me two days ago you'd do everything possible to assist me in this procedure. And now this unacceptable—to me—request, that you have this operation without anesthesia."

Looking deeply into the eyes of the troubled surgeon as his attendants prepared him for the operation, Reb Yisroel could not—or dared not—find the words to explain why he refused the anesthesia. (And he would not be the last to refuse. According to Reb Ben Zion Shenker, a well-known Modzitzer *chasid* and composer of classical *niggunim*, there was once another *gadol*, the first Rav of Brisk [Brest-Litovsk], Reb Yoshe Ber Soloveitchik,[5] who needed a similar operation, and he also declined to have anesthesia. It's only conjecture, but it's likely, from what we know about the infancy of anesthesia, that it might damage one's mind, and since few people understood its powerful effects—or could control them—it was not considered safe.) Perhaps these very doubts were also in the mind of Reb Yisroel, who declined it.

The operation had to go on, and seeing how determined his patient was, the surgeon proceeded.

Who knows what pain the Rebbe felt, if any. Yet, as the story shows how far Reb Yisroel removed himself from his pain, and thus helps us even now to transcend his pain, and ours, we know that during that time, the Rebbe composed one of the most monumental and God-given songs ever given to man—yes!—"*Niggun Ezkerah Elohim Ve'ehemoyah.*"

"God, I remember and I moan when I see every city built on its high pedestal, while the city of God is cast down to the depth of the abyss; yet despite all this we worship God and our eyes are toward God." Gone was Berlin, gone Warsaw, gone all the clay cities of man. From that moment on, the City of God was forever begun.

It's also been said that during the amputation the Rebbe composed the whole *niggun*. But that is in general dispute. More likely, it was begun then, although, according to Ben Zion Shenker, "Actually he had begun work on '*Niggun Ezkerah*' two years previous to that time, where on the same *posuk*, he had composed a *niggun* to those words but he had felt he was as yet not satisfied with the results. He had so many thoughts on the same subject that he knew until that very moment nothing was settled about that. He was determined to start anew under the knife. If Reb Yisroel had merely composed the first part of his *niggun*, it would surely have been acclaimed for its beauty and spirituality, but as it turned out, fortunately, he composed thirty-six parts of the *niggun*. It takes about a half hour to sing. Pretty long," admitted Ben Zion Shenker. "Yet it's hard for me to believe that Reb Yisroel composed all of it during the operation. I would suggest that he composed the opening part of it at that point and later on developed it."

Another mystery: While recuperating in Berlin, Reb Yisroel decided to take a ride in the fresh air through the city of Berlin. Accompanying him in an open carriage were his son Shaul Yedidyah Elezer[6] (who would later succeed Reb Yisroel as the Modzitzer Rebbe), another son, and a son-in-law. When they came to a busy traffic to clear up, a German *goy* passed the carriage, saw Reb Yisroel and his entourage and shook his fist at them.

"Jews, what are you doing here? Go to Palestine where you belong!"

It was an unprovoked remark, and who knew how much the

ailing Rebbe took it to heart! Yet, to raise purpose from Berlin's dust, we know that, at that point, the Rebbe told his children, "According to a *posuk* in *Tehillim*, 'I rejoiced when they said to me, "Let us go to the House of *Hashem*"' [Psalm 122], and he paraphrased it by saying, 'I rejoice when they tell me, "Jew, go to Palestine." Now is the time to sing *"Ezkerah."*" It was then that he introduced the *niggun* to his children and cleared up the mystery that separated his other thoughts from his family.

And who can explain this? World War I broke out. Like hundreds of others, Reb Yisroel was caught in Berlin at the time. Directly, from there, he had no way he could return to Poland, which at the time was in Russian hands. Aided by family members, he made his way by train to Denmark, then by ferry to Sweden, and thence to St. Petersburg, Russia; the final step would take him by train to Warsaw, hobbling most of the way on crutches—an exhausting trip. Yet, as unforeseen things have their own life, he almost missed the train to Poland, which was pulling out of the station as he and his family arrived. Everyone started running to catch the train. It looked as if they'd make it; the train was moving slowly forward, but the hobbling Rebbe started to fall further back from his party. This is where another mystery came in. Suddenly a large man appeared out of nowhere and said, "I'll help you, Rabbi." He picked up the Rebbe and ran with him toward an open door of the train. There, he safely delivered him into the waiting arms of the Rebbe's family on the train. However, by the time the Rebbe turned around to thank the man, the man had disappeared. Who was the man with the saving grace? No one really knew, nor even saw his face in the darkness. All they knew was that he vanished into thin air.

When Reb Yisroel returned to Warsaw, his *chasidim* held a *se'udas hodo'ah* for him, giving thanks for his life. There he revealed to them the whole story about *"Ezkerah"* and all his experiences. He told of his experience in 1911 when he was walking through the streets of Carlsbad, Czechoslovakia, also a highly regarded beautiful city, and having many thoughts on the same subject of "'*Ezkerah*.' And yet I felt I hadn't said everything I had to say on this theme, and I attempted a few other times to compose something which I felt was what my heart and soul desired, but I couldn't bring it to fruition. Of course it had its own life, *Rabosai*, which is known as '*Ezkerah Hakoton*' ('Small *Ezkerah*') At one point, a grandchild almost drowned and I was taken much aback at the incident.

Over the past few years there were many other incidents that distracted me.

"Then, *Rabosai*, came this crucial time in my life where my own life was in the balance and I felt compelled to bring out all my thoughts in this song. Now, I am completely satisfied."

But that was only the beginning. Although Reb Yisroel lived on for another seven years, he began a dynasty of Modzitzer Rebbes whose music lives on forever, shrouded in ancient Judaism. Yet, as the author Isser Frenkel wrote about the second Modzitzer Rebbe (which aptly describes Reb Yisroel's music, too), "Simplicity was also the basis of all his music. Music which is not simple, he would say, is not worth singing. It is not understandable to the simple ear. Music must be made for the simple ear of a simple Jew so that he, too, may reap the benefit.

"Simple but concentrated. These were the two requirements—or more correctly, the two ingredients—which made Modzitz music different from others."[7]

Although "*Niggun Ezkerah*" is sung in Modzitzer *shuls* certain times a year, it has not yet been recorded electronically. But to hear the glorious song in its entirety is to walk through the City of God. Let me say no more!

16

Jail House Rock

This story begins very slowly.

The Riker's Island (New York City) jail room had been silent for a long time. Suddenly, in a corner of the ceiling, a spider ceased weaving its web as a key turned in a lock. The door opened. In filed several men with guns in their holsters. Already seated in the room was a man in black hat and black coat, who smiled at the guards. None of the armed men had ever seen him before, but they had been briefed about his mission. So they smiled back and unobtrusively took their seats around the perimeter of the room. One of them spotted the spider and its web as he looked up at the ceiling. Nobody knew what to expect.

Soon, other sounds filled the room. Thirty men entered. Coughing. Scuffling sneakers. Chewing gum. Sneezing. Moving chairs. Then the silence fell again. The spider went back to its work. All eyes were upon the man in black hat.

It was not at all unexpected that he opened his mouth to say, "*Sholom Aleichem.*"

"*Aleichem Sholom*," the Jewish inmates said back to him. The man in black introduced himself. He introduced why he was there. He introduced the story of Chanukah. He introduced the subject of *niggunim* (wordless chasidic songs), which was another way to introduce the inmates to their Jewish souls, although, in truth, some of them, who already wore *yarmulkes* and *tzitzis*, needed no introduction.

Still it came to most of them as a culture shock that this man in black, who had come there as part of an ongoing prison outreach program sponsored by Lubavitch Youth Organization (L.Y.O.), had arrived a week before Chanukah and was telling them what, of all things, a *niggun* was.

He told them the story behind the "*Shpoler Zeide's Niggun*," which in its way touched every man in that room.

As one version of the story goes, the Shpoler Zeide[1] wanted to save a Jew who was thrown into a deep pit in prison for not paying his taxes. In those days—the eighteenth century—it didn't take much to jail Jews and to throw away the keys. The way to determine the guilt or innocence of a Jew, decided the lords of the land, was to bring a Jew to a big tavern where lords and cossacks sat in judgment. There, dressed in a bearskin, the Jew was forced to outdance his opponent, generally the best handpicked, exquisite dancer in the tavern. If the Jew fell first, he was guilty and would be whipped and put to death. If the cossack fell first, the Jew would go free.

"You can believe it when I tell you," said the man in black, "no Jew had a chance against such accomplished and energetic dancers."

According to legend, one night the Shpoler Zeide was visited by Elijah the prophet in a dream. The angel instructed him in the fine art of dancing, in order to outlast the cossack, and taught him what was to become forever known as the "*Shpoler Zeide's Niggun*." "The same *niggun* that I'll sing for you shortly," the man in the black coat said to the prisoners.

The Shpoler Zeide went to the prison, drank *mashke* with the guard until the guard fell asleep, then lowered himself into the pit. Whereupon the Shpoler Zeide exchanged clothes with the other Jew and told him to leave the prison unnoticed, which promptly the Jew in the Shpoler Zeide's clothing did.

Finally, a messenger from the nobles and cossacks waiting in the tavern arrived with the bearskin and threw it down into the pit. The Shpoler Zeide donned the bearskin and pulled himself up by the rope. Then the messenger led him to the tavern, where he was greeted by everybody there with jeers and hoots.

At once the musicians started playing song after song, the cossack and the Jew danced, and as the hours went on everyone could see how evenly matched the dancers were. Never had a Jew danced so hard and so excellently. Never had a cossack met his match. By now the lords and cossacks had stopped laughing and sat there stunned.

Finally, the musicians got tired, and even the cossack dancer was willing to stop. Not so the old Shpoler Zeide with his white beard hidden under the bearskin, who started singing the *niggun* and danced as he had never danced before, and the cossack felt obliged to pick up the dance, too.

Slowly the *niggun*, slowly the dance. Without realizing it, the dancers, caught up with the rapidly accelerating tune, moved faster and faster and faster and faster and faster and faster and faster—the Shpoler Zeide dancing with astonishing ease—until they reached a pace that was so fast they couldn't make out their own singing and dancing of the *niggun*.

That's when it happened, according to one chasidic version: the cossack dancer's heart gave out and he fell dead. So the Shpoler Zeide won, and his fellow Jew was freed from prison.

The story was not quite over; there were other details to be told, yet the excited inmates had heard enough. All they wanted was to hear the "*Shpoler Zeide's Niggun*."

So the man in black stood up and started slowly to teach them the *niggun*. Within moments, as the guards nervously fingered their guns, the Jewish inmates began to sing and leaped up off their chairs to form a large circle, and they danced with all their hearts and souls. Never had the guards witnessed such a sight.

Thirty men, some with their *tzitzis* dangling in the air, others holding onto their *yarmulkes* with one hand, singing, "Deyamam mamayayayayayayayayayayayyadedeyi. Aiyidedeyiyiyidedeyiyi—up cossack."

"Part of the song means 'Up, Cossack, jump, Cossack!'" explained the man in black, quickly losing breath, as he danced with the inmates.

"Dadadadadadadadadadadeumpdadadadadadadadeump."

And the tune got faster and faster, and the Jews were singing and dancing until they reached a pace that was so fast they too couldn't make out the *niggun*. And the spider quickly deserted its shaky web and sought refuge in a crack in the wall.

Later, the man in black was to tell his fellow Lubavitchers who also visit prisons through L.Y.O., "What energy these prisoners had! Some of these Jews hardly had spent more than five minutes with another Jew outside. Nevertheless, in this long-silent room with a heart, their Jewish spark was kindled, and they all were thoroughly involved in this dance with me. Hardened criminals some, others I never would have taken to be Jewish, these people were dancing around and around and around and around, and somebody shouted, 'Hey, I think I see the Shpoler Zeide in the circle opposite me,' and another one said, 'Yeah, I think I see him too,' and others amiably agreed to join in on the fun: 'Yeah, he's right here.' 'No, he's over there.' 'Hey, he's holding my hand.' There was no doubt," added the man in black, "these inmates were being touched by the hand of God."

Finally the prisoners and Levi Reiter, the man in the black coat, fell back exhausted onto their chairs, perhaps leaving the Shpoler Zeide to continue the dance till the end of time.

The other part to this story also starts slowly.

It's Chanukah party time at Riker's Island. Very early in the morning, Jewish men and women inmates are gathered from their cells all over the metropolitan area and bused in to a big correctional room on Riker's Island. It is one of the few times each year that Jewish inmates come together, and nobody really fully knows what to expect. But the Lubavitcher prison outreach volunteers plan and hope for the best, and so do the prison officials.

As the buses make their way to Riker's, scheduled to arrive at 9:30 A.M., already Jewish *bochurim* have arrived and are setting up chairs and tables. Once that is done, they lay out *kosher* salami sandwiches, sour pickles, cole slaw, and potato salad. Soon they are joined by Feygah Sarah Friedman and the other volunteers.

One of them complains that there is no *mechitzah*. "How are we going to separate the men from the women dancing?" she wants to know.

One of the *bochurim* suggests that rows of chairs, stacked two or three high, serve as a *mechitzah*, and everybody, although not entirely happy with the makeshift alternative, pitches in to set up the *mechitzah*.

By 9:25, the music equipment is set up. The female volunteers are looking forward to the dancing, although by no stretch of imagination is the big, dreary room designed to bring out the best in dancing.

"I bet even Fred Astaire and Ginger Rogers would have trouble tripping the light fantastic here," quipped Mrs. Friedman.

Finally, promptly at 9:30, the doors of the big room are opened. Entering first are armed guards who bring in separately the groups of female and men inmates, each wearing a band around his or her wrist saying "KOSHER" or "JEW," which is a standard procedure in prison to separate *kosher*-food eaters from non-*kosher*-food eaters. They are followed by family members and numerous other people, including some Orthodox rabbis, Jewish prison chaplains, and prison officials. The group also includes Rabbi Josef Baruch Wircberg of Yeshiva Hadar Hatorah in Crown Heights. At the right moment, he'll give a special talk to the inmates.

But right now it's getting time to eat. After that, there will be plenty of time for one-on-one talks between prisoners and families, between prisoners and rabbis, between prisoners and volunteers.

When 11:30 comes, *kosher* lunch is served to everybody. During that time, Rabbi Wircberg talks about the joys and significance of Chanukah.

By 12:30, with a half hour left of the Chanukah party, everybody feels the need to dance. They rise from their tables, see the makeshift *mechitzah*, and separate themselves, the men to one side of the room and the women to the other side, forming two circles as they hold hands. As yet the music hasn't started. With their feet and hands poised for dance, they still have time to look around and take in an eyeful of the big, dreary room they're in, the armed guards looking at everybody with suspicious eyes. This is the last place, many of them feel, that they can dance and sing freely, but that's all they've got for now. So they intend to give the dance their all and dance as they never danced before.

Men will forget women, women will forget men, and everybody, it's hoped, will forget the prison.

When the *bochurim* play chasidic dance music, all the inmates and family members and prison outreach volunteers pour their entire souls in the dance; they dance for the sake of dancing, for the pure ecstasy of it, for rejoicing exclusively in its movement and energy. The men—and the women in their own "room"—interlock arms, each man holding fast to his neighbors' shoulders. The circle is joined, a simple melody breaks forth from the throats of the male dancers, and the circle begins to turn with an ever increasing velocity. The onlookers almost feel sucked into the swirl. Here and there a pair of interlocked arms gives way, a new dancer thrusts himself into the gap, and the dance widens and quickens to ever new feet. Then the circles dissolve, and in a few moments re-form, as some dancers join the onlookers. A new dance begins, faster than the previous one. Then another dance, even faster.

Gone is the prison, gone the dreary life. The cup of joy overflows. The dancers are light of heart as they whirl around: things are moving forward in their lives, in their newfound *Yiddishkeit*. What more is needed to be happy, even in prison! For those brief moments the prisoners are no longer prisoners but Jews: they dance as Jews, with Jews.

"We've outlived Haman and Rome and Nazi Germany," somebody sings to the music, "and we'll outlive all the enemies of *Hashem* that fight against us."

"Yes, yes," shouts another male inmate, "yes, we're going to live, sing, and dance. And there can only be one answer: to remain loyal Jews as long as we breathe. Jail or no jail!"

Then abruptly the music stops, the two circles dissolve, and all the Jews breathlessly look at one another, and smile. In the end, the guards lead the inmates back to their cells, and everybody else files out to various destinations. The Chanukah party is over; the prison room regains its dreary silence.

But somewhere in the room, the jail house rock goes on, and the Shpoler Zeide, the greatest dancer in chasidic history, continues dancing till the end of time.

17

Leonard Bernstein Unbound

By their furtive glances, they were waiting for somebody, these thirty persons, fifteen men and fifteen women, seated in the comfortable living room of Professor Bloch's home. On this hot summer night, if anyone felt a bit warm in the house, it was probably from the stoked expectations of who would walk through the front door and stand there in living color next to them for the first time. Professor Bloch had promised them a big surprise—"a dear old friend," as he had put it—although the name mentioned, Leonard Bernstein, meant nothing to two men dressed in black suits and black hats; as far as they were concerned, if this "friend" did not show within the next fifteen minutes, before sundown, it would be too late for him to participate in the religious activities, including putting on *tefillin* (phylacteries).

Undeniably, one of the so-called black-hatters, Shmuel Spritzer, couldn't help noticing that all the men—and women—had one eye on the *tefillin* and one eye on the door. If this were "770," his *shul* back home in Crown Heights in Brooklyn, New York, he was certain that all eyes would be on the Rebbe.

But it wasn't 770. He and his fellow Lubavitcher *yeshivah* student, Chaim Jacobs, were some 3,000 miles distant, outside Portland, Oregon, in the expensive-looking split-level house of a well-known music professor and composer of the area, who, himself recently turned on to Jewish music through the records of Shlomo Carlebach, had invited them there to hold a *farbrengen* (chasidic get-together) for Jewish people from his college. True, the Lubavitcher Rebbe had sent them there—years before his emissaries had established themselves all over the country and the world. In those days of 1969, dressed in dark suits and black hats, the two *yeshivah* students were briefed for the last time on their mission, which was then part of the so-called "Jewish Peace Corps." Initiated in 1950 by the Lubavitcher Rebbe, the Jewish Peace Corps continued to send out emissaries, two to each state, to carry the message—"We remain with thee, our Torah, for life or death—and bring the gifts and truths of *Yiddishkeit* closer to home."

So they came to Portland, Shmuel Spritzer, now a rabbi and one of the major forces behind the national prison outreach program of the Lubavitch Youth Organization, and Chaim Jacobs, now the Rebbe's emissary in Glasgow, Scotland. Both twenty at the time of our story, their tasks that summer, for a period of three weeks, included acting as traveling emissaries of the Lubavitcher Rebbe, selling Judaic books by the Merkos L'inyonei Chinuch (the educational arm of Lubavitch) to individuals, religious organizations, schools, and institutions, and increasing in any manner Jews' observances of Judaism.

"To help us," said Spritzer, "we brought along Jewish reading materials, which we'd leave after we met with a person or a family, and I brought along my favorite record album of *niggunim* to enchant people like Professor Bloch, whom I was scheduled to meet."

In Oregon the sun sets late. By 8 P.M., partway through their *farbrengen*, the pair of Lubavitchers asked all the men to put on *tefillin*. "As you know," Spritzer explained to the men, "it's an obligation to put *tefillin* on in the morning. But for a man who doesn't put on *tefillin* in the morning he still has the opportunity to do *tefillin* anytime during the day before sunset." All the men obliged.

Afterwards, as Spritzer and Jacobs were elaborating on the joys of *Yiddishkeit*, in "walks a guy, and the whole room becomes quiet,"

Spritzer said, in recalling the incident. "All eyes go toward the direction of the door, toward the guy coming in, and I look at my
watch and I realize we have about fifteen minutes left before sunset.
So now I geared my mind in only one direction, to get this guy to
put on *tefillin*. I introduced myself: 'Shalom, I am Shmuel Spritzer
and this is Chaim Jacobs, and you are . . . ?'"

"I am Leonard Bernstein."

Spritzer, who had thitherto been totally immersed in Torah studies, didn't know Leonard Bernstein from Elmer Bernstein. "To me
Leonard Bernstein meant nothing out of the ordinary. I said to him,
'It's nice meeting you. We would like to put on *tefillin* with you.
We only got fifteen minutes left.' He said, 'I don't want to put on
tefillin.' So I said to myself, 'If a guy doesn't want to put on *tefillin*,
and everybody else did it already, you go to the next step and try to
draw close to him through understanding where he was coming
from.' So I asked him what he does for a living."

"I'm a conductor," he responded.

"Maybe," Spritzer thought to himself, "this man is like a conductor on the IRT subway in New York. But of course I won't say
anything that way to him." Instead he said to Bernstein, "Very nice.
What kind of conductor are you, Mr. Bernstein?"

"I conduct music."

Almost in the same breath, Bernstein asked the two black hat-
ters if they knew how to sing, and both said, "Sure."

"*Chasidics* know how to sing?" Bernstein was pleased to hear.
"Then sing something."

Spritzer turned to Professor Bloch. "I'm not going to sing a
solo here, but maybe we should put on a record of mine."

The professor agreed, and Spritzer asked him to put on the
fourth song of the fourth record in the album he had brought with
him. In looking back at that time, Rabbi Spritzer said, "The reason
I asked to put on '*Shamil's Niggun*'[1] was, when I was a young *bochur*
I had heard that when '*Shamil's Niggun*' was recorded on record in
1962 the man who played the violin at the recording was a Gentile.
In those days there weren't too many Jews playing music. As the
goy played his violin, at the recording, something astonishing happened to him. He began to sweat to the point that his whole body
was bathed through and through, so deeply was he affected by the
music. Not even taking time to wipe his brow or dry his eyes and
hands, the *goy* played as he had never played a violin before. Later

he admitted that he had experienced the full power of the '*Niggun Shamil*.' So I said to myself, as I then stood before Mr. Leonard Bernstein, if it touched a *goy* to the core, then maybe it'll touch this Jew. This was my reasoning. And it proved to be the case."

"You know," confided Bernstein to everyone in the living room, "being a Jew myself, I carry a lot of music in my soul."

"Jewish?" asked Spritzer.

"Some. I have deep roots, each different from one another . . . I can only hope it adds up to something you could call universal. Still," he sighed, "it would be nice to hear someone accidentally whistle something of mine, somewhere, just once."

"Then, Mr. Bernstein, you're in the right place."

"How do you know that, Rabbi?"

"Because even your sigh has been recorded in the heavens, just as God heard the sighs of Shamil."

"Shamil? Shamil?" Bernstein looked puzzled. "Who's Shamil?"

Putting on a record from his collection of *niggunim*, Spritzer said confidentially, "You'll know him from his song. You and he have a lot in common."

"Was he too a conductor?" Bernstein said.

"In a way, Mr. Bernstein."

Spritzer said no more. He wanted the music to speak for itself. Heaven always remembered. And thousands of miles across the sea, across the span of forgotten time, a man, although perhaps now not quite the man he once was, still languishing in a prison that has been forgotten by everyone except heaven, indeed in a place that one would be hard put to find on any map any longer, he too heard the sigh of Leonard Bernstein—"It would be nice to hear someone accidentally whistle something of mine, somewhere, just once"— he too was a leader of his people, and cried aloud for a just God to release him from his bondage.

His song, "*Niggun Shamil*," begins in war-torn Georgia, more than 100 years ago. There lived a leader of the Georgian people in Russia who then inhabited the Caucasus mountains. His name was Shamil. The Russian army engaged the Georgians in battle, seeking to conquer them and deprive them of their freedom. The Georgians fought valiantly against the invaders and could not be vanquished. The Russian army leaders then proposed a false peace treaty and by this means succeeded in getting the Georgians to lay down their arms.

However, immediately afterwards, the Russians lured the Georgian leader, Shamil, and confined him to a prison.

Staring out of the window of his small, narrow cell, Shamil reflected on the days of liberty in the past. In his current exile and helplessness, he bewailed his plight and yearned for his previous position of freedom and fortune. He consoled himself, however, with the knowledge that he would eventually be released from his imprisonment and would return to his previous position with even more power and glory. It is this thought that is expressed in this melancholy, contemplative, yearning *niggun*.

Leonard Bernstein heard it all, every note of "*Niggun Shamil*"— "I never saw anybody listen to music like that; it was like Bernstein and Shamil were bound up as one," said Spritzer—and almost wept. So moved was he that after hearing the *niggun* he said, "I love that song, I love that song! I feel tied up in knots about that song, I cannot explain it, yet at the same time I feel released."

And Spritzer, very aware that the clock was ticking away, said, "I'll explain it to you, why you may feel that way, but first, would you like to put on *tefillin* now?"

"I must know one thing," Bernstein said. "I noticed that you chose the song—'*Niggun Shamil*'—from the middle of a record, yet there were other songs on the record. Why didn't you choose them?"

As he prepared the *tefillin*, Spritzer said, "Because I like it, and I felt you had to hear it."

"You have a feeling for music," Bernstein said. "If you promise me that you will take up music for your future, I will put on *tefillin* right now."

"It's a deal," Spritzer said, later confiding to Chaim Jacobs, "Why did I say that? Because every Lubavitcher takes on music as part of his *Yiddishkeit*. Every Lubavitcher sings continually."

So in front of a hushed group of men and women, Leonard Bernstein put on a pair of *tefillin* for the first time in his life, and that too was recorded in heaven.

And after the sun was down and darkness finally fell outside, the two young *yeshivah* students enlightened the guests about *Yiddishkeit*, with Bernstein asking many questions of his ancient religion. Then Spritzer explained the special significance of Shamil to Bernstein. He spoke of the descent of the soul to its abode in the human body, in which it becomes adjusted to the physical, and the mundane becomes the "prison" of the soul, longing for spiritual fulfillment, striving against its "exile" within its earthly pleasures and pining for its freedom, which it feels it can attain only through complete adherence to the divine Torah. And Bernstein took it all in and recorded it in his prison—and his heaven.

After an hour, Bernstein excused himself; he had to go home. Before he left Professor Bloch's house, he said to Spritzer. "Rabbi, I want you to look me up in Radio City in New York City so that we can meet again."

Spritzer agreed to the invitation, not knowing in the least where Radio City was. "I marked it down in my notebook and that was it," said Spritzer. "Later on, even before we got back to Brooklyn, New York, we heard and spoke much about Leonard Bernstein. People said, 'Leonard Bernstein put on *tefillin*—wow!'"

A few weeks back into New York City again, Spritzer started checking around about Radio City, and someone said, "Yes, it's a place in Manhattan." When he asked how he could get there, he was told he had to buy tickets. "The night Leonard Bernstein was supposed to perform I found out I could get a ticket for $20. Twenty dollars? Forget it. That was the end of Radio City for me. I consoled myself with the thought that if Leonard Bernstein wants to see me he'll let me in for free."

The two never met again, but like Bernstein and Shamil, Bernstein and his Jewish rabbi friend were tied forever through the cords of heaven.

About ten years later, Leonard Bernstein was approached by a traveling Lubavitcher rabbi, in Boston, to put on *tefillin*. Bernstein, this time, readily agreed. As the rabbi helped wrap the *tefillin* around Bernstein's arm, he said to him, "This is probably a first for you, eh?"

"No," Bernstein said solemnly, "this is not the first time. I did it once before in Portland." And he recalled his dear, beloved friend, Professor Bloch, who had passed away by then, and Rabbis Shmuel Spritzer and Chaim Jacobs, and all those supportive Jews in that living room in Portland, and he said, his voice cracking, "Somebody finally accidentally whistled something of mine, somewhere, just once."

"What do you mean?" asked the inquisitive rabbi.

"Something took place ten years ago, at a *farbrengen*, as you call it, one summery night, when I heard the plaintive song of Shamil."

A slight smile broke out on the face of the rabbi. "*'Shamil's Niggun'*—ah yes."

"You call it a *farbrengen*," said Bernstein. "I call it something else. I heard the deep calling unto the deep. I heard Shamil. I heard myself. I heard . . . and, rabbi, that's when I put on *tefillin* for the first time in my life."

It is also recorded in heaven that the Lubavitcher Rebbe, *shlita*, Menachem Mendel Schneerson, once said, "All that is necessary is for a person to perform one small act and God will help him and lift him above all things. This is enhanced by the influence of a chasidic *farbrengen* which—as revealed in the note that descended from heaven—can achieve more than the influence of the angel Michoel."

Don't ever say that Leonard Bernstein died in 1991. Not true at all. In the end, Bernstein became Shamil unbound! Bernstein's Jewish soul lives, in the flesh and blood of God's song.

18

The Songs that Almost Weren't

Sitting among the other passengers in a bus as it motored along the streets of Riverdale, the Bronx, New York, one early week-day morning, an elderly man began to whistle a tune over and over. Some of the other passengers, attracted by the wistful sounds, turned around to give him encouragement; others, absorbed in their own daydreams, kept their eyes and ears straight ahead in anticipation of their destination. But one man, a rabbi at a local *yeshivah*, was more than intrigued by the song so familiar to him that he put down his prayer book and ceased praying. What was it about that song he was hearing? Who in the bus was singing it? He had to find out. Looking around the bus, which was filled with people of many races, the rabbi couldn't imagine anybody on the bus singing such a tune—a *niggun* composed by the former Modzitzer Rebbe many many years ago. The rabbi himself had heard it frequently in his life, but not for a while.

Moved by more than curiosity, he strolled the aisle until he reached a seat where a black man sat. There was no doubt he was the one whistling the *niggun*.

To the black man, who might have been twice as old as the *niggun* itself, the rabbi said, "How do you know this tune?"

"I don't know," replied the black man, "but somebody gave me this tape and I enjoy it!"

"I know this song too," said the excited rabbi, "from my childhood." As he then thanked the black man for his song and went back to his seat, he thought to himself, "It just goes to show that even people who have no *Yiddishkeit* are affected by *niggunim*."

For the rest of the journey the black man continued whistling some more of the *niggun* while the rabbi carried the song all day in his prayers.[1]

This is the story of hundreds of songs that almost weren't, and it surely had its beginning in a resort town, Otvotzk, in Poland, in the year 1939, when that populous town was filled with many Jewish tourists and rebbes and their *chasidim*. At that time there were two particular rabbis, two old friends with dark clouds over their heads, who were destined to change the commitment of *Yiddishkeit* the world over—one with education, the other with song.

"But when, *Moshiach*, when will you come?" asked the Baal Shem Tov.[2]

And the *Moshiach* answered: "When your spring will run over, when your teaching will cover the land."

The two old friends, ever mindful of *Chasidus* and knowing full well of the onslaught of the German Luftwaffe and invading German and Russian armies catching Poland in a pincer, knew nothing Jewish would be safe or sacred any longer in Poland. The end of all Jews was possibly close at hand. In a few days there might not be a *shul* left in Poland. Each rebbe asked the other where he'd go. The Rabbi of Lubavitch, Yosef Yitzchak Schneersohn,[3] said he had made arrangements to travel to America. For the Rabbi of Modzitz (Shaul Yedidyah Eleazer Taub[4]), there was only one possible escape route: toward Russia and beyond.

The best of devised plans notwithstanding, even they, on separate paths fleeing alongside thousands of other displaced Jews, were not prepared for the German onslaught, which was coming on land, sea, and air like a plague of deadly locusts, to ravage Poland and kill Jews. "I was born to bring rejoicing to the hearts of Jews," Reb Shaul often said, but for Reb Shaul, who came into the world on the Hoshanah Rabba of 1887, born to the sound of music, the day before the jolliest of all Jewish festivals, Simchas Torah, he wondered where he'd be on Rosh Hashanah, a matter of a week away. Just at the time when Modzitz music had attained its peak of popularity in Poland, it was silenced. A week before Rosh Hashanah 5700 (September 1939), he had to flee his villa at Utwocziec. As he was endeavoring to reestablish his *yeshivah* in the local *beis hamidrosh* of Otvotzk, German planes appeared over the town and a rain of death fell on the city.

Miraculously, Reb Shaul survived unhurt, and he took refuge in a haystack from which later, under cover of night, he and his family fled to Vilna, Lithuania. Fleeing the Germans, he and his family would be forced to be on the road, under bridges, in barns, hiding in bushes, walking through forests, wading rivers and lakes, across mountains, along side roads under the cover of darkness—anything to avoid the bombs of the Luftwaffe that were raining down on the countryside. There was no avoiding them; merely just to survive them was all that anyone could hope for.

This was not the best of times for soul-searching. The road to Vilna was fraught with hideous terrors and shocks, beyond all regrets, yet music guided Jews' souls through the darkness. It is clearly written: "Nevertheless He regarded their affliction . . ." And when? . . . "when He heard their cry" (Psalm 106:44). The Lord heard their cry and knew they were hurt but were trying to hide their pain by singing.

Reb Shaul encouraged his *chasidim* to flee wherever and however they could—even if it meant traveling on *Shabbos*. When a Modzitzer *chasid* from Radom cried to Reb Shaul about his desecrating *Shabbos* to escape the Germans, Reb Shaul answered him, "Don't cry. I did the same myself."[5]

During this trip, as a musical diary of his travels and hardships, Reb Shaul began composing "*Min Hameitzar*," which is a part of Psalm 118. "From out of distress I called upon the Lord; He answered me through the breadth of divine relief. The Lord was with me, therefore I did not fear; what can man do to me?" Perhaps "composing it" is a weak way of putting it. He lived it, he experienced it, he was prepared to die for it. Listen to the song the way Ben Zion Shenker sings it and you are there, with Reb Shaul and his family, with bombs and shrapnel bursting around you. The music the way Reb Shaul composed it and later in Vilna notated it is to hear the German bombs falling as if they were meant for your head only and there was no way to escape that fate. Listen and you can hear Reb

Shaul praying from the innermost parts of him to the innermost parts of heaven. Listen to section 17, "I shall not die, but I shall live and recount the works of the Lord," "*ki yechyeh vaasapeir maasei Koh,*" and you'll hear the wailing of thousands of Jews along with Reb Shaul caught in the strafing of German warplanes breaking up peace into pieces. Lift up your eyes and ears, O listener of "*Min Hameitzar,*" to experience the terror and cringing of a people torn between east and west, traveling between a hard rock and a stone, fleeing east to Russia because there was no other choice. Perhaps at another time a wooded area or forest was a pleasant picnicking experience, table-cloths laid out neatly on wooden tables or on the grass, the wine and cool, fresh water, the potato *kugel,* the roasted chicken, bowls of fresh herbs, spinach and lentil soups, and stuffed tomatoes, and inevitably everyone's favorite desserts; this, however, was no such time. Nobody could afford the luxury of a lengthy meal, what with the German war machines bearing down from the skies and land. But Jews being Jews, they still took the time—wherever they were— to act like Jews and not animals, to *daven* and *bench,* to give thanks to *Hashem,* and to help a straggling Jew back on his feet.

No one can say how many notes of "*Min Hameitzar*" Reb Shaul composed as he lay face down in forests or on dirt roads to avoid detection. There is a time for everything, and such was the time for Reb Shaul to note his complete journey from Otvotzk to Vilna and beyond. But such a journey would be "*Min Hameitzar.*"

It probably would not be farfetched for a listener to this *niggun* to experience without knowing when those few moments in time, along the way, out of the living hell called Poland, when, according to Reb Shaul's son, Rabbi Chaim Yitzchok Taub, they heard a *shofar* that Rosh Hashanah, days into their escape. They were aware that a hidden saint, who visited Reb Shaul on occasion, lived in a forest near Dubenka, where they were wandering. Suddenly, they heard a blast of a *shofar.* Following the sound, "I saw a little hut filled with burning candles," said Rabbi Chaim Yitzchok. "The *nistar,* dressed in white, was blowing the *shofar,* unaware of all that was going on outside his immediate environment."[6] This is also recorded for posterity in the *niggun.*

Likewise no one knows what it took for Reb Shaul and his family to reach Vilna safely.

"From out of distress I called upon the Lord; He answered me through the breadth of divine relief.

"The Lord was with me, therefore I did not fear; what can man do to me?"

It's all there, in this *niggun* of twenty-five parts, if you listen intently for it and get beyond the specter of death and fire lurking everywhere in this travel. Listen hard, and you'll conjure up the time that the Rebbe and his family spent Yom Kippur in the town of Kamin, near Kovla, in Russian-controlled territory. How sweet it was—to be among Jews, perhaps a little like the hidden saint of the forest, taking time to acknowledge the Living God. Yes, you can surely hear as two local Jews ask Reb Shaul to lead the *tefillos*. Yes, you can see how Reb Shaul responded, in that little heaven on earth, when he saw two men—two of his *chasidim*, former *talmidim* of his *yeshivah* in Otvotzk—enter the *shul* in the middle of *Musaf* and then faint at the sight of their Rebbe. Later they explained, "We've been on the run since Rosh Hashanah. We thought that the Rebbe and his family had, *chas vesholom*, perished in the bombings. Suddenly we heard our Rebbe's voice! We thought for sure that we were dead and had come to *Gan Eiden*! Thank God, we are still alive and hearing the Rebbe!"

And listening even more closely, the listener to this *niggun* will hear the words again: "The Lord was with me, therefore I did not fear; what can man do to me?" And as the Lord told Jacob, "You shall ascend and not descend," so the Rebbe told his *chasidim*, "Your enthusiasm for that which is sacred will not wane even after you discover the sufferings and hardships which you have to overcome to attain it."

Still not out of harm's way, the Modzitzer Rebbe, his family and followers arrived in Vilna, Lithuania, sometime after Sukkos. It was there that he made the decision to notate his *niggunim*—"I was born to bring rejoicing to the hearts of Jews," he was wont to repeat. Not all of his *niggunim* could be recalled—he and his family left most of his belongings in the depths, and such is total regret. But he did recall about 300 of them, which, with the help of his followers, were carefully written down.

"*Min Hameitzar*" is not an easy song to sing, remarks Reb Ben Zion Shenker, who has sung and recorded many of the Modzitzer Rebbe's *niggunim* over the past forty years. "The Rebbe had a very beautiful voice, with a large scale of notes in his range, so it was easy for him."

"*Min Hameitzar*": not an easy song to sing nor an easy song to live. Reb Shaul made it through nine months of Vilna where, whenever he held a *tisch*, "the *shul* was packed by *chasidim* and *misnagdim* alike, all pushing to get as close to the Rebbe as possible. . . . On *Kislev* 19, 5700, Reb Shaul spoke at the *farbrengen* of the Lubavitcher *chasidim* in Vilna.

"Wherever he went in Vilna he was greeted by all Lithuanian Jews, who had always been the most virulent opponents of Chasidism. Thousands of such Jews came to his Court and participated with him in his learning and singing."[7] "I try," Reb Shaul said at that time, "to introduce the chasidic ability to laugh and cry at the same time, in the music I compose. In terrible times like these, it especially needs both."[8] At another time he said, "When a Jew has a problem, he is so confident of God's mercy that he sings about His salvation before it happens."[9]

For Reb Shaul, it only took nine months to become disillusioned with Russian-occupied Vilna and to make plans with his family to travel to America via Japan. All this time the *niggun* "*Min Hameitzar*" traveled with its own set of ears and eyes. It recorded the meeting between Reb Shaul and his interview by the N.K.V.D. in Vilna. It noted the resistance on the part of the Soviet government, which was not particularly inclined to grant exit visas to Polish refugees, even if they had entry visas for other countries. According to a Modzitzer *chasid*, Yehuda Nathan, "Reb Shaul decided to challenge this policy and applied at the Intourist office in Vilna." According to another Modzitzer *chasid*, Ben Zion Shenker, the Modzitzer had been forewarned by his friends: "Dress very simply, take off your hat, yes, your *yarmulke*, too, and don't say anything to offend them." It was obvious by his attire that day that he paid this advice no mind. Reb Shaul showed up in his most luxurious, dark velvet *yarmulke* that covered the entire top his head. In his finest clothes, he made an impressive sight. "No one knows for certain what effect that had in the eyes of the communists, but . . . his inquisitor, a Jew, charged that the Torah was a capitalist document. Reb Shaul answered that the Israelites in the *midbor* (wilderness) were the first true socialists, as they had no need of material gain. In addition, *Halachah* (Jewish law) is designed to protect the poor. He requested that his socialist comrades award him an exit visa so he could live in a country where he could practice his religion."[10] The communists were not too eager to give him a visa. He used diplomacy, and they liked what he said.

He had to show them he was with them. And they told him when he comes to America he should not give them a bad name, otherwise he'll affect the other Jews left behind. "His replies to the many searching questions were so excellently and cleverly worded [that] he managed to parry every one of them without actually saying or arousing the suspicions or animosity of his interrogator."[11] The N.K.V.D. agent relented and issued visas for him and his family. To repeat, nobody knows for certain how effective was the attire of the Modzitzer on that day, but he was the first person to stand up to the communists—with a *yarmulke* on his head—and he was the first person to receive an exit visa from Lithuania to the United States. In effect, he opened the flood gates. Many other Jews followed,[12] including Rabbi Aaron Kotler, founder and *rosh yeshivah* of the famous Lakewood (New Jersey) Yeshivah.

By way of Shanghai and Japan, Reb Shaul and his family arrived by ship at San Francisco, thence by train to New York City, where he finally settled in the Williamsburg section of Brooklyn. There, he established a chasidic center. Together again with his old friends from Poland, Rabbi Yosef Yitzchak Schneersohn and Rabbi Shimon Kalisch of Amshinow, he formed a threesome dedicated to the spiritual uplift of American Jewry.[13] And, as they say, the rest is history. Jewish America has never been the same again, and thank God for that!

We finally come to the place where this musical diary ends. Ben Zion Shenker recalls the day—he was there at that momentous occasion, at that astounding moment in time. It was *erev* Pesach *matzoh* baking in 5701. "I happened to be there at the time they were baking hand *matzohs*, in a *matzoh* factory, and the Modzitzer Rebbe was sitting there, leaning on his cane (not because he needed it but because it was traditional for rebbes in Poland to walk with canes; a trademark, as it were). He was deep in thought. Suddenly he began tapping with his cane and foot and humming, so I knew something was coming up. Then, just as suddenly, he ceased the tapping, looked up at all of us *chasidim* in the room, and said, '*Baruch Hashem*, I finally finished "*Min Hameitzar*."'"

It had taken him this long to finish it; the act of making *matzohs* was a sign he was out of danger and his mind could relax enough to finish the *niggun*. It was an appropriate moment, for Pesach *matzohs* were being made for the *seder*, and it was time to say *Hallel*. It was then that Reb Shaul composed the culmination of the song, the last part of which says: "This the day the Lord has made; let us rejoice and be glad of it."

All this happened oh so long ago, yet his songs—the cherished *niggunim* of the Modzitzer Rebbe—are still sung and hummed at special occasions and not-so-special times all over the world.

Perhaps right now, you, sitting at the window of a bus as the sun rises, are humming one. Perhaps it's the only *niggun* you know. Perhaps, but sing on. And when you stop singing, take a moment out to say, "Thank God for the songs that almost weren't." That, too, is a prayer answered.[14]

19

A Fair Exchange

There once was an exchange of letters between Napoleon and Cherubini.

Napoleon: My dear Cherubini, you are certainly an excellent musician; but really your music is so noisy and complicated that I can make nothing of it.

Cherubini: My dear general, you are certainly an excellent soldier; but in regard to music, you must excuse me if I don't think it necessary to adapt my compositions to your comprehension.[1]

Such an exchange of letters could also have occurred between Josef Stalin and one of the great Jewish leaders of his days—Benzion Shemtov—that is, if Stalin knew where the elusive Shemtov was.

If nothing else, Rabbi Benzion Shemtov was a foot soldier who single-handedly captured a Russian army with one hand tied behind his back. How did he do that? By being a composer for the right hand—he wrote one song—the right one!—beyond the comprehension of the Soviet Union, which could not figure out Shemtov and was determined to first catch the elusive rabbi, then lock him up and throw away the key.

His crime? No, not the song, which he had not yet written. His crime was his passion for Torah, his passion for *Hashem*, his passion for the Jewish people. In short, he was, in his own way, an excellent soldier and an excellent musician.

There is, however, nothing more difficult than talking about music, so let's talk about the composer. In the 1920s, at a secret meeting, Rabbi Benzion Shemtov joined the then Lubavitcher Rebbe, Yosef Yitzchak Schneersohn,[2] to form a group of dedicated Jews—a *minyan*, as it were—who would work for the preservation and promotion of *Yiddishkeit* in Russia, even at the ultimate risk of life. In those days, working for *Yiddishkeit* carried severe penalties of imprisonment and even sentence of death. This *minyan* undertook this work with total disregard of self, with complete *mesiras nefesh* (self-sacrifice) for *Yiddishkeit*.

In carrying out his tasks, Rabbi Benzion Shemtov outran and eluded the Russian secret police for a long time. During that time, while he was occupied in this work and "a wanted man," being sought by the authorities throughout Russia, a young Jewish woman, Esther Golda, came into the rabbi's life. Herself an activist and closely identified with his ideology, she was undeterred by the risks, and they soon became engaged.

In 1927, before they were married, Rabbi Shemtov was arrested and sentenced to seven years in Siberia for his *Chabad* activities.

And what of Reb Benzion's song—"The Armies of Our Rebbe"? Many years later, the Boys of Lubavitch Schools-London put out a record and cassette called "*Mi Armia* . . . Linking the Treasured Jewish Past with the Vibrant Jewish Future." The record jacket reads: "The theme song, '*Mi Armia*,' is adapted from an old Russian army march. The late Rabbi Benzion Shemtov heard it when he was exiled in Siberia for his efforts to bolster Jewish education. He composed words expressing our pride at being soldiers in the army of *Admurie* (our Rebbe), working to spread light and spirituality, in spite of any obstacle, until we bring about the ultimate redemption of *Moshiach*."

In English, here is the song, "*Be'ir Mi Armia Admurie*," that for more than a thousand times seventeen days shook Russia—and the world:

We are the army of our Rebbe,
And the whole world is talking about us:
About the time, during the days of terror,

We crossed the Red border
Armed to the teeth with ammunition
And united as one, all ready.
We are a young guard of a white-haired people,
Our slogan is the study of Torah
Our slogan is in the service of our Creator.
Our call is "Be ready, be ready!"
Through spying and deceit and treachery
Our wicked enemy has oppressed us.
But we march united as one family.
We keep our banners of Lubavitch students high.
N.K.V.D. has dealt us blow after blow
But we did not give in to this lopsided battle.
With faith in the victory of the Era of Redemption
We are continuing our work.
Many of our friends are in jails and exile
And not one of our heroes fell in battle.
We are the young guard; we went to replace them.
Our leader is the world's hero.
Under the pressures of enemy persecution and terror
Our brotherly union of young *chasidim* grow stronger.
In response to the persecutions we are everywhere
Our call is, "Be ready, be ready!"

We know from two of his children, Mendel and Israel Shemtov, two leading figures in the Lubavitch New York community of Crown Heights, that their father was jailed sixty-five years ago (as of 1992). In 1992, as the Lubavitcher Rebbe, Rabbi Menachem M. Schneerson, *shlita*, celebrated his ninetieth birthday, so too would have Benzion Shemtov celebrated his ninetieth.

Ninety years ago (as of 1992), their grandfather lived in a small place called Dulia, near Vilna, in Lithuania. Recalls the son, Mendel Shemtov, "My grandparents had a goodly size number of children; some of them died very young. And when my grandmother was pregnant with my father (my grandfather was not a Lubavitcher, but she was, having come from a Lubavitcher family) she went to the village of Lubavitch, to the previous Lubavitcher Rebbe's father, Rabbi Sholom Dovber.[3] And she told the Rebbe she was expecting a baby. She also told the Rebbe that she had lost several of her babies and didn't want to lose this one. She then asked for a blessing.

"The Rebbe told her that when she will have the little boy (the Rebbe foretold it would be a boy) for up to seven years she should not buy clothes for him; instead he should only wear hand-me-down clothing. He further stipulated that the clothes should be made of linen. Finally, the Rebbe told her the baby must be named 'Benzion,' which means 'son of Zion.' That is all that the Rebbe told my grandmother."

The mother, said the grandson Mendel, went back home and had "my father, and she carried out the Rebbe's words. And when my father was ten or eleven he visited the village of Lubavitch. That was the turning point for him. Chasidic legend tells us many *chasidim* consider their first birthday the moment their eyes fell upon Lubavitch. So my father stayed there. When he became older the Lubavitcher Rebbe (then Rabbi Yosef Yitzchak Schneersohn) made him, in combating communism, one of his emissaries, and he was involved in educating Jews in Kharkov in the Ukraine. There he taught little children till the communists came and arrested him. At the time he was engaged to my mother; still, they sent him off, without his *kallah*, to Siberia for years. Why? Because he was teaching Torah to little boys in the big *shul*, and the Reds didn't like that."

After a year he was voluntarily joined by his *kallah* Esther Golda. You know how they married in Siberia? He needed a ring. They took a silver spoon and, with the help of a blacksmith, fashioned a wedding ring. For obvious reasons they had no trouble gathering a *minyan* of Jews to witness the blessed event. As for the *mikvah* (ritual bathing place), they used the ice-cold ocean. Benzion was about twenty-eight and Esther Golda was about twenty-three.

Siberia: the place of frozen dreams for so many Jews. But no matter what, no matter where Benzion Shemtov was, the rabbi was always working for the Rebbe, in spite of the sacrifices and dangers. Countless other Jews never returned from Siberia.

Some say Rabbi Shemtov composed his *niggun* in jail, some say in Siberia, still others say he composed it after he and his family were safely out of Russia. There's no doubt, however, that his *niggun* did jail time with him. You have to read between the lines of the *niggun* to know the true story of the Jews' exodus from Russia, but it's all there. Some people live on the run. The *niggun* is the story of one man who lived thus, but it's also the exacting suffering the Jews of the Soviet Union willingly paid on the road to ultimate victory, as it is said, "All the people arose as one man."[4]

From the time of his release from Siberia until he and his family left Russia in late 1946, Rabbi Shemtov, although constantly sought and harassed by the Russian authorities, continued his work of inaugurating Jewish religious schools throughout Russia. These schools were illegal. Countless Russian Jews received a Jewish education and were provided with religious amenities only through the efforts of this dedicated band—the Lubavitcher Rebbe, *shlita*, and his *minyan* of *chasidim*. Especially during that period, Mrs. Shemtov was a vital force and a source of encouragement in her husband's endeavors, whilst at the same time raising their young family— Mendel, Yisroel, Berel, Abraham, Fradel, and Bessie—a task made infinitely more difficult by having a husband "on the run" and being constantly harassed and questioned by the Soviet Secret Police, the dreaded N.K.V.D. The survival of Judaism there and then was largely a result of their efforts—and other dedicated Jews like them—inspired by the indefatigable direction of the Lubavitcher Rebbe.

Another story about Benzion Shemtov: When his children were young, he arranged a teacher to come in and learn with them; fortunately, he had a very sympathetic landlady. She set up a never-ending game of checkers, so when the secret police came to the house looking for the father, she and the teacher would hide the Jewish study books and pretend they were playing checkers as the kids watched. It was the only game in town where nobody won or lost— and provided a good cover.

By anybody's account, it was a very big miracle that the Shemtovs were allowed to leave Russia. "When we left Russia," said Mendel Shemtov, "we didn't know if we were going to go to Poland or directly to jail. And, in fact, later we found out, other Jews trying to leave the Soviet Union in '46 and '47, after us, were jailed."

It was also a big victory for *Chabad Chasidus.* For thirty years the soldiers of the Lubavitcher Rebbe had put up a great fight to educate Soviet Jewish children, fought for *Yiddishkeit*, and, for their efforts, had often been thrown into jails. And now "in the middle of the day like the Jews coming out of Egypt," said Mendel Shemtov, "we Jews were leaving Russia. This had to be a great victory for all Jews, a new start."

From Russia, the previous Lubavitcher Rebbe sent the Shemtovs to Poland, Czechoslovakia, Paris, then to London. There, together, Rabbi and Mrs. Shemtov initiated the Lubavitch movement in England (you can read all about it in the book *Challenge—an Encoun-*

ter with Lubavitch-Chabad). Apart from *Chabad*'s normal activities, they opened a *Talmud Torah* in their own small home for Jewish children whose families had no religious affiliations. Some of the pupils of that small *Talmud Torah* are now *sheluchim* of the Rebbe, *shlita*, in other centers around the world. In sum, Rabbi Benzion Shemtov was the first *sheliach* in England. His wife started the first *neshei* women's group in London. In addition to her many other accomplishments, she was a talented authoress of a number of books of English short stories published in the United Kingdom. Many of these stories have as their theme *hashgochah perotis* (divine providence), as illustrated in her own eventful life.

Finally, Rabbi Shemtov carried his song with him to the United States. There, one day, as his family drew close to the Schneersons, he sang the *niggun* in front of the Lubavitcher Rebbe's[5] mother, Chana. Deeply impressed with the song, she asked Rabbi Shemtov to put it on a tape for the Rebbe to hear. When the Rebbe listened to it, he asked the rabbi to sing it in front of the *chasidim* at *farbrengens* (chasidic get-togethers). Forever since, it's been sung regularly after *farbrengens* when the Rebbe gives out *mashke* (strong alcoholic drinks).

As for further insights into how Rabbi Shemtov wrote such a *niggun* that has inspired generations of Jews, nobody can say. He was a private man who "never discussed his personal insights into the *niggun*," said his son Mendel. "Yet if anyone ever wanted to study the whole exodus of Jews from Russia, my father surely put it in the form of a song, and the *niggun*, considering what is happening today, right now as we're sitting here, is as fresh and as relevant as when he composed it. As the song says, 'Our call is, "Be ready, be ready!"' The only difference is, from then to now, there's more of us marching in the armies of our Rebbe."

Rabbi Shemtov's *niggun* is a song without end.

Part of his song includes his being one of the first rabbis to recognize Rabbi Menachem Mendel Schneerson as the Lubavitcher Rebbe, *shlita*, after the passing of the previous Rebbe.

Another part: he originated the compiling of *sichos* (collected talks) of the Rebbe's speeches during his weekly *farbrengens* during *Shabbos*. Rabbi Shemtov: "We had to have something for each person so he could learn something very easily every week." What he began in his own house soon mushroomed into a worldwide organization. Nowadays there's hardly a Jew in this world who can't get to read the words of the Lubavitcher Rebbe, if he or she wants to, thanks to the tireless efforts on the part of one dedicated Jew, Rabbi Benzion Shemtov.

Hashem sees and hears all. Nothing is lost.

When Rabbi Benzion passed away in an accident in 1976, his son Mendel sat *shivah* in Kfar Chabad, Israel. "A man came to pay a *shivah* call," remembers Mendel, "and the man said, 'Listen. The Lubavitcher Rebbe is like Dovid Hamelech. Why? Because King David was a big *tzadik* and a very big Talmud scholar; he was such a king, he was running a war, he was running a whole nation, and yet he found time to make *Tehillim*, not for kings, not for learned people, but for plain Jews like me.

"'And the Lubavitcher Rebbe is also such a big *tzadik*,' said this man, whom I had never met before and have never seen again. This man said to me, 'And yet he [the Rebbe] finds time to make such little *sichos* that are good for me also. *Tehillim* are for plain people. *Sichos* are like little *Tehillim*. Something special for plain Jews. That's a fair exchange, as I see it.'"

Hearing that, the son, grieving for his beloved departed father, found himself smiling. After all, his father, through a sole *niggun* and countless efforts, had inspired thousands in many countries to elevate their spiritual standards, to be big enough and to be humble enough to follow the guidance and directives of the Rebbe, *shlita*, in his outreach efforts to spread the essence of Judaism throughout the world. It was a fair exchange. Even Napoleon and Cherubini couldn't have said it any better.

20

Embers midst the Ruins[1]

Rabbi Yisroel Spira,[2] the late chasidic Rebbe of Bluzhev, of blessed memory, was heir to the dynasty of the B'nai Yisos'chor, Harav Tzvi Elimelech of Dinov and the grand rabbis of Bluzhev. Before the war, Rabbi Spira was Rav of Prochnik.

Then came World War II. His *rebbetzin* and their only child— a daughter, her husband, and their children—were among the Six Million. Rabbi Spira suffered for nearly five years in a succession of labor, death, and concentration camps. His personal travail began in the ghetto in Lublin, a camp that was commanded by a notorious sadist. Out of perhaps half a million people who passed through the Lublin ghetto, there are only fourteen known survivors.

Rabbi Spira had many memories. They are a panorama of tribute to the Jewish people. They are tales of strength, courage, faith, resistance, self-sacrifice, holiness. They are expressions of people— great and simple men and women, religious and nonreligious—who knew that their cause, and not the murderers', would ultimately prevail, people whose great wish was that they not lose their inner strength and that they not be forgotten. One such memory, like others, paints a picture in which pride overcomes pathos and light banishes darkness.

In the Bluzhever Rav's *beis Midrash*, as in hundreds of others, each *Yom Tov* ends with *ne'ilas hachag*, a soulful, joyful gathering of refreshment, song, and Torah. But the Bluzhever *beis Midrash* in Brooklyn is different. *Ne'ilas hachag* always concludes with a lively singing and dancing of "May they all come to serve You," from the Rosh Hashanah-Yom Kippur liturgy. That "*Veye'esoyu*" goes back to 1941 in the ghetto of Lublin. Tens of thousands of Jews were crowded together in the ghetto square waiting for their own Final Solution.

The Bluzhever Rav was one of them. The Gerrer *Rebbetzin*, wife of the late Reb Yisroel,[3] and her son Reb Leibel were there. They and other great and ordinary people spoke to one another, giving each other strength as they prepared to go together in sanctification of the Name. (After the war, the Bluzhever Rav wrote to the Gerrer Rebbe, informing him of the greatness of spirit with which his nearest ones faced their end.)

Another person in that group was Rabbi Yehuda Leib Orlean, who was one of the key figures in the establishment and growth of the *Beis Ya'akov* movement.

Rabbi Orlean said to the Bluzhever Rav, "Tonight is Shemini Atzeres. We have no *sefer Torah* with which to rejoice, but at least we can say the '*Ato Horeiso*' prayer."

With that, Rabbi Orlean raised his beautiful, powerful voice in the words that had always signaled the outbreak of joy, the tingle that was the prelude to the *hakofos* (Torah circuits) of Shemini Atzeres and Simchas Torah.

"You have been shown to know that *Hashem*—He is God. There is no other beside Him!"

Thousands of voices repeated after him in a crescendo of devotion. If this was indeed to be their last *Yom Tov*, then they would surrender their souls with unflinching proclamation that there was none but Him; that *Hashem*, the God of mercy, might assume the attribute of *Elokim*, the dispenser of uncompromising justice, but He still remained the God of Mercy whether or not we understood his ways.

The verses continued: first Rabbi Orlean serving as cantor, the largest congregation he ever led, repeating after him. Tears flowed like a river. "*Ato Horeiso*" was concluded, but Rabbi Orlean had another thought. Again he turned to the Bluzhever Rav.

"The Nazi soldiers saw us and heard us. They think we were crying because we fear them. Let us show them the truth."

He began singing "*Veye 'esoyu*" with a lively, infectious tune. What a beautiful liturgical poem! It foretells the End of Days when everyone, including the most distant of nations, will come to the Mountain of God to pledge their devotion to Him, to serve Him, to proclaim Him as King. It concludes "and they will give You the crown of sovereignty."

He sang and others joined. Hands clutched one another and feet began to dance. It was Shemini Atzeres and Jews rejoiced. More—under the muzzles of German rifles they sang that even the hated murderers, the most degraded and bestial of men, would one day acknowledge the kingship of *Hashem*. They sang and danced until the SS commandant arrived and the death march began.

Hardly anyone survived that horrible night. But the Bluzhever Rav was spared, and that "*Veye'esoyu*" and that tune is recalled at the end of every festival in the Bluzhever *beis Midrash*.

21

Travels of Two Niggunim

Traveling together has always been a great test. Ask any Jew since the days of Moses, and he'll probably tell you that the time to enjoy a 220-year enslavement in, and freedom flight from, Egypt is about forty years after you unpack. Since then every Jew continues to travel in order to come home.

It's no wonder then that on the nights of Passover, any *chasid* worth his soul on fire is already there, or on the way, wherever his rebbe holds court to honor the idea of freedom. Whether the *seder* table is set by the Modzitzer or Lubavitcher or Kalever Rebbe, there you must be. This *gadol hador*, or rebbe, as he is frequently called in bonding to his *chasidim*, has a unique relationship with them that can never be severed. This bond is so powerful that when the *chasid* is happy so is the rebbe. Such interaction is illustrated in the following story.

In the year 1948,[1] during the second Passover *seder*, held in Brooklyn, New York, seated at table were the previous Lubavitcher

Rebbe, Rabbi Yosef Yitzchak Schneersohn (1880–1950), and his close *chasidim*. The minds and bodies of these holy men were reliving the Israelites' deliverance from enslavement more than 3,200 years ago, as recounted in Exodus.

In the ancient language of Aramaic, the Rebbe opened the *seder* and intoned:

"This is the bread of affliction that our fathers ate in the lands of Egypt. All who are hungry, let them come and eat; all who are needy, let them come and celebrate Pesach with us. Now we are here; next year we may be in Israel. Now we are slaves; in the year ahead may we be free men."

Who during those brief moments didn't think of the plague that afflicted the firstborn of the Egyptians! And who during that time didn't think it was his own journey out of Egypt to the Promised Land! During this long night of the Jewish Souls, the Rebbe and his *chasidim* marked their path, remembering all of Israel's firstborn children, ever grateful to be alive.

As the evening drew on, the *chasidim* continued talking late into the night, when all of a sudden the Rebbe did an unusual thing. Instead of turning to Reb Shmuel Zalmanov,[2] as he usually did at such times, he turned to a certain *chasid* and asked him to choose a song to sing—a *niggun*.

The *chasid* chose the "*Mitteler Rebbe's Kappele.*"[3] This *niggun*, always a favorite choice of chasidic singers in the village of Lubavitch, was composed by an ensemble of musically gifted young men, divided into two groups—vocalists (*baalei shir*) and musicians (*baalei zimra*)—who composed, sang, and played *niggunim* in the presence of their rebbe, the Mitteler Rebbe, Rabbi Dov Ber of Lubavitch.[4] Although he himself never composed melodies, the Mitteler Rebbe nevertheless conducted all aspects of his leadership in a royal way, and no less, in his eyes, was the royal performance of a *niggun*.

But whenever the Mitteler Rebbe requested the *niggun*, the "*Mitteler Rebbe's Kappele,*" his orchestra of *chasidim* smiled with utmost eagerness and supreme gratitude. At such a time they played their hearts out, as if it were a matter of life and death. And indeed this special melody is, and will always be, a lifesaver. When the musicians played it, they knew they'd prevent the Mitteler Rebbe from departing from this world through his longing after God (*kelos hanefesh*). Some *chasidim* explained that through listening to *niggunim* played by musical instruments, the Mitteler Rebbe maintained his existence in this world. Others said that in his supreme service to *Hashem*, the Mitteler Rebbe could have literally expired into Godliness. This *niggun* without words is a musical composition divided into four sections, symbolizing the four rungs on the ladder of approach and devotion of man to Godliness.

Gladly, then, in the presence of the previous Lubavitcher Rebbe, did the *chasid* chosen sing this melody in honor of the Mitteler Rebbe. Who knew! Maybe it would keep a Jewish soul from expiring that very night. After he finished the *niggun*, the *chasid* sat down and closed his eyes for a while. When he finally opened his eyes again, he noticed that everyone was still in the room and the night of the second Passover *seder* was still going on. Nothing physically had occurred. Yet, who knew!

During the course of the evening the Rebbe asked the same *chasid* to choose another *niggun* to sing. This time he chose "*Lechatchilah Ariber*," or, as it's come to be known, "*Einz-Tzvei-Drai-Fir*." Everybody was baffled by the Rebbe's actions—including this particular *chasid* himself. No one dared question the Rebbe's actions, but their queries were short-lived. For, as soon as the *Yom Tov* was over, this particular *chasid* received a telegram at the *seder*, wishing him *mazel tov* on the birth of his first grandchild—a boy—a firstborn.

While this *chasid*, whose name was Reb Mordechai Dov Ber Teleshevsky, was singing those two *niggunim*, his granddaughter gave birth to her son—the great-grandchild—whom she named Menachem Mendel Popack.

Over the years, now Rabbi Menachem Mendel Popack had his own travels, finally arriving in Cape Town, South Africa, and continuing to serve as *sheliach* there. There also lives his son, Dovid Eliezer Popack.

"Yes," says Dovid Eliezer Popack, "at the moment that my great-grandfather was singing those two *niggunim* in front of the Previous Rebbe, my father was born. My great-grandfather brought my father into the world with two special *niggunim*, and my father, with *niggunim* in his own heart, has brought me here. All the more reason to celebrate Passover. It's my journey, too."

Yes, since the days of Moses, every Jew continues to travel in order to come home.

22

Rebbe Hoppin'

Growing up in the year 1949 in the Williamsburg section of Brooklyn for this on-again, off-again Jewish boy wasn't easy. Caught between the outside secular world and the inside chasidic world, neither section I felt comfortable with, I was left to my own devices: daydreaming and daydreaming about my daydreams.

Once, a Jewish teacher in a local high school, frustrated from teaching me how to play piano, told me a story about music. "One summer, the eighteenth-century Austrian composer Joseph Haydn ('Papa') and his group of musicians had been entertaining at the summer estate of the Duke of Esterhazy. By then the musicians were homesick: The summer had been long, they missed their families, and the duke, whom they worked for, didn't seem ready to return to the city.

"So, sympathetic Papa composed the *Farewell* Symphony, his Forty-fifth. Outdoors, under a calm night sky, the duke and his family and friends assembled to hear the new work. One by one the musicians took their seats on the stage, each lighting the candle at his music stand. Haydn appeared on the stage, bowed to the duke, then turned to face the orchestra.

"The music began: As symphonies go, the music typically consisted of four related movements. But something unusual happened in the final movement: Suddenly, as if timed to last precisely the length of the movement, each musician, one by one, stopped playing, blew out his candle and immediately left the stage. Twenty musicians, 19, 18, 17, 16, 15, 14—the duke was flabbergasted, turning his head this way to his wife, then that way to his friends—13, 12, 11, 10, 9, 8—twisting and turning his head so much, the tired duke finally sat back and waited for the inevitable, and it came—7, 6, 5, 4, 3, 2, 1—when the last musician stopped the music before the final notes, he blew out his candle and left the stage. It was then that Papa Haydn turned to face his audience, and bowed low, with an appropriate smile on his face, to the duke.

"Smiling back, the duke got the message. The next day everyone returned to Vienna."

That was the first and last story the music teacher ever told me. Why this story at that particular time? I don't know, but he—perhaps it was his way of saying farewell—stopped teaching me to play the piano. I went back to daydreaming and daydreaming about my daydreams.

Now, after so many years away from Williamsburg, I know that everybody has a farewell in him. Which brings to mind another story, this time occurring inside the chasidic world while I was nearby tripping over piano keys. It was told to me by Akiva Greenberg, now a rabbi and teacher at Yeshiva Chanoch Lena'ar in the Crown Heights section of Brooklyn, New York.

Once upon a time (and don't get me wrong; this is a true story!)—once, a singular man came to this country and was quickly heralded as the Hungarian who assumed the principalship of Yeshivah Torah Voda'ath (at that time located in Williamsburg) in 1923. Who was this man who was personally responsible for most of the advances and innovations in American Torah education until his untimely death in 1948? A self-effacing idealist who loved to be called "Mister"—anything but "rabbi"[1]—he knew how to reach Jewish children in very special ways.

During the *yeshivah*'s fledgling days, "Mister" came out to the street one day and saw some Jewish boys, and, so the story goes, he said, "Come, boys, I'll buy you ice cream." Off to the local *kosher nosh* store Reb Shraga and the boys went, after which they sat on a stoop as he told them funny Jewish stories. The next day he met the boys again outside for ice cream and stories. A day or two later, the boys couldn't wait for the rabbi, and to show their enthusiasm each brought a friend. This time, as expected, Reb Shraga, he who was born to teach the teacher, appeared and bought all the boys ice cream. But he pulled a switch. Perhaps because there were too many boys to sit on one stoop or perhaps because the rebbe planned it that way, he brought the ice-cream boys into a classroom in his *yeshivah*, saying, "Come, my young scholars, I want to teach you something." Once inside, the boys never left, becoming *bochurim* right then and there, and, says Rabbi Akiva Greenberg, who joined the same *yeshivah* the next year, after Reb Shraga's death, "that's how the famous 'ice-cream *yeshivah*' got off to its great start. Rabbi Mendlowitz was very interested in seeing that his *yeshivah* boys should not become rabbis, but teachers. He saw the work he had to do in America, teaching young Jews, and he went right to it."

Yeshiva Torah Voda'ath, Reb Shraga's open prayer, was to be for teachers. But there were moments—better yet, hours!—when the *yeshivah* was filled with the sounds of heavenly *niggunim*. Day and night, *bochurim* walked the halls of the *yeshivah* humming tunes, exchanging songs like baseball cards, sometimes at the expense of Torah-learning time. Was this *yeshivah* for teachers? openly wondered the *yeshivah* rebbes. Or was this a school for cantors? Where on earth did these *bochurim* learn such *chasidishe* songs? These *niggunim*, as far as their *yeshivah* teachers were concerned, had no place in an *American* institution dedicated to the furtherance of Jewish education. *Oy,* if Reb Shraga were alive today this would never happen! Never!

But it was happening.

Now the inside story can be told, of how part of a generation of Jewish *bochurim* learned to be rabbis, teachers, and *chasidim* of *rebbeim*. As it is written, "Each person expresses himself on three levels—thought, speech and deed. When a *chasid* carries out his rebbe's directives, he unites with the rebbe's actions. When he learns *Chasidus*, he unites with the rebbe's facet of speech. But when he sings the rebbe's *niggun*, he becomes united with the highest of the three levels—the rebbe's thoughts."[2]

Reb Akiva remembers: "In Torah Voda'ath, the guys loved to sing. And you can be sure we didn't pluck these airs from the air.

What did we do? On Friday nights, we knew the rebbes in the area held *tischen* (chasidic get-togethers), and so we did the following: After we ate our *Shabbos* evening meals in different houses—always outside our *yeshivah*—we regrouped, thirty to forty guys, at a designated place and went rebbe hoppin'.

"In those days, the years after World War II, most chasidic rebbes from all over Europe emigrated to Williamsburg, Brooklyn, a few to the Lower East Side in Manhattan. But Williamsburg, thanks in part to the great name of Reb Shraga Feivel Mendlowitz, was *the* place for a Jewish lad to be. There was a time, when I was a *bochur* in Torah Voda'ath, when it could almost be said that on every street in Williamsburg there was a lamp post and a rebbe. And you can be certain that the rebbes gave off greater light."

Reb Akiva also made a journey. At the age of sixteen, he left his home in Canada because he wanted to study in a *yeshivah*, first enrolling in Torah Voda'ath in Brooklyn, New York, then traveling to *Eretz Yisroel* where he enrolled in a famous *yeshivah* in Bnei Brak. "Those," he said, "were some of the happiest years in my life."

Reb Akiva loved *niggunim*, and so did every other *bochur* he knew in those days. Unbeknownst to the *yeshivah*, which would have frowned on such activity because it had nothing to do with the *bochurim* becoming teachers in those days, the *bochurim* put their collective heads together and figured out exactly, every Friday night, when each rebbe would make his entry at a *tisch* where his *chasidim* gathered for the night to continue celebrating the *Shabbos* Bride with song, prayer, and story.

"We had it down to a science," says Reb Akiva. "We knew when this rebbe came in, when this rebbe went out, when this rebbe came in. And we'd arrive at the beginning of the *tisch* and learn one or two *niggunim* every week by this method. Our friends never failed us; always we were alerted which rebbe was about to teach a new *niggun*. So we went and listened. From one *tisch* to another and to another, we went and listened and listened and listened. That was it for us. Not to learn any *Chasidus*. Just a *niggun*—that's all we wanted—preferably two, every *Shabbos* night."

Then, about 2 or 3 A.M., when the rebbe hoppers had a few "great *niggunim*" under their belts, they returned to their *yeshivah* and sat for an hour in somebody's room, usually on the first floor in order not to disturb the students who were fast asleep. "We'd sing and recall in every detail each *niggun* we had learned that night," says Reb Akiva, "and the next day, *Shabbos*, even having been up all night, we would eagerly teach them to the other students in the *yeshivah* who were interested in learning; then all week long, the *bochurim* of Torah Voda'ath spent a lot of time singing *niggunim*. It was the thing to do. I tell you, there were always new *niggunim* coming up, and you'd walk into the *beis hamidrosh* and you thought you were walking into a *beis hamidrosh* specializing in *chazonim* (cantors), because the guys would be singing *niggunim* along with *Gemara*. We *yeshivah* guys thrived on *niggunim*, and it was a beautiful experience."

It's said somewhere, "In the path a Jewish person wants to go, that is the way *Hashem* will lead him." Or, as secular people may put it, "Bring the body and the mind will follow." So, too, the inevitable happened to these *bochurim* who kept showing up at *tischen* just to snatch a *niggun* or two for their repertoire. As they started the rounds of rebbe hoppin', week by week, suddenly a *bochur* would beg off exiting with his chums. "Look, you go, I want to hang out here for a little while longer. Catch up with you. Later."

Such statements increased as time went on. In those days there was no Krazy Glue adhesive, but somehow a *bochur* here and a *bochur* there seemed glued to one rebbe's *tisch* or to another, and subsequently dropped out of Yeshiva Torah Voda'ath to take his place among the other *chasidim* of the rebbe. Of course, Krazy Glue notwithstanding, this did not sit well with Yeshiva Torah Voda'ath, but what could they do!

"What did these guys see in these *rebbeim*? What did I see in my own rebbe, the Vizhnitzer Rebbe?[3] I'll tell you. A lot of things, or often one thing that separated one rebbe from another. Maybe they liked his appearance, his outfit, his hat, the company of *chasidim* he kept, his songs—oh yes, his *niggunim*, definitely that!—or his *tischen*, his Torah comprehension, his personality, his deep chasidic thoughts, his love of *Kabbalah*. Even his *ahavas Yisroel*. Eventually all of us were caught up with a special rebbe, and his spiritual wonders, and we dropped off to join him."

"Then," added Reb Akiva, his eyes flashing with excitement, "in 1949 there was a kind of occurrence in Williamsburg, the likes of which I'll never forget. Two rebbes—the Modzitzer Rebbe[4] and the Vizhnitzer Rebbe—both of whom had *chasidim* in America, left *Eretz Yisroel* for a visit and arrived on the same boat, reaching Williamsburg at the same time."

"That *Shabbos* thousands of Jews from all over the country arrived in Williamsburg. It didn't matter what kind of *chasid* you were—for this historic moment was not to be missed. And so the *yeshivah bochurim* also found out when the *tischen* were. Think of all the new *niggunim* we might learn! Think of dancing and singing in the rebbes' presence. Think of what we would tell our sleeping buddies at the *yeshivah* later!

"Through our connections, we found out that the Modzitzer Rebbe would hold his *tisch* early, in what was then known as the Polish *shtibel.* When his *tisch* was over—and his *tisch* was not long— you'd think a bomb had blown up the *shul.* Not a single pane of glass was intact in the windows. Not a single chair—nor a table— stood on its legs. The only thing that was not touched was the *aron hakodesh.* Otherwise the place was a complete and total wreck. So many Jews had danced so hard, bursting into song after song, on tables, chairs, benches, on top of each other, jumping up and down, with the dancing spilling out into the streets. Why? What was the big deal? The Modzitzer Rebbe simply—hah, simply!—had introduced a new *niggun.* He sang the *niggun* and taught us the *niggun,* and then we started to sing and march, march and sing and dance to the *niggun,* and everybody suddenly went wild, haywire, and in their —mine too—spiritual excitement the *shtibel* came apart at its seams."

Here, Reb Akiva Greenberg paused to catch his breath.

Then he went on. "After that, everybody went to the *tisch* where the Vizhnitzer Rebbe held court, at the *beis hamidrosh* on Ross Street, next to where his son then lived, before he moved to Monsey, New York."

The same thing happened all over. The Vizhnitzer Rebbe introduced a *niggun*—"and later that morning we left the *shul,* or what was left—minus windows, doors, tables, benches, anything only good for firewood, if that," Reb Akiva said.

"As we headed back to our *yeshivah,* we left thousands of *chasidim* dancing in the streets, humming one *niggunim* after another, and, I might add, a number of our *bochurim* were lost happily in the *chasidishe* crowd forever. Who cared—our task was to bring *niggunim* home to our sleeping buddies."

Then one day it happened—7, 6, 5, 4, 3, 2, 1—when the last musician stopped the music before the final notes, he blew out his candle and left the stage. So it was with the "musician" Rabbi Akiva Greenberg, who left eventually to become a *chasid* of the Vizhnitzer

Rebbe in Israel. Why? "For the love of his *niggunim*," said Reb Akiva. Since then he has had only joy. "With a song in my heart every day, I am both a rabbi and a teacher."

At that, even "Mister" Shraga Feivel Mendlowitz in heaven— he who had been born to teach the teacher—must be smiling with pride.

23

The Dreamer Who Never Sleeps

From his hard, plastic seat, Moshe Goldman, an observant Jew from Borough Park, Brooklyn, watched the Mormons come and go at the Salt Lake City airport. Always there was a seat and destination for them. For him, too, there was a seat, indeed, an airport of choice seats, but he had no place to go. Not a plane, bus, train, or even a donkey was headed in his direction. As for returning to Los Angeles, whence he came after completing business in Anaheim, that was out of the question. He had flown from L.A. to Salt Lake City only to be told there were not enough passengers to make the trip to the East Coast.

For the next twenty-four hours, then, he was stranded at the airport. In a way it didn't matter. It was *erev* Tisha B'Av. He couldn't—wouldn't!—travel on one of the saddest days in Jewish history. With his luggage to lean his head on, Moshe Goldman sat tight, perhaps feeling distressed and alone, a man dressed all in black—suit, hat and beard—among strangers. But that's the way it was.

Don't feel sorry for Moshe Goldman. Know that he is a Jewish composer of *niggunim*. Asleep or awake, he is a dreamer of the day—in other words, a realist—who always acts upon his dream with open eyes, to make it possible.

In the airport twilight of dozing off, he sees sharp or amorphous shapes of his present life and his past. He sees the ten to twelve hours he was supposed to stay over in Anaheim to adjust a plastic machine turn into four days. He sees his wife phoning him, looking forward to his coming home. He sees his kids, all wanting to speak to him on the phone—at the same time. He sees the Bobover *yeshivah* in Bat Yam, Israel, where his fellow *bochurim* huddle together there in a bomb shelter during the Six Day War. He sees all the boys at Bobover Camp Shalva, in the Catskill Mountains of New York, who inspired him to compose more than six tapes of *niggunim*. He sees a dear friend, the camp's head counselor, pushing a wheelchair with a boy who has only one leg.

Having to fast for the next twenty-four hours, he sees Tisha B'Av. He sees the divine decree (1321 B.C.E.) that the Jewish people remain in the desert for forty years till that generation dies out, after they cried over the twelve spies' false report of the land. He sees Nebuchadnezzar the Babylonian destroy the First Temple . . . the Romans under Titus raze the Second Temple. He sees the last fortress of the Bar Kochba rebellion destroyed, with terrible loss of Jewish life . . . Jerusalem plowed up and turned into a non-Jewish city—Aelia Capitolina (about 1253 C.E.). He sees more than 300,000 Spaniard Jews leave Spain on the 9th of *Av*, 1492. He sees the First World War begun on that date, how it uprooted large Jewish populations and threw most Jewish communities into chaos. In its wake came the Russian Revolution, which systematically crushed Judaism, the Cossack massacres of Jews throughout the Ukraine (1918–1921) and the conditions that gave rise to Nazism and the Holocaust. Moshe Goldman sees . . . he sees everything . . .

But then he sees no more; instead he hears a tinkling of sound. A bar or two—that's all. Is he asleep? Is he awake? He wakens . . . he falls asleep again . . . he's never certain of the state of things as he sits restlessly in the airport; yet the tinkling of sounds goes on, day, night, twilight, dawn, sleeping, yawning, staring into the nothingness of the airport setting. The sounds never leave him.

"My mind," said Moshe Goldman, "was certainly dwelling on all the sadness of this day. Suddenly *Hashem* sent me a few bars of a song. And it kept running through my mind all day and night; I slept a little bit, I wakened, I slept—the bars pitter-pattered through me. Da—de—da—de—da—da—de—da—de—da—de—da—da. De—da—da—da—de—da—de—da . . . By itself I had no idea what it meant."

Finally he forced his eyes wide open. He could still hear the sounds. What did it mean? Knowing what he had to do, he leafed open the *siddur* he had with him. In one of the *tefillos* from Rosh Hashanah, his eyes fell upon the words: "Is Efraim not My Beloved Son, from the beginning of creation; is he not a precious child that whenever I speak of him I recall him even more? Therefore My inner parts stir for him, I will surely have compassion on him, says the Lord" (Jeremiah 31:39). *"Habein Yokir Li Efraim im yeled sha-ashu'im ki mehday dabri boh zochor eskerenu od al kein hamu ma'ei lo rachei arachamenu ne'em Hashem."*

There he had it. "I fit these few bars into these words from the *siddur*," said Goldman, "and I created the most satisfying piece of music I ever wrote. Immediately I made a beginning and I made an end. The result was '*Habein Yokir Li Efraim.*'"

"Why am I telling you this story?" Goldman asked. "Because every *niggun* is a story by itself and ofttimes has a tale within a tale or . . . well, hear this story out. About a half year ago a young fellow visited me. It seems he was searching for the composer of '*Habein Yokir Li Efraim.*' Was I related to this Moshe Goldman who made a tape with this *niggun* on it? he asked me. I said yes. 'I am he.'"

"Then," said the young man, "I've come to tell you a story about your *niggun.*"

"I'd like to hear it," said Goldman.

The young man nostalgically told Goldman about his *bubbe*. Descended from a well-known rabbinical family, before she passed away the grandmother totaled over 200 grandchildren and great-grandchildren. Deep into her nineties, she had terminal cancer and was finally treated in a hospital in San Diego.

One day, the *bubbe* expressed a strong wish that all her relatives should visit her on a particular *Shabbos*. She had something to tell all of them, she said.

So the trek began. From all over the country, mostly from Borough Park, and from other parts of the world, the *bubbe*'s relatives flew to San Diego and rented a nearby hotel for the occasion.

When she saw all her "children" assembled around her at the

Se'udah Shelishis (the third meal eaten after the afternoon service on *Shabbat*) the *bubbe* wept with joy. And all her family, not knowing what to expect, were thrilled to see her. Bittersweet were the feelings. They awaited her words. In a faint voice, she finally turned to the young man and asked him to sing the *niggun*, Moshe Goldman's, "*Habein Yokir Li Efraim.*"

Soon all the other men joined in the song. The *bubbe* was beside herself with joy. This is what she wanted to tell everyone, to share with them in her last moments. In Yiddish, in Hebrew, the family men sang the song.

"This is for you, my dear family," she said, "something to remember me by. *Shabbos*, a flavor of Paradise about it, as it is written, 'I have a good gift in My treasure-house—it is the Sabbath, says God.'"

The singing of the *niggun* slowly continued, hesitatingly. It was as if nobody wanted it to end. Each word was clearly enunciated: a song by itself. The feeling was sweet, the tears were bitter. Beyond that, who knew! It was only a song picked out for a solemn occasion. It was only a song—or was it only that? "Is Efraim not My Beloved Son, from the beginning of creation; is he not a precious child that whenever I speak of him I recall him even more? Therefore My inner parts stir for him, I will surely have compassion on him, says the Lord."

"I will surely have compassion on him, says the Lord."

So be it: this was the last line of the *niggun*, and when it was laid to rest, the *bubbe* passed away. But life, as you well expect, carried on in this large family, for as the young man told Moshe Goldman, they now sing his *niggun* wherever two or more family members gather to celebrate their *bubbe*'s *yahrzeit*. It was a *Shabbos* gift, a hint of life everlasting in a world full of rest and repose. For one family, the *bubbe* carries the song and the song carries the *bubbe*.

Another dream: By now Moshe Goldman is forty-two years old, and he's been composing since the age of thirteen. At first he kept his *niggunim* private until he found an audience. That happened at the Bobover *yeshivah* in Bat-Yam, outside Tel Aviv, where *niggunim* are sung for every sacred occasion. One day, the *yeshivah* cantor mentioned aloud he'd like to sing a new *niggun*, "something different," as the cantor put it. Moshe Goldman came forward, offering one of his. Immediately it caught on, the *bochurim* picked it up like a bear to honey, and from then on the composer never stopped. "One thing led to the other until in a short period of four to five years I composed about fifteen *niggunim*."

Then the Six Day War came. Quickly the students and their teachers huddled together in the bomb shelter below the *yeshivah*. It was a difficult time. Trying to study, trying to stay alive. The fear of the war gripped everyone; terrified of what would be before the war, terrified during the war, they shuddered at the bleak future. Even when things took a good turn, the possible capture of Jerusalem, for instance, nobody rejoiced. There were too many uncertainties; the radio didn't help. No good news—definitive!—was heard. Stay tuned—the radio said—which they did. Nobody could concentrate on books and learning. Nobody could sleep. The *bochurim* took turns straying outside the shelter to see if others needed their help. After a while everyone got anxious because it took over twenty-four hours from the time they captured Jerusalem till the news came out that everything had been secured. Here and there still was pocket resistance, and the streets were considered unsafe, according to the radio. The last thing the Israeli authorities wanted was to create a panic among its own citizens, so, understandably, the news was sparse.

Moshe Goldman the *bochur* felt and saw it all. "We felt like we were in a pressure cooker. Rumors were starting to abound."

To uplift everybody's spirit in the shelter, the dreamer of the day began to sing a *niggun* he had finished secretly. Now was the time to bring it into the open. "*Beis Elokim neileich*"—"Let us go to the House of the Lord. Our feet were standing within your gates, O Jerusalem; Jerusalem that is built like a city in which [all Israel] is united together."

As more *bochurim* caught onto the song they started to sing it like a fugue. A pair of students started it; within moments another pair picked up the song, and then, shortly, another and then another and then another. Finally, at the end of the *niggun* everybody joined in to sing the last refrain, "Jerusalem that is built like a city in which [all Israel] is united together."

When they stopped singing, an inexplicable thing happened. A newscaster on the radio suddenly started shouting: "Jerusalem is ours! Jerusalem is ours!"

The *bochurim* broke out again into the song, and now, whenever Bobovers from Bat-Yam meet anywhere in the world, they break out into that song.

After that, in the United States, Moshe Goldman got married to Chaya Eisen. Currently they have nine children. During these family-oriented times, he was named director, in 1975, of a boys' Bobover summer camp, Camp Shalva, in South Fallsburg, New York. Meeting the 600 boys, aged six to thirteen, was a challenge, which was triggered by a question the camp manager posed to him: "How come you don't teach new things to the children?"

The next day, into the dining room marched Moshe Goldman, armed only with his *niggunim* to entertain the boys. If he had any doubts about himself, they were dispelled by the boys' overwhelming response.

"That gave me encouragement," he said. "Later that summer the head counselor came over to me and said, 'How about making a record of Camp Shalva *niggunim*?' I really liked that idea, and so I made my first tape. Now I have six cassettes, all very good sellers wherever *niggunim* are sold. Some call my music Camp Shalva, some people call it Bobover, some call it Moshe Goldman's songs. They seem to have universal appeal."

There's one *niggun* associated with Camp Shalva that Moshe Goldman will never forget. An image of the *niggun* remains within him forever.

Since that first year, Moshe Goldman, ever inspired by the campers at Shalva, has returned every year. One summer, he arrived and, entering the campgrounds, he saw his old redheaded friend, the head counselor, pushing a wheelchair. In it was a frail, thin boy. Not thinking beyond what he superficially saw, he approached his old friend, whom he hadn't seen since the year before. When he reached the head counselor, Goldman gulped. In the chair was the counselor's seven-year-old son with only one leg. Cancer, he was told, had taken the other. Not once had Goldman suspected the boy's condition. He knew the boy from previous years. Never had the father let on. What could he say? What could he do? The boy had cancer, his leg had to be amputated to save his life, and now after Goldman had sputtered out his sorrow, the man, an old thirty-five years old, slender, with a reddish beard, truly once the spirit of the camp, wheeled his son along the road. All the time Moshe Goldman had stood near the wheelchair, speaking to the father, he couldn't help notice the once bright eyes of the thin, white-complexioned boy looking up to heaven. The way Goldman saw it, "He had a look on his face as if he were begging for something; the boy's eyes were looking up for relief from his life, wishing he could be like other children, and yet he couldn't." It was a sight that immediately began to haunt Moshe Goldman.

Because of it, on the way home to Borough Park, Moshe Goldman composed another *niggun*: "*Elokai Neshomah*"—"My God, the soul which You have given within me is pure. You have created it, You have formed it, You breathed it into me, and You preserve it within me. You will eventually take it from me, and restore it within me in Time to Come. So long as the soul is within me, I offer thanks to You, Lord my God and God of my Fathers, Master of all works, Lord of all souls. Blessed are You Lord, who restores souls to dead bodies."

Moshe Goldman likes to link stories. Here is such a story. During the taping of an album, which contained "*Elokai Neshomah*," Moshe Goldman utilized an adult choir of five singers and the Camp Shalva choir. The music was mixed digitally by Michael Marciano, a Gentile with thirty years' experience in the music business. During the recording of "*Elokai Neshomah*," an unusual thing happened. One of the singers facing Marciano in the booth saw him crying incontinently and mentioned it to Goldman. Turning to Marciano, Goldman was at first puzzled by what he saw. Why was he weeping so? Had a terrible tragedy just happened to Marciano? After recording, he determined to speak to him.

He didn't have to wait. Immediately, Marciano approached him to ask, "Mr. Goldman, you've got to tell me what the words of that song mean. My eyes are streaming with tears, my heart is bleeding, and I don't even know why."

Goldman explained the words of the *niggun* "*Elokai Neshomah*" to the Gentile, but how could he adequately express his feelings about the counselor pushing his own son in a wheelchair along the darkening road? How could he express the ineffable? Some things he would never be able to put into words, he said, "so thank God for a *niggun*. That a song, with such Jewish power, can affect even a non-Jew, who didn't even understand a word of it, continues to keep me in awe of *niggunim*."

God has a lot of names, all known by Jews. One of the names is *Chuzuk*, which means "very strong" or "strength." Generally we pray to Him (*Chuzuk*) every *motzoei Shabbos*. We ask the Strong One to fill our requests; the Firm One to implement our prayers; and we ask that He will bless our work in the coming week with success.

In every man's life anything can happen at any time. So far, Moshe Goldman has handled his events with *niggunim*. A few years ago his first son, Avraham Yehoshua Goldman, a *yeshivah* rebbe in Toronto, Canada, was about to become engaged. In getting ready for the *simchah*, Goldman, as all dutiful husbands do, had to wait for his wife to finish dressing the children and herself. "Just five minutes more, Moshe," she said. He said okay.

While waiting for her, he turned to one of his young sons, who inherited Moshe's musical talents, and asked him to give him a D minor on the keyboard. "I'll try to come up with a *niggun*," Moshe said.

The boy began to play on the keyboard.

As soon as Goldman opened the *siddur*, his eyes fell upon the words "*Chuzuk yemalei mishaloseinu, omeitz yaaseh bakoshoseinu, vehu yishlach bemaaseh yodeinu, berochah vehatzlochah.*" "O Strong One . . . bless our work . . . with success."

"For the past few years," Goldman said, "this highly successful, recorded *niggun* in our Bobover circles is always sung at weddings and *bar mitzvahs*. All because I was so excited about my son's *simchah* and because my wife asked me for only five minutes."

These are some dreams of the day—and the dreamer who made them come true.

24

The French Don't Have a Word for It

nd the controversy goes on.
　　One year they want to scrap "the Marseillaise," the former, the present, or maybe the never-again French national anthem. Another year they want to slow it down. Next, change the lyrics. Next, put new emphasis on the tempo. Next—*Vive la France!*—they don't want to touch it at all. Next, they want to replace the word *war* with *peace, blood* with *love*. Next, who knows, they may plan to mount a national referendum—similar to what the U.S. Post Office did awhile back when they couldn't decide which Elvis Presley (the young Elvis or the older Elvis) to put on a commemorative stamp—and let the French people themselves choose the anthem. Tempers have flared, faces reddened, voices shouted, editorials condemned or praised, sometimes both in the same article; some teenagers, it was reported tongue-in-cheek, were seriously considering—well, maybe it was just talk—storming the Bastille again (nobody told the teens it no longer exists). All this controversy in a time of great peace in France—about their beloved national anthem?

What's going on in France that is making the French act like "mad dogs and Englishmen out in the noonday sun"? Why are they, because of one adopted Jewish *niggun*, willing to change their "swords" into "plowshares"?

In the words of Jewish writer Gitty Stolik:[1] "A number of years ago [1974] a large group of Jews from France who were looking into their roots came to Crown Heights [Brooklyn, New York] to acquaint themselves with the Lubavitcher movement. At the *hakofos* [of Simchas Torah], they were unable to join in with the singing, being unfamiliar with the melodies of the *niggunim*. Suddenly the Lubavitcher Rebbe, *shlita*, Rabbi Menachem Mendel Schneerson, began to sing a tune they knew well, that of the French national anthem (*'La Marseillaise'*), accompanying it with the words of a prayer, *'Ho'aderes Veho'emunah'* ['power and trustworthiness']. The singing began softly, as most of the chasidic multitude were unacquainted with the song. But the momentum built up and before long, French guests and bearded *chasidim* were singing the rousing march in unison. As the Rebbe kept them going, over and over, the newcomers and *chasidim* picked up in fervor, and soon the anthem was transformed into an outpouring of emotions. Suddenly the newcomers felt that all these bearded people were not strangers at all, but brothers, with one soul, one purpose and one God binding them all together. Feelings of love and yearning toward God were welling up and gripping them with their intensity.

"The singing stopped, but its echoes continued to resound in the hearts of these newcomers to Judaism. The indelible stamp the experience left on them gave them the strength to endure all the travails of a *baal teshuvah* (a returnee to Judaism) beginning a completely new lifestyle.

"Outsiders that heard this story, though, could not understand. What? Singing a secular tune at the Rebbe's *hakofos?*

"What is a secular song anyway? There are *chasidishe* melodies incorporated from the Baal Shem Tov onward that were originally composed by lonely shepherds tending their sheep in pastures. The tunes were picked up by his holy disciples who used to travel incognito from town to town. A great rebbe or even a particularly devout *chasid* had the power to redeem the holy sparks in it and uplift the songs to the elevated status of what is called in chasidic terminology a *'niggun memula'*—a song rich in spiritual content, with a meaningful message, and in particular one which will enhance the quality of a *chasid*'s prayers, enabling him to *daven* with complete and utter concentration and feeling."

Meanwhile the French are befuddled. They don't know quite what to do, with or without their anthem. They recall their *"Marseillaise,"* from the French Revolution of 1789, and nobody denies nowadays that the words of the song are too abhorrent even for the French because of its revolutionary flavor, calling, as it does, for blood and revolt.

So to some Frenchmen, it was perfectly okay when the Lubavitcher Rebbe, Rabbi Menachem Mendel Schneerson, in 1974 officially introduced their anthem to his *chasidim* and watched as it was adopted as a *niggun*. And it was also okay when the French government in turn, a year later, considered changing the fast tempo to a slow tempo—or perhaps dropping the song for good and coming up with a new anthem. After all, the French were then seriously considering joining the ECC, the European Common Market. "The *Marseillaise*" was too radical, some Frenchmen said; an anthem should befit a peace-loving nation, not one where the guillotine and blood-letting and war raise their ugly heads.

Simmering but never too far from the hearts and minds of the French, the anthem controversy was again raised on Bastille Day, July 14, 1989, the two hundredth anniversary of the French Revolution. On that day a very famous author, Marcel About, went to see the French president to prevail upon him not to change the anthem. He said he personally would compose a new version with modern lyrics. What the French author Marcel About came up with didn't sit too well with many Frenchmen: He called, specifically, for "boys and girls" to leave behind the old bywords like "war" and "suffering" and to bring on the new ones—"peace," "harmony" and "love."

When the French newspapers got wind of the new switch, one journalist[2] wrote, "To Rewrite the *Marseillaise*? . . . Poor *Marseillaise*!"

Before François-Maurice Mitterand became the French president, Valéry Giscard d'Estaing found it ("the *Marseillaise*") too warlike, and imposed a controversial new beat. Since Mitterand, the national anthem has again found its original power. One could hear it even in the voice of Jean-Pierre Chevenement, then minister of education (was he, amusingly mused the journalist, perhaps already thinking of future responsibilities as head of the army?), who began to insist that the war song should resound in the classrooms of the republic without any changes.

"Oh," mused the French journalist, "how beautiful our France would be if we hadn't used a guillotine on our king, decapitated and massacred so many innocents during our grand Revolution! How beautiful our country would be if we hadn't dirtied our hands so in colonial wars and the collaboration. Ah, how sweet things would be if the French didn't carry any responsibility for the deportation of the Jews! . . ."

Poor *Marseillaise.* Poorer French.

As of 1992, it came down to this: In a recent, revealing explanation from Rabbi Menachem Mendel Schneerson, delivered at a *farbrengen* (chasidic get-together) on *Shabbos Parshas Vayeishev,* 5752 (1992), he spoke about a miracle in today's world: the transformation of the French national anthem into a chasidic *niggun.*

"There are many who complain that the present era is different from previous ones. In the previous eras, the Jews saw open miracles, and no such miracles have been revealed in the present era. This complaint has no basis, and it can be disproved by drawing attention to something that has happened in France.

"I once spoke of the miracle to be mentioned to a *chasid,* and he replied that in Lubavitch, it was said that the principle of publicizing a miracle is relevant in regard to Chanukah and Purim, but not in regard to other miracles. On the contrary, one should not divert one's attention from Torah study to speak about miracles.

"Subsequently, I made mention of the matter at a *farbrengen* and the *sichah* [talk] was even printed up. But the matter was not noticed and the record of the *sichah* became part of people's bookshelves and not their thoughts.

"What is the miracle in question? Just as every nation has a flag of its own, every nation has a national anthem. Similarly, France possessed a national anthem, a melody which was sung during the French Revolution in which the country was freed from the rule of its monarchy. This melody was a symbol of the French spirit which the Alter Rebbe [Rabbi Shneur Zalman of Liadi] opposed.

"And yet, shortly after the melody was adopted by *chasidim* and used as a chasidic *niggun,* it was no longer sung as the French national anthem. Indeed, the older *chasidim* said that it is as if France willingly gave over its national anthem to the *chasidim.*

"This is an inconceivable miracle, that a country change its national anthem and particularly a national anthem that is so intrinsically related to its history. Moreover, today, in many places, it is not even known that this melody was ever the national anthem of France. When people hear the *niggun*, they assume that it is a chasidic *niggun*, like other *niggunim*. For there are various different melodies composed in all eras of our people's history, including the present.

"The recognition of this miracle is significant, firstly as a factor in its own right, but also as part of the process of hastening the coming of the Redemption. Our sages relate that God desired to make King Chizkiyahu the *Moshiach*, but because he failed to recite songs of thanksgiving and praise after the miraculous defeat of Sancheriv, God withheld this from him. Thus, taking notice of the miracles that occur to us is a fundamental aspect of the process of speeding the *Moshiach's* [Messiah's] coming.

"Within the context of publicizing miracles that have happened to our people, it is significant to mention the importance of publicizing the Chanukah miracles. In this context, chasidic *farbrengens* or other gatherings where Jews will meet in commemoration of the festivals should be arranged which will gather together and unify Jews from many different sectors.

"At the gatherings, efforts should be made to inspire increased observance of the Torah and its *mitzvos*.

"Furthermore, may our talk of the imminence of the Redemption hasten its actual coming. And then we will merit that 'those who lie in the dust—all the *rebbeim* from the Baal Shem Tov to the previous Rebbe [Rabbi Yosef Yitzchak Schneersohn]—will arise and sing' and proceed with us to *Eretz Yisroel*, to Jerusalem, and to the *Beis Hamikdosh* [the Holy Temple]."[3]

Whether 40 million Frenchmen take to the streets to prove that "the *Marseillaise*" is all right by them again, there is another *chasidishe* instance when a rebbe used the power to redeem the holy sparks in a French song and gave it elevated status. As you may know, it is traditional with Lubavitcher *chasidim* to sing the *niggun* "Napoleon's March" at the conclusion of the *Ne'ilah* service on Yom Kippur, before the sounding of the *shofar*. "This practice has its origin in an incident in 1812 when Rabbi Shneur Zalman of Liadi[4] heard this march played by the armies of Napoleon when they crossed the

Russian border near Prussia. The Rebbe left his native town when the enemy was approaching, and after his escape he designated 'Napoleon's March' as a song of victory. Singing the tune to this day at the *Ne'ilah* service symbolizes the victory of the Jewish people over Satan, the certainty that all the prayers they uttered on the day of Yom Kippur have been accepted."[5]

In the end, as the late David Ben-Gurion once said, "It doesn't matter what the *goyim* [non-Jews] say, what matters is what the Jews do."

"The *Marseillaise*"—anthem or *niggun*? Perhaps the French no longer have a word for it, but, rest assured, when the Messiah comes, there will be no question to whom "the *Marseillaise*," or "Napoleon's March," belongs: to God. Then, "the *Marseillaise*," with or without its bloody past, will be one of the purest songs imaginable.

25

Jerusalem on Her Mind

The morning after Cantor Boris Pevsner sang at a private Russian Jewish wedding in a small town in White Russia, he received a letter requesting his appearance at the KGB headquarters that afternoon at 2 P.M. By itself a letter from the KGB, in the year 1975, would make any Jew shudder, but coming so quickly after Pevsner had applied for emigration to the United States, he felt panicky until he came face to face with the local KGB official in a highly decorated office in the middle of the town. Then it was clear what the KGB wanted from him.

"For your information, Hebrew and Yiddish are forbidden languages in this province. Speaking, singing, writing. I know you are aware of that, eh?"

Pevsner nodded.

"We know that you performed and sang Yiddish songs at a Jewish wedding last night. Don't bother denying it—we know you did."

"Okay," said the cantor.

"We now warn you. Continue singing in Hebrew or Yiddish and you face grave risks. Will you stop before this occurs?"

"Y-y-yes. I will."

"Excellent."

The official showed Pevsner to the door.

Four years later, in 1979, the cantor and his family were allowed to leave the Soviet Union. Among the Jews, if you ever wanted to hear a talented young Russian-born singer and entertainer who could easily charm an audience with songs in Yiddish, Hebrew, English, Italian, and—let us not forget—Russian, Boris Pevsner was your singing man. He had attended the Music Institute of Minsk, and he performed frequently as soloist, particularly with the Riga Philharmonic Orchestra.

But to the officials of the Soviet Union, Pevsner was just another Jew, and they were happy to get rid of him and his "baggage." During that year, 50,000 Jews took their baggage, too, and left for parts known—in short, anywhere outside the biggest communistic state.

Once outside the Soviet Union, Boris Pevsner and his family, parents and grandparents included, stopped over in Vienna as part of the immigration processing system. They were told that their stopover would consist of fifteen days and were directed to a friendly hotel for that period. Not surprisingly the Pevsner family was lumped with two other families, all fifteen persons in one large room with eight rows of bunk beds. Each family divided up the sixteenth bed for its suitcases. As it was not too different from their situation back home, they managed well.

There was one problem. One of the two other families, both headed eventually to Australia, had a six-year-old daughter who seemingly never stopped crying. Day and night she wept and moaned. All the adults in the room tried everything they could do to mollify her, but nothing worked. She wailed and whimpered that she wanted to go home, she missed her friends, she didn't like it in the hotel, and she generally gave voice to whatever else she could think of to make her unhappy. Those fifteen days were a torment to the room's occupants.

Until Boris Pevsner had an idea. On the fifth day of their stay, he announced to everyone in the room that he was going to hold a concert. "Come on," he said in Yiddish, which was the common language amongst the families. "Come, sit on your beds and I'll stand here and entertain you."

Fortunately, the little girl was in between crying jags, so she, too, responded well to the request.

When everyone was seated on the beds, Cantor Boris Pevsner said in Yiddish: "Four years ago the KGB demanded that I stop singing Yiddish songs. So today my first song"—and here he directed his happy eyes at the little girl, who again looked as if she were on the verge of tears—"will be in Yiddish called 'Jerusalem of Gold.'"[1]

Before he sang, the cantor spoke about the divided *Eretz Yisroel* separated from its beloved Jerusalem, before the Six Day War. The situation in the room they were in, Pevsner pointed out simply, was also very much like Israel before the Six Day War. "All Israel was in tears, and they couldn't stop weeping. For thousands of years, their tears had flowed. They were homesick, and they wanted to go home. Like Chana, the little girl on the bed over there, we too are crying because we miss our home and especially the holiest place in the world—Jerusalem. There is no beauty like the beauty of Jerusalem. There is no home like the home of Jerusalem. And yet now, after the Six Day War, we now have our beloved Jerusalem. If I forget thee, O Jerusalem, let my right hand wither! Let my tongue cleave to my mouth if I remember thee not, if I prize not Jerusalem above all my joys! But we have not forgotten Jerusalem, we remember!"

Then Cantor Pevsner sang the song "Jerusalem of Gold," and there was not a dry eye in the room—except for the little girl who smiled for the first time in recent memory—and never stopped smiling, even giggling with glee. Cantor Pevsner had found the right song for this little daughter of Jerusalem. The concert of Yiddish songs went on that afternoon in a crowded, stuffy hotel room in Vienna far, far away from the Jewish homeland.

Chana the little girl never cried again in that room, and ten days later was off with her family to Australia.

Now, many years later, Cantor Boris Pevsner still often thinks of that little girl, and he prays she always feel joy by letting Jerusalem come into her mind.

26

The Night a Jew Sang
for His Supper in the Kremlin

adies and gentlemen, be seated.
　　"In memory of the biggest stars this side of the Iron
Curtain, Lenin, Stalin, Khrushchev, Andropov, Gorba-
chev, we . . ." reads the master of ceremonies, holding a
program close to his eyes: "now bring you directly from the convention hall in the Kremlin . . . Cantor Berele Zaltzman.
　　"A Jew? Wait a minute."
　　Before the announcer can say another word, Cantor Berele
Zaltzman on stage opens his mouth to sing. "We are the *Chabadniks*. . . ." The announcer wants to say something else—a protest?—
but he's shushed down by the audience who, hearing a composition
of music they've heard all their lives, are also stunned in their own
way. This music: an orthodox communistic military march. These
words:

We are the *Chabadniks* emerging from the pain of the earth.
We bring you the Tablets of Moses.

At this point, we also bring you a truth about this story: the M.C. of the concert never spoke such lines; all the rest, however, is true: the words of hope, the sparks of redemption, the cantor and his song, and Jews openly weeping in the audience.

> What is our secret?
> How come we endure and endure and leave the graves of our enemies behind us?

The cantor's voice rises. With outstretched arms, he asks his people:

> Where does our power come from?
> Our power is the Torah. Our power is God.

Somehow, in spite of the overwhelming applause that drowns out a word or two of his song, the cantor manages to make his point clearly: *We are the Chabadniks. God has seen to that. The Soviet Union is relegated to a grave of the past.*

The cantor sings on. To his right is a large *menorah*, with the first night's candle lit. If this were some underground *shul* in Moscow how easily the Jewish audience—all 10,000 of them—could have accepted the situation, keeping one eye on the cantor and one eye out for the secret police. Nothing so radical as they beheld in front of them could really be taking place, in the Kremlin of all places. Yet, as it is written in Ladino, whatever has not happened in a thousand years may happen the next moment. Still, some Jews in the Kremlin audience pinch themselves. Any moment they expect the secret police to overwhelm them all and by tomorrow morning be on their way to Siberia. But as the minutes go by, Cantor Zaltzman takes on a new reality and the audience, gaining strength and hope, cheers him on. He's singing their song. He's singing of their Torah.

> We are the *Chabadniks* . . .

The year is 5752, December 1991, Chanukah. In the wings wait other Jews—Mordechai ben David, Avraham Fried, Sandy Shmueli, and the spirit of Soviet Jewish composer Dimitri Pokras, who composed the song the cantor now sings.

As the cantor sings and the audience reminisces, let us return to the past, away from the good of the concert, back to the bad old days of the Soviet Empire, where Berele Zaltzman and his brother

Hillel would have never been so daring. Oh yeah? Hear it now: It was in 1961 that the two brothers came up with a plan to turn the tables on the Ruskies. They would turn an evil song into a holy song.

Such a decision did not come easily. For some *Chabadniks*, living life on the run was common. For others, living the Jewish life had to be underground. Big Russian Brother had a million eyes. But the eyes of *Hashem* were on Cantor Berele Zaltzman. Born in 1936, into a Russian Lubavatich cantorial family, as a youngster, Zaltzman's musical talent was soon evident, and in the "underground" synagogue where the family prayed, a great future was predicted for him.

For fourteen years, Cantor Zaltzman prayed in underground synagogues. During his last three years in Russia, he was the chief cantor of a *shul* in one of Russia's largest cities. Although he was invited to be the chief cantor of the Great Synagogue in Moscow, he declined, fearing that this would hinder his endeavors to get to Israel.

Sometime in 1961, brothers Hillel and Berele seized upon transforming a communistic song to a holy Jewish song. Berele recalls the time he used to live in Moscow and had to pass Red Square: "I was afraid even to look in the direction of the Kremlin. Yet one day I forced myself to look, even to silently thumb my nose at it, and somehow after that I knew I had found a new strength to resist the communist regime.

"Together with my brother Hillel, I became a *Chabadnik*. I was ready to fight. The idea of rewriting that song was my brother's. We were at once angry and sad that a beautiful song composed once by the Soviet Jewish composer Dimitri Pokras had been forced out of him and communistic lyrics—words, thank God, I never have to hear again—that praised communism and denigrated everything Jewish, were added. How could they have added such words to a holy melody! Profaned the sacred?"

But—in 1961—were the Zaltzman brothers really willing and ready to suit the actions to their thoughts? For every thought in a Jew there's a history behind it: Behind this thought are the words of Rabbi Abraham Isaac Kook:[1] "Holiness should be built on a foundation of the secular."

The die was cast. The Soviet military march was forever then known in English as "We the *Chabadniks*." The Song of Songs is Solomon's, but the Song of Zaltzman became the Jewish underground national anthem. In the years to come many Jews listened raptly with tears in their eyes as Cantor Zaltzman sang the song in underground *shuls*—shades of things to come, as it is written, "Whatever God created has a spark of sanctity in it."

The spark had to wait a few years for the big fire. Indeed, sometimes it seemed as if that very spark was in danger of being snuffed out. There were days—on *Shabbos*—when the underground observant Jews would alternate the services at one house or another. What marked these underground *shuls* to Jews, who were in the know, was the ubiquitous dog each house owner had in the front yard. Why in the front yard? For two reasons: It alerted the Jews inside that an unwanted person was outside, possibly a governmental official, and by telling the unwanted person that the dog was ferocious and that it had to be put in the backyard before the person could enter the house, it gave everyone in the house enough time to hide the Jewish prayer books and run for cover—in the closets, under the bed, in the cellar, wherever. Often such occurrences happened week after week, especially involving Soviet schoolteachers who kept checking up on delinquent Jewish children absent from school on *Shabbos*.

Such things are, thank God, over now, sighs Berele, thinking back to his song, "We the *Chabadniks*," and his underground *shuls*. Now he laughs at his past, lucky that he and his family escaped the close calls. And he also laughs about how he and his family pulled the wool over the eyes of the governmental officials: "We had such a little dog, yet they believed it was ferocious. It's said, in the Torah, that not a dog shall snarl. But ours did."

We are the *Chabadniks* emerging from the pain of the earth.
We bring you the Tablets of Moses.

Ten years after they wrote their *niggun*, Cantor Zaltzman and his brother Hillel were permitted in 1971 to leave the Soviet Union, fulfilling his lifelong wish of emigrating to Israel, together with Berele's wife and six children who, despite great emotional hardships and mental strain, were educated as God-fearing Jews.

On Rosh Hashanah of that year Berele visited the Lubavitcher Rebbe, *shlita*, Rabbi Menachem Mendel Schneerson, in the Crown Heights section of Brooklyn, New York, and he was invited to sing at the services. Several Jews in attendance said: To witness his *Musaf* prayers in "770" [the Lubavitch Synagogue, at 770 Eastern Parkway, in Brooklyn] was an unforgettable experience, bringing tears to the eyes of the more than 5,000 worshipers there.

After that, brother Hillel settled in Crown Heights and Cantor Zaltzman toured the United States and Canada, where he gave concerts, and though he was invited to remain as cantor in large communities, he declined all offers, as the Lubavitcher Rebbe had told him to live in the Holy Land, in Nachlat Har Chabad. This was in accordance with Cantor Zaltzman's lifelong wish to live in Israel, where he lived for nine years. Currently, he is a *sheliach* of the Lubavitcher Rebbe and lives temporarily in Salem, New Jersey, heading one of the Lubavitch centers there, at Bris Avrohom Shul, until one day he finishes his work there and once again moves to Israel.

As it is written here, Cantor Zaltzman sang the song in underground *shuls*—shades of things to come, as it is written, "Whatever God created has a spark of sanctity in it." We need to repeat this here, because the shades of things to come have arrived, and once more Cantor Zaltzman is singing "We the *Chabadniks*" to the 10,000 Jews in the Kremlin, who finally know they are hearing the true words to the song. Forget the lyrics of the past. Remember the Torah, and that deep things are songs.

Such are the words of "We the *Chabadniks*":

> We were born under the blackest cloud in Russia
> In the little town of Lubavitch
> And under the most difficult times
> We yearned for our leaders who were in gulags.
> Yet we followed our beliefs.
> We are *Chabadniks*—we're dedicated to our Torah.
> We came through the pain of the earth.
> We bring you the Tablets of Moses.
> To help the blind people to open their eyes to the truth:
> That is what *Chabad* is about.
> We'll open the ears of people who cannot hear the truth.
> We'll open the mouths with a prayer for people
>   who cannot talk anymore.
> And for people who are too tired and sick to fight,
>   we'll give them the strength to go on.
> We are the *Chabadniks* and we come through the pain
>   of the earth.
> We bring you the Tablets of Moses.

What is our secret?
How come we endure and endure and leave the graves
    of our enemies behind us?
Where does our power come from?
Our power is the Torah. Our power is God.
How fortunate we are to have such a heritage!
We are the *Chabadniks* and we come through the pain
    of the earth.
We bring you the Tablets of Moses.

During the eight days of Chanukah, at seven concerts (none was held, of course, on *erev Shabbos*), 30,000 Jews in seven major Soviet cities wept and cheered through the songs of Cantor Zaltzman, Mordechai ben David, Avraham Fried, and Sandy Shmueli. Every opening night the cantor began with his song, sung in Russian. It was not unusual for grown Jewish men, scientists, rabbis, educators, lawyers, men with white hair, to grasp the cantor's hand after the concert, with tears in their eyes, to thank him for helping to restore a Jew's dignity again.

At another concert, at another time, a thirty-five-year-old man with his young daughter shook hands with Cantor Zaltzman. "He started to kiss my hand," remembers the cantor; "he wouldn't let go of my hand. And as he was holding my hand and kissing it, I felt my hand was very wet, and I realized he was crying, his tears falling on my hand. I tried to calm him down. Then he told me, 'You have no idea how you affected me. You transformed me. I never believed that such things existed or could ever again exist that I heard today from your lips. I never thought I'd hear in my homeland such Jewish songs and music.'"

There was nothing more Cantor Zaltzman had to say to the man. He who is touched by Jewish music, he who has known that all of exile is like a furnace of fire, he who is a *Chabadnik* emerging from the pain of the earth, bringing his fellow Jews the Tablets of Moses, he is the one who knows for certain that whatever has not happened in a thousand years may happen the next moment.

As it is written, tears unlock gates, songs tear down walls.[2]

27

A Twice-Told Story

or safekeeping, this has to be a twice–told story.
Many know his art, but not too many know much about
the famous artist Baruch Nachshon himself, or the *niggun*[1]
that helped him guarantee his everlasting Jewish inheritance.
A soft-spoken man filled with determination, intensity, and with a
fire burning in him, he was born in Haifa in 1939 and grew up in a
mizrachi—a religious-Zionist home. His parents came to Israel from
Poland. As a teenager, Nachshon became interested in *Chabad* through
what he terms "divine providence."

"I heard a *Chabad niggun* melody on the radio. It was so deep
that it shocked me. I had never even heard of *Chabad* before. Maybe
I had read that there was such a movement as Chasidism which existed
200 years ago. But I never knew any *chasidim*."

As Nachshon puts it, those were the days before the word
Chabad was a household word in Israel. Not too many chasidic
Chabadniks lived there; those who did were concentrated in the small
agricultural village of Kfar Chabad.

"It occurred to me, by divine providence [after hearing the *niggun*], to go to Kfar Chabad and meet the *chasidim*."

To Kfar Chabad he went, with some friends, and found himself especially captivated by the "light and vivid eyes of the children."

Still, his first trip to Kfar Chabad did not affect him as much as he yearned for—until a while later. "When I heard the same [*Chabad*] melody that had touched my heart before," said Nachshon, "I understood that I belonged to this group. Without any philosophy or spiritual difficulties, convincing, or talking," he came to his conclusion.

Through a simple *niggun*, and once, for a period of forty days, every night, of reciting the Psalms of David (whose poetic lines form the basis of many a *niggun*), Nachshon has never lacked for artistic inspiration.

"I found the balance between myself and the Creator."

The art of Baruch Nachshon continues to show all the best that *Chabad* chasidic art can offer.

This has to be a twice-told story for safekeeping, and you can look it up in its first telling, as told by Yehudis Cohen in the June-July 1987 issue of *Wellsprings* magazine, vol. 3, no. 5.

II

Path Two

Whenever my little friends Mendel, Chaya, and Rivka Blau, separately or together, ask me to tell them a story, they inevitably and invariably ask, "Is it a true story?"

On Path Two, I continue to hear their voices in my head asking me the same question about the short stories I wrote for this section. "Are they true stories?" Yes, I answer them (and myself), they are true. No, they are not true. How can I say both things? Because the best of the retelling of chasidic life in the past involves both truth and poetry. Or, put another way, "Where there are no longer words for prose, poetry begins."[1]

Yet you'll find no obvious poetry here along Path Two. Look, instead, for nine more or less true stories—short stories—historical fiction, if you will—based on a lot of research. Have I taken out a poetic license? Only within the confines of what makes sense and gives order. All the important words quoted by rebbes are theirs. Sometimes it seemed as if I had to pluck their quotations, like a rabbit, out of a hat, but thank God, I found them, like magic, cited in many books.

Here, on this path, you'll see why there was nothing more the Baal Shem Tov wanted than to see Jews in *simchah*, in joyful prayer, singing and dancing in the fellowship of *chasidim*, the necessary background for a life of Torah and *mitzvos*. Why the saddened Ropshitzer Rebber, near the end of his life, returned to the *sukkah* of his heart as often as he could, to await the arrival of his beloved friends, Avroham of Ulanov and Reb Yid. Why, when the Egyptians were drowning in the Red Sea, the angels wished to sing for joy, but God silenced them, yet He let the Israelite men led by Moses sing what we now know as the "Song of the Red Sea." Come along with me and find out why the Baal Shem Tov called the *Maggid* of Zlotchov "the sweetest singer since King David." Why a *goy* decided to be the best *golem* he could be—and guided by the spirit of a *niggun*—dramatically blurted out for all the world to hear, "I am a Jew—by choice!" Along Path Two you'll find out that you are definitely what you sing—so be careful what kind of songs you sing! Note how a boy's pure whistling in *shul* was once responsible for all the prayers of the *shul*'s worshipers being hastened to heaven at that very moment! Experience also along this way the power of *chasidim* coming together in chasidic get-togethers and bringing forth their ancestors through the power of *niggunim*.

After reading these stories, I have a feeling you won't ask, as my little friends Mendel, Chaya, and Rivka Blau still do, if they are true stories. For Path Two, in truth, is lit by the stars of *Chasidus*. This is as it should be. Fortunate are we Jews!

So, now, enter these pages and let's be on our way . . .

28

The Purpose of Life

He had tried everything, and everything had tried him. "What can I do?" Nosson the inept tailor, peddler, common laborer, tinker, farmer's helper, shoemaker, weaver, butcher, barrel-maker, and blacksmith asked himself. Fired from everything, or simply letting the businesses fail, he was beginning to think he'd never fit in or support a family adequately. For years he had dared to prevail in the ghettos of his life in Galicia. Yet he followed suit with all the other Jews who were in the same "boat on the sand."

For Nosson, there had never been the one thing that made the big difference in his life. There had never been much Torah learning. "I admit that," he said. And he also openly admitted he had never put on *tefillin*—"not yet," he added. Not that not reading Torah, doing *mitzvot*, or *davening* properly were unimportant—or important—matters in his life. He knew that when the time came he would embrace his Jewishness with all his heart and soul. After all, he had yet to find his purpose in life. He was still telling himself that when he reached his thirty-sixth birthday.

At the local *shtibel*, he met another man, Nathan, who was cele-brating his own thirty-sixth birthday; after *Maariv*, they went to a popular place and drank themselves into a deep sleep on the same bench. Hours later, under cover of dark, their wives came for them and dragged them back to their homes. After that, Nosson and Nathan became comrades in arms; even when Nosson made up his mind to seek out "the Master of the Good Name," he vowed he would never forget Nathan, and Nathan vowed never to forget him.

Three months later, he set out to seek the Master, namely Yisroel ben Eliezer—the Baal Shem Tov. In effect, Nosson had left his wife and children to serve God in his own way, but, let us be blunt about it, his family, surrounded by many relatives, was only too happy to see him go so that he could, to use a modern phrase, get his act together and stop whining his life away.

Along the way to Medzibosh, where the Baal Shem Tov was, Nosson, who had long yearned to meet him, decided that he had to be a *chasid* of the Baal Shem Tov—that surely was his calling! Wher-ever he was each day, he borrowed another's Jew's *tefillin* to put on his arm and head. Buying a *siddur* with the little money he had, he learned how to *daven* properly—with fervent enthusiasm, intense concentration, and awareness of God's presence. This journey to the Master of the Good Name was more than Nosson expected. He began to feel certain that all else in time would be revealed to him. He was right.

When he finally asked the Baal Shem Tov, "How shall I make my living in the world?" the Master responded: "You shall be a can-tor."

But I can't even sing!" the other objected.

"The pastures are clothed with flocks; the valleys also are cov-ered over with corn; they shout for joy, they also sing.[1] I shall teach you a *niggun* and bind you to the world of music," said the Baal Shem Tov.

At that moment, Nosson's old chum Nathan appeared out of the shadows and the two embraced. Nathan confessed that he too, without telling anyone, had journeyed alone to see the Baal Shem Tov.

When it was time, the Baal Shem Tov said, "Now you two both are bound to the world of music."

Nathan said to Nosson: "It is true as the Master of the Good Name says. My singing voice changed in a trice and now I sing bass."

He grabbed his friend's arm and they danced, forming a swirling half-circle, their other arms waving in the air, in front of the Baal Shem Tov. The Baal Shem Tov tapped his right foot and clapped his hands, urging them on. There was nothing more the Baal Shem Tov wanted than to see Jews in *simchah*, in joyful prayer, singing and dancing in the fellowship of *chasidim*, the necessary background for a life of Torah and *mitzvot*.

"Nosson," Nathan said breathlessly, "I wouldn't have believed it for a minute, until I learned a *niggun* from him"—he pointed to the Baal Shem Tov—"and now I can sing for more than my supper."

After he learned the same *niggun* as Nathan had learned, Nosson sang it aloud.

From that moment on, Nosson became a singer without peer, and far and wide they called him the cantor of the Baal Shem Tov. Eventually, Nosson and Nathan moved their families to Medzibosh, where they too joyfully admitted that Nosson had finally gotten his act together.

But as the years went by, Nosson still had an unmet yearning; he wanted to serve God in a special way. As it is written, "There are people whose fame goes before them—and others that follow their fame."[2] Neither one was Nosson's choice. To be the Baal Shem Tov's cantor was a great honor, but Nosson still had to find his purpose. Advising him, the Baal Shem Tov told his *chasid* to visit another of his disciples, Rabbi Elimelech of Lizhensk[3]—the *No'am Elimelech*, and there he would find his life's purpose. Nosson agreed to go, and Nathan the bass singer accompanied him.

Why did the Baal Shem Tov send Nosson to Reb Elimelech of Lizhensk? For one thing, the Rebbe was one of the leading figures of *Chasidus*, having developed the idea of making the holy personality of the rebbe the focal point of a *chasid*'s existence.[4] For another, there was in Reb Elimelech's soul a gift only Nosson could receive. From one singer to another singer, a *niggun*. Yet would the Rebbe give Nosson the gift? Would Nosson know how and what to ask for? These were unanswered questions, which remained unspoken between the two friends.

In their journey to Lizhensk, Nosson and Nathan had heard many stories about Reb Elimelech. As one story goes, at the *mikvah* (the ritual bathhouse), Reb Elimelech met a *chasid* who had arrived from faraway Hungary to spend *Shabbos* at his table. Said the Rebbe to his unsuspecting guest: "You came all the way from Hungary to spend *Shabbos* with this no-good charlatan, this liar, this impostor?"

"How dare you insult my saintly rebbe like this!" the Hungarian *chasid* said in a fit of anger.

That evening, at the Rebbe's Shabbat table, the *chasid* recognized Reb Elimelech. His entire body trembling, he begged the Rebbe's forgiveness. "I am deeply sorry for speaking to you in the *mikvah* with such disrespect and irreverence," said the *chasid*. Taking the *chasid*'s hand in his hand, Reb Elimelech comforted him: "Don't worry about it. You told me your truth, and I told you mine."

But would the truth be told this time? Could Nosson be certain that *this* time his purpose in life would be revealed to him? The only thing certain about this is, there was some truth to all of this. For a long time, the Rebbe and his son Rabbi Eleazer could not make up their minds to let Nosson and Nathan sing with the chorus in their synagogue on *Shabbos*. Why? Reb Elimelech feared that the artistry of their singing might disturb his devotions. But Rabbi Eleazer argued that because of the holiness of the Baal Shem Tov, it would not be right to withhold the honor from the men, and so it was agreed that they should sing at the inauguration of the Sabbath.

The honor—his purpose in life!—had finally come to Nosson. But when he began, Rabbi Elimelech noticed that the great fervor of his singing flowed into his own and threatened to drive him out of his mind, and so he had to retract his invitation. This was not unusual; all the *chasidim* were used to it by now. As *Shabbos* began, the Rebbe could not endure the voices proclaiming it. He had to stop up his ears to keep the holy thunder of the *Shabbos* from deafening him.

Where did this leave the two men? "I'm patient," said Nathan. "Well, I'm not," Nosson muttered. "I came here to find my purpose in life. And what do I find?" That question also remained unposed and unanswered out of respect for Reb Elimelech.

Rising above his frustration, Nosson the cantor, and Nathan the bass singer, remained after *Shabbos* was over. It was not for naught, as the Rebbe paid them both many honors.

Later in the night, the Rebbe invited Nosson to his house again. When he was greeted by Reb Elimelech at the door, Nosson couldn't help notice how tall the rebbe was—or was that because he wore a short coat and a straw belt around his waist—or was it from the way the lamps back-lit him in the doorway? Once they were seated, Cantor Nosson said, "Rebbe, I came to you for something very important. My Rebbe, the Baal Shem Tov, told me you were the only one who could give it to me."

"Well, did you get it?" smiled the Rebbe.

"No, I didn't." Nosson didn't know whether he should smile with gratitude or frown with gratitude.

"Then maybe you got something better."

Nosson shook his head. "Only *Hashem* knows for certain. I surely don't."

"Did you learn a new *niggun* during *Shabbos?*"

"Yes," was Nosson's emotionless response.

"There you are. Certainly a thing of beauty forever!"

The cantor seemed beyond satisfaction.

"Rebbe, I'm in search of purpose—the purpose of my life."

"Is that what you want, what you're really after?"

"Yes, and I'll keep saying yes till I find it."

"Allow me to ask: Will that purpose be absolutely necessary when you get to the Gates of Heaven?"

"Yes, yes, yes," insisted Nosson. Your own brother Reb Zisha[5] said it best."

"Zisha?" The Rebbe's face lit up.

"He said, may I humbly remind you, 'When I shall face the celestial tribunal, I shall not be asked why I was not Abraham, Jacob, or Moses. I shall be asked why I was not Zisha.'"

Reb Elimelech sat back on his cushioned chair. "Those truly are my brother's words. But, dear friend, I see things very differently from him. How can I aid you in finding your purpose when I keep avoiding my own purpose?"

"How so?"

"Not how so, but so how I am. In heaven, they will ask me if I was just; no, I shall say. Then they will ask me if I have done all the good I could have; again I will say no. Did I devote my life to study of the Torah? No. To prayer perhaps? No again. And then, finally, they will pronounce the verdict: 'You told the truth. For the sake of truth, you deserve a share in the coming world.'"

The cantor gave out a long sigh.

"Rebbe, I'm a simple man with unfortunately a complicated

sense of being. As far as I'm concerned, you and your brother already have staked out your places in the Garden of Eden."

"Isn't that what you want, too, Nosson?"

"Doesn't every Jew? Where else will I see the likes of Moses, Avroham, Yaakov, and Sorah? Yes, that is a wonderful goal, but give me a cup of wine to say '*lechaim*,' a song to sing, and a real purpose in my life, and I'll show you the real Jew in me."

"On earth, my friend," said Reb Elimelech, "I know only one way to get you on that road."

"And what is that, Rebbe?"

"Come, Nosson, tell me about our holy Baal Shem Tov, the light of Israel."

Suddenly Nosson's eyes kindled with new life, and it was clear that there was new life in his throat and in his heart as well. What came out of his mouth about the Baal Shem Tov was divinely inspired. He spoke—no, he sang. Until now he had been bottled up, not being allowed to sing; now he spoke with all the fervor in his heart that he usually poured into his song. Music flowed into his spoken word. Suddenly, the night "stars sang together and all the sons of God shouted for joy"[6] and somewhere on the road leading from Medzibosh to Lizhensk was the divine chariot that Ezekiel once saw.

"Reb Elimelech, I was there, in the *shul*, during the hours when the soul of the Baal Shem Tov rose to heaven. Terrified, I touched the Baal Shem Tov, and I could see that his body remained behind, as if dead. Nathan pulled my hand away and calmed me down.

"'The Baal Shem Tov's soul is in the right place,' said Nathan to me. 'I'm certain he's in the inner recesses of heaven at this very moment and—'

"'Yes,' I said excitedly to Nathan.

"'And his soul is speaking to Moses and King David and *Moshiach* [Messiah].'

"'Yes, Nathan,' I said over and over, carried away with this wonderful thought. 'And he's asking anything he wants to, and all his questions are answered.'

"'Perhaps,' Nathan said to me, 'the Baal Shem Tov is speaking right now on behalf of both of us. You'll see, my beloved friend, you'll get your wish.'"

"Yes," said Nosson, "the Master of the Good Name speaks to each creature on earth in its own language, and to every heavenly being in its own language. He hasn't forgotten us."

Stretching for the first time, in the early hours of the morning, Nosson suddenly heard something outside. Rushing to the window, he cried out.

"What, my boy?" said the Rebbe.

Nosson shook his head in disbelief. "A chariot is outside there."

The Rebbe joined him at the window.

"My boy, it is a chariot all right."

"Look, Rebbe, who the driver is!"

"Who else but our light, the Baal Shem Tov!"

"Rebbe, what does this mean—the Baal Shem Tov riding a chariot?"

"Not just any chariot, my boy, but the chariot of God!"

"I think I'll go outside and greet it."

"Yes, go, my boy, your purpose in life has finally arrived!"

Nosson rushed out the door, almost tripping once or twice.

When Reb Elimelech looked out the window, his face glowed.

Not once during the rest of this long night did the Rebbe and the ecstatic cantor ever bring up what had happened outside the room. The sight was for all Jews, but the message was only for Nosson's ears. As quickly as it had appeared to Nosson the singer, the chariot made tracks in another direction. For the truth was, it had many places to go before the light of morning arose. As for Reb Elimelech, he took the coming and going of the chariot in his holy stride, as it is written, "When a *chasid* speaks in praise of *tzadikim*, this is equivalent to dwelling on the mystery of the divine chariot which Ezekiel once saw." It is also written, "For the *tzadikim* are the chariot of God."

When finally Nosson arose from his chair again, the room was bright with morning. In a voice still lilting with music, he told the Rebbe that he and Nathan the bass singer had once received the Torah "through the mouth of the Baal Shem Tov as Israel had once received it at Mount Sinai through the sound of thunder and trumpets. No, Rebbe, the voice of God is not yet silenced on earth, but endures and can still be heard."

"Yes, Nosson," agreed the Rebbe, "that is why we need chariots of God and singers like you."

Shortly after his visit to Lizhensk, on *Shabbos*, Nosson, the cantor of the Baal Shem Tov, lay down and died. Thirty days after that, and again on *Shabbos* night, his friend Nathan came home from the *mikvah* and said to his wife:

"Summon the Holy Burial Society quickly to see to my remains. In *Gan Eiden*, Nosson has finally found his purpose. They have commissioned him to sing for the inauguration of *Shabbos*, and he does not want to do that without me."

Then, Nathan, too, lay down and passed away.

29

Reb Yid

From a window, Rebbe Naphtali[1] watched several of his disciples exiting the *sukkah* outside his modest home, and he began to weep. Outside the *sukkah* his disciples spotted their Rebbe through the window, smiling—or was it laughing? Laugh—cry. In a few, short hours, Simchas Torah would be here, and he was not looking forward to it, or at least to last year's memory impinging on the present holy day. Last Simchas Torah, Rabbi Avroham of Ulanov, his dearest friend in the world, had passed away unexpectedly. More and more, since then, Rebbe Naphtali began retreating into an invisible *sukkah* in his heart; seated there, with a cup of wine in his hand, he awaited Avroham; but he never came. He never came, but Rebbe Naphtali, jester of Ropshitzer, masterful concealer of pain, was a patient man.

Suddenly there was a knock on the door.

Rebbe Naphtali turned away from the window and said, "Come in."

When the door opened he could see it was young Rabbi Feyvish.[2]

"You wanted to see me, Rebbe?"

"So, Feyvish, you really are leaving us?" said Rebbe Naphtali.
"Yes, Rebbe, right after Simchas Torah."
"That soon?"
The young rabbi was about to respond, but Rebbe Naphtali
interrupted. "Who will recite for us 'Lamentations'[3] like you? Who
will I find in all of Ropshitz who takes himself as dead seriously as
you? We're all clowns here, but poor or not we laugh. You—you're
my perfect foil, Feyvish. I laugh, you cry. I make a joke, you feel
you're the butt of the joke."

"Rebbe," he blurted out, "for now, I must seek out Rabbi
Avroham Yehoshua Heshel—the *Oheiv Yisroel*—of Apta."

Rebbe Naphtali enveloped the young man's right hand with
both of his hands. After a long nod, he said, "Yes, the Apter Rav is
a good man, but he'll not teach you to weep any more than you do
now."

"I'm not going there for that."

"Then," Rebbe Naphtali broke out into a good laugh, "to teach
you what—to laugh?"

Feyvish shook his head and removed his hand from the grasp of
Rebbe Naphtali. "I really don't know how to answer your question."

"Of course not. With all due respect to my honorable colleague
from Apta, either way he'll ruin you."

"Rebbe!" protested Feyvish. "Please don't say such things."

"Dear, dear boy. With all my strength, here I've tried to keep
down your fire. With the Rav of Apta, you will be a burnt offering
in the conflagration of his heart."

Feyvish sensed he was fighting a losing cause, arguing with
Rebbe Napthali. Unlike the Rebbe, he didn't have it in him to be
biting and argumentative. For all the time he had spent studying
under this Rebbe, he kept things serious—a sure bet to throw off
balance the sharp wit of the Ropshitzer. Feyvish wanted a clean break
from him, and a new beginning, that was all. "I leave two days after
Simchas Torah," he said.

Suddenly the Ropshitzer beamed like a soul on fire. "If that is
so, may God be with you all the way."

Feyvish seemed relieved. "I'm glad there are no ill feelings."

"Why, of course not," said Rebbe Napthali, raising his voice,
to begin a sing-song. "Feyvish is going to Apta, Feyvish is going to
Apta, and the breath of all that lives shall bless your name. Feyvish
is going to Apta, Feyvish is going to Apta." Grasping his disciple's

hands, Rebbe Napthali danced a little dance with his partner, spinning them around together on "and the breath of all that lives shall bless your name." It did not go unnoticed by either that this was the first time Feyvish ever danced as a *chasid*. Perhaps, after all, he was onto something happy. Certainly the young rabbi was dancing with a big smile on his face, surely reflecting what he saw on the rebbe's face. As for Rebbe Napthali, he was weeping.

When Rebbe Napthali saw his young follower to the door, he again embraced him. "God willing, I'll see you tonight at Simchas Torah. Dance, sing, be happy for once in your life."

"What do you mean, Rebbe?"

"Forget 'Lamentations' just for tonight."

In his own way, Rebbe Naphtali that day fired up each and every *chasid* for that night. They were going to have a *simchah* on Simchas Torah, for, after all, said Reb Chaim of Sanz[4] to the other *chasidim* peeling potatoes in the kitchen, "We have another reason to celebrate—Rabbi Feyvish is leaving us."

"Yes," said Reb Shalom of Kaminka,[5] "We must give him a good send-off—even one he'll have something to smile about."

That evening, all eyes were on the private quarters of Rebbe Napthali. So far he had not emerged from them to begin the *hakofos* (the sevenfold procession of circuits Jews make with the Torah scrolls in their arms in the synagogue on Simchas Torah and accompanied by singing and dancing). So far the *chasidim* and the townspeople, milling about, exchanged holy pleasantries, sang songs, chanted ancient prayers. Even Rabbi Feyvish, taken aback by all the unwanted attention he was getting, kept a smile on his face. As soon as Rebbe Napthali appeared, *hakofos* would begin. As time went on, the Rebbe remained in his room. Two hours went by and he still didn't appear in the *shul*. *Hakofos* had to go on, everyone agreed, but without their Rebbe? Nobody quite knew what to do.

That evening, something blew into Rebbe Napthali's slightly ajar window, the same one he had looked out at the *sukkah* in the morning, and found the darkest corner in the room to hide in. As it moved, it made a sound. A human sigh? What was it? Why do we need to go to such lengths to describe a nonhuman once-human supernal being? Who is to say where it came from? A fiery ball in its last flicker. The end of life as a dandelion knows it. A purple aura fading into darkness. Once a human life. Surely it once had a *pintele Yid*. Once a beating heart. Once a master? Once a peasant's mouth, once a shepherd's ear. Whatever. In the beginning it was in the darkest spot in the darkest corner of Rebbe Naphtali's room, and suddenly he heard it. Standing up, he thought he recognized it. Suddenly he fell against a wall and gasped.

"Avroham, my loving friend. It's you. Thank God, you've returned! I knew you would. You had to." Tears started flowing down the Rebbe's face. "Nothing's gone right since you left me. Nothing. You have no idea how much I had to pretend to be happy—just for my people. But you, Avroham, I could always cry in your presence. I never had to pretend joy. And, oh, did I cry the day you left me. On this joyful day last year, I—but, of course, you weren't there—how could you know, Avroham? I—even now I tremble at remembrance—recall it all!"

Last Simchas Torah, the Ropshitzer stood at the window and saw how the *chasidim* celebrated and danced in the courtyard. He was in an exalted mood and his countenance was illumined with great joy. Suddenly he moved his hand as a signal that they should cease. They saw that his face had become pale and they were stricken with great fright. Gradually he recovered himself and cried out with great enthusiasm: "Are we not at war—at war with destiny, with the entire world? And if a commanding officer of the army falls, is the battle broken off? Does one run away? No, one closes ranks and fights even harder. So close your ranks and dance, dance, with more vigor than ever; dance like you've never danced before!" At that moment his friend and disciple, Rabbi Avroham, had breathed forth his soul in Ulanov.

Now Rebbe Napthali of Ropshitz wept openly in the room. "Speak to me, my beloved friend," he cried out. "I know it's Avroham. I would have gladly given my life to save yours. Speak. Come into my arms and we shall have a sumptuous meal in my *sukkah*. It's not the one you're used to, but I think you'll appreciate it as no one else can. Come with me to my *sukkah*. For one last meal."

For a long time there was silence. Rebbe Napthali continued holding up his arms in the air and staring at it in the dark corner.

Finally: "Rebbe Napthali?"

"Yes, Avroham?" the Rebbe said hesitantly.

"I'm not Avroham."

"You're not?"

"I'm not even from Ulanov."

"Are you trying to make a fool of me?" Rebbe Napthali asked.

"Far from wanting to do that," it said.

"Then come out from that dark corner and show me your true colors."

"I have none, Rebbe."

"Of what are you made then? Who sent you here? I was about to join my followers in the festivities outside, and here you came—no, I can't say, returned—to haunt me. Yet I don't even know who you are—or what you are."

"I am it. Once I was a man. The worst kind of sinner, yet I was a very intelligent man."

Rebbe Naphtali stretched his neck up, rolled his eyes, and clapped his hands, smiling for the first time that night. "You know, Reb Yid, if I may call you that . . ."

Reb Yid, in response, said yes, he'd been called many other things in his time, but "Reb Yid," he admitted, gave him a bit too much dignity for his own good, although, he quickly added, if that was what the Rebbe chose to address him with, he said he would accept that.

"Well, Reb Yid, as I've said before, and you may as well know it too, I would rather sit near a man of intelligence in purgatory than near a fool in paradise."

"You certainly have a sense of humor, Rebbe. I've heard much of it. You've certainly chosen well in speaking to this lost soul—a short time out of purgatory and trying to get to paradise."

"Yes." Rebbe Napthali sat down at table, never leaving his eyes off Reb Yid. "But who are you?"

The voice drifted closer to the Ropshitzer and moaned, "Holy man of Israel, have pity on a poor soul, which for the past ten years has been wandering from eddy to eddy. I don't deserve pity."

"Anger? Scorn? Abuse? Ignominy?"

"Yes, yes," moaned Reb Yid.

"Well," Rebbe Naphtali stood up and beckoned it to come back to the dark corner. There, Reb Yid found its place and Rebbe Naphtali sat in the corner, in the darkest spot. "I'm with you all the way, Reb Yid."

"Forgive me, O holy man of Israel, I never heard of a saint sitting down with a sinner."

The Rebbe broke out into a guffaw. "You make me laugh. You really do. So now I am to address you as Reb Yid the Sinner. Well, I won't."

"Thank you."

"Reb Yid, my sitting here in this corner is symbolic. It's part of my *sukkah* that dwells here." He pointed to his heart. "I was hoping to meet my friend Avroham, but I am sincerely happy to meet you. Welcome to my humble abode, Reb Yid, but pray, tell me who you are."

"I cannot say. I've lost much of my memory about my body's life."

"What are you then?" Rebbe Naphtali by now was sincerely interested.

Said Reb Yid: "This I can tell you, because some words stay with you till the end of time. It's said: 'When a thief has no opportunity for stealing he considers himself an honest man.' Such an honest man I never was or let myself be. I sinned and when there were no such opportunities to sin, I created new ones. I could not let it be said I was a hypocrite. I could not let myself think there was an honest bone in my body."

"And what, pray tell," asked Rebbe Napthali, "was your big sin?"

"In a word, flattery." It sounded as if Reb Yid were wringing his hands.

"Flattery?"

"Flattery." The word groaned out of Reb Yid.

"I'll tell you something only Avroham knew—or at least at first knew. I was loath to accept a rabbinical post, inasmuch as I believed I would have to resort to flattery. I despise flattery. Then I observed that everyone must practice flattery, whether he be tailor, shoemaker, or storekeeper. Hence, I said to myself: 'Since flattery is an unavoidable and universal necessity, I may as well be a rabbi.'"

"Rabbi, my flattery has doomed me."

"That's not for you to say. Look at Boaz. Had Boaz become angry when Ruth sought him out, he would not have married her, and Dovid Hamelech would not have been born."

Reb Yid's voice became a tear. "Can you help me gain a place in paradise?"

The Rebbe nodded. "I'm sure you didn't travel this far to hear me sing."

"What do you mean?" said Reb Yid.

"This is my *sukkah*, here in this dark corner. I brought you here, Reb Yid, because only someone who has dwelled in the desert, long endured by the ancient Israelites, has a right to seek a tent with such intensity. To rest. To breathe. To dream. What is this *sukkah* if not to bring you to redemption, to the Promised Land?"

"But how?"

"Reb Yid, what have you learned in your travels?"

"We are told that the universe was created six thousand years ago, yet astronomers claim that there exists one star that is visible once every thirty-six thousand years!"

"So what?" said the Rebbe, "God can be found in this mystery, too. Look for Him—not for the star."

"Rebbe, may I confess something?"

"Reb Yid, anytime you're ready. But, as I counsel preachers, make the introduction concise and the conclusion abrupt—with nothing in between."

"Suddenly I recall what I did last on earth?"

"Finally—what?"

"I was a musician," said the voice. "I played the cymbal and I sinned like all wandering musicians. Those sleepless nights, traveling from one town to another, alone in bed by myself, all those lies I told women that I loved them—you know, the whole catastrophe."

In wonderment, Rebbe Napthali shook his head. He had heard such stories, but he himself led a life of a contemplative—well, let's not get too carried away. Still, he understood the lost soul, the lost body, the lost heart. "Well, Reb Yid, it still rings true: flattery will get you everywhere, including the place you're now in: my *sukkah*."

For the first time, Reb Yid began to cry. "But holy man of Israel, I want to be in paradise."

"My dear friend Avro—I mean, Reb Yid, I shall get you there." The lost soul stopped weeping when he heard the Rebbe say: "Tell me . . ."

Shortly, the door to the Rebbe's room opened and he emerged. Immediately *hakofos* began, and Rebbe Napthali led off with a *niggun* nobody had heard before. The *chasidim* danced and tried to sing along with the *niggun*. When the second circuit came, surprisingly the Rebbe continued to sing this unusual, haunting *niggun*. Reb Chaim of Sanz was the first dancer to catch on, and he slowly hummed parts of the melody. Then, Reb Yisroel Dov Gelernter,[6] who generally picked up a tune at first hearing, suddenly saw the light, and he passed it on Reb Yitzchak Eizik of Ziditchov,[7] and he passed it on to Reb Yaakov Tzvi Jolles of Dinov.[8] By the third circuit and surely by the fourth all the other wildly ecstatic *chasidim*—except for Rabbi Feyvish, who watched the goings-on from the sidelines—caught on to this *niggun* that seemed, that night, inseparable from Rebbe Napthali's lips and heart. The fifth circuit was the turning point. Everyone in the synagogue carried the tune to greater glory.

Through the whole night, Rebbe Naphtali and his followers unerringly sang this *niggun*. The tone of the night was set. There was something special about this tune. Perhaps the heart of this melody could never be put down on paper. Perhaps the angels sang other *niggunim* praising God, but in many minds there was no doubt that *en famille* they sang this *niggun* to *Hashem* to celebrate man's devotion.

At the end of Simchas Torah, the *chasidim* asked, "Rebbe, what is this *niggun*?"

The Rebbe, with renewed, gladdened heart, explained: "When I was in my room a Jewish soul came to me for help. I had never met one, but I greeted it as my long-lost friend.

"'Rebbe,' he said to me. 'It's been three hundred years since I died, and I am stuck in limbo.'

"'Why is that?' I asked.

"'Because I can't go back to where I came from; I did terrible things in my life. Please, Rebbe,' he said to me, 'can you help me?'

"This lost Jewish soul moved me to tears. I had to help him. 'Did you do any good deeds?' I asked him. 'Did you make another Jew smile? . . . Did you give charity? . . . Did you ever lend someone money to save him from ruin? . . . Did you observe the Sabbath? Did you . . . Did you . . . Did you? . . .' To whatever I asked, the Jewish soul said, 'I lived a life of dishonor and shame, that's all I can say.'

"You, my dear *chasidim*, were waiting patiently for me outside in the *shul*, yet I felt compelled to save this poor soul. There had to be something! No Jew is merely a man of words; in his life he has to do something of value. Yet, as the Proverbs [10:19] teach us, 'When words multiply, sin is not wanting.' Between me and this lost soul were, in the end, words, and I had to find the right word to abolish his sins.

"Suddenly I asked him an obvious question. What did he do for living?

"'I was a musician at Jewish weddings.'

"Aha, I had hit on something. I proceeded further. 'You were a *klezmer?* Maybe you have a good *niggun?*'

"'Yes, I do,' said the soul.

"'Then teach it to me.'

"The *neshomah* agreed, teaching your Rebbe the *niggun.*"

"So, *Rabosai,*" said the Rebbe, "I finally came out to you, and then I sang this *niggun.* Even more important, we all sang this *niggun.* In doing so, we all gave honor to the Torah and in turn to *Hashem.* And now I know that we helped that poor soul by singing his *niggun* on Simchas Torah. His good deed is done."

Two days after Simchas Torah the Rebbe stared through his window deeply, longingly at the spot where the *sukkah* had been dismantled.

A knock at his door startled him for the moment. Quickly the Rebbe turned around, went to the door, and opened it. It was Rabbi Feyvish, in traveling clothes.

"Do come in," Rebbe Napthali gestured.

Entering the room but preferring to stand, Feyvish said: "Bless me, Rebbe. I've come for that."

"Of course," said Rebbe Napthali. "Go, Feyvish, go away from your land, and from your birthplace, and from your father's house, to the land that *Hashem* will show you."

Then the Rebbe said something unexpected.

"Feyvish, bless me, too."

"I—I don't understand," stammered the young rabbi. "You want me to bless you. What have I to offer you? You are the Rebbe. No, I refuse your request."

The Rebbe looked him straight in the face. "The jokes are over, Feyvish. You're no longer my *chasid.* I treat you with utmost—"

"Then why are you still making fun of me—asking me, of all people, to bless you."

"I am very serious." The Rebbe's deadpan face showed it. "This I tell you: Before the Jew of Pshiskhe[9] became known, I asked for his blessings. To my disciple Reb Yehuda-Tvi of Razdal[10]—he came a few years before your time—I said to him, 'One day you will be Rebbe. You will have to offer blessings to people. So start with me.' Reb Yehuda-Tvi refused. 'You are wrong,' I told him. 'You see, when I was your age, the great Levi Yitzchok of Berditchev[11] pleaded with me for the same favor, and I also refused. And I regret it to this day.'"

Suddenly they embraced, this time Feyvish leading the Rebbe

in a short dance, humming the *niggun* of the past night. When they stopped dancing and singing, they held hands, and with bated breath, Rabbi Feyvish blessed the Rebbe.

That was the last time the two men saw each other alive. Within a few months Rabbi Feyvish died in the synagogue of the Apter Rav, during the prayer, "The breath of all that lives shall bless your Name." After that, Rebbe Napthali returned to the *sukkah* of his heart as often as he could, to await the arrival of his beloved friends—Avroham of Ulanov and Reb Yid.

30

The Journey

W ho is this Maria Theresa to say such terrible things about us?"

"Rebbe, I don't know, but I'm certain that if we go to her on behalf of all the Jews she'll change her mind."

Reb Shmelke broke out into a noisy laugh, and it seemed that the very room they were in followed suit. The windows pitter-pattered from the falling rain and snow, the fire crackled in the fire-place, the wind swirled to and fro from the chimney, all making strange sounds. Even the Rebbe's closest disciple, in turn, forced a false smile on his face as he heard his mentor say, "My dear, dear, young Moshe Leib, always the optimist, always the compassionate. A lot of Danube water has passed under the bridge. Why do you think she'll listen to us after all this time? Are we madmen or two Jews?"

"Moshe and Aaron were more than enough for Pharaoh. I feel certain, with *Hashem*'s help, we can win her over."

For a few moments, the Rebbe Reb Shmelke of Nikolsburg (1726–1778) paced the floor of his large, low-slung personal quarters; then suddenly he turned around in dead seriousness. "To me, she remains an enigma. Sometimes I think she is—or can be—a friend of the Jews. Other times she seems more like a sworn enemy. But I'll tell you—" The Rebbe sternly rapped the little three-legged table he was standing by, then came closer to his disciple Moshe Leib.[1] "You know what she did barely a few months after you were born?"

"What?" asked a smiling Moshe Leib.

"What?" said Reb Shmelke, who was not at all pleased with the smile on his *chasid*'s face. "My dear Moshe Leib, you were still in swaddling clothes, in '45, when Maria Theresa, empress of the Holy Roman Empire, lover of all mankind except those she was taught to hate, ordered the expulsion of Jews from Bohemia and Prague. That was twenty years ago, and she's at it again. With a stroke of the pen she can annihilate at least five hundred thousand Jews in Poland. She must be stopped."

"But, Rebbe, at that time, she was barely twenty-nine years old, ill advised by counselors with their own agendas to carry out, and surrounded by Jew haters. That doesn't make her one now. She needs to be counseled by the right people—that's all." From an earthen pitcher, Moshe Leib poured himself a drink into a pewter cup. He looked up to the Rebbe, who shook his head. "Drink, drink to *Hashem*, Moshe Leib. Drink—He will help us win over the empress—God-willing, of course."

". . . *Shehakol* . . ." Moshe Leib finished the blessing, drank the water, and wiped his lips. Then he said, "Some Christians say that Jews had something to do with her father's death in 1740."

"Yes, no doubt," said Reb Shmelke. "It makes sense—only if it's natural that the dead shall praise the Lord."

"I'm sorry, Rebbe."

Reb Shmelke was taken aback. "Sorry—for what, my boy?"

"For bringing up that base rumor about my fellow Jews. It's the worst kind of *loshon hora*. Forgive me," he said as he bent down to pick up a log to throw into the fire. "I'm still wet behind the ears, and I should know better than to say—or listen to—anything derogatory about any Jew." Moshe Leib made certain that the log found its rightful place in the fire.

"Dear young friend, without sin, there can be no forgiving. Your heart was in the right place. As for Jew haters, fire consumes fire.

Maria Theresa eventually will feel the heat and repent. She's already, I've learned from my court friends, growing weary of her old advisers and wants to do something to appease the Jews."

"What, Rebbe?"

"I don't know, but I hear it's coming. Things already are happening to her. The news of Francis I's death this year shocked and elated her. With her chief rival out of the way, she seems ready to make concessions—especially when there's talk from her court that she—or her enemies—plan to divide Poland and annex Galicia. Then, she'll have a lot more of us Jews on her hands."

"Yes," Moshe Leib said, "but the wild card is her eldest son, Joseph, who was just named as emperor and coregent with Maria Theresa. He's not for us—yet no one knows if he's against us."

The Rebbe shrugged. "*Hashem* will provide for the Jews. He always has."

"Rebbe, do you know when we Jews will get a reprieve? I'll tell you," he said without stopping, "when we—you and I, master and student—go to see the empress and tell her what she must know. That the dangerous plots against the Jews must stop; as *Hashem* is our witness, she will suffer the same miserable fate as all those other petty tyrants who have plotted against the Jews. We must make her realize that the deep shadows of the hills around her are all Jews. Now, we come in love and wisdom. Now, we come to sing the song of our Lord on alien soil."

Reb Shmelke took a long, admiring look at his favorite student— Moshe Leib, the future Sassover Rebbe. How proud he was of him!

After *Minchah*, the Rebbe turned to Moshe Leib to say: "We shall journey to this Gentile female ruler and may *Hashem* help us help her see the light." After *Maariv*, the pupil said to his teacher, "If we are convinced that we are trusted servants of the supreme King, we have true cause for rejoicing. This is a wonderful opportunity for *simchah*."

The Rebbe and all his *chasidim* ended the night with song and dance in praise of God.

In a week's time, the pair of Jews began their journey from Nikolsburg to Vienna. The freezing weather seemed to separate Jews from non-Jews. For some reason many Jews were on the roads during that time. Could it be they were placed there to cheer on these two holy men from Nikolsburg? Hardly likely, but they were there on the road, determined to get to their safe havens. Still, as it is said,

"Better a traveled fool than a stay-at-home sage." Whatever their makeup, the Jews, dreamers and wise men, greeted one another warmly, sharing supplies, food, and tales to keep one another spirited and warm. In the depths of winter, they had found an invincible summer of Torah and *mitzvot*.

Along these hard roads came dreams of good times and revelations. Along these icy roads they arrived at the town of Brody, where Moshe Leib's father lived. This time it would be different. Different from what? The memory for young Moshe Leib was acutely fresh. Trenchant. Incisive. Three years ago, the eighteen-year-old Moshe Leib left his father's home to join Reb Shmelke. So enraged at this, Reb Ya'akov, his father, a hater of Chasidism, in every sense a *misnaged*, put aside a cat-o'-nine-tails whip for the day when his son would return. Two years later, the son went home to visit the father, but the father couldn't find the whip, nor could anybody else either. As the mother stood to one side, wringing her hands, tears rolling down her face, father confronted son. He wanted to make him pay dearly for the desertion and pain he had caused him. But the whip was nowhere to be found. As for Moshe Leib, he could not bear his father's frustration, so he went to look for the whip. When he found it he came to his father and said, "The Torah begins with the words: 'In the beginning, God created.' This means, Father: The first thing to know is that God is the sole Creator of everything. Here now is the whip." At that moment the father openly wept. At that moment he made up with his son and with Chasidism.

This time the visit was different. Reb Ya'akov warmly embraced both his son and his son's Rebbe. After a few days of rest the two were again on their way.

Along the way their pack animals died from exposure to the cold. They themselves narrowly missed being captured by a band of brigands. And, finally, part of the way, they traveled on a small ship, which a dangerous storm threatened to destroy at one point. Rabbi Shmelke rushed over to Moshe Leib and saw that he was dancing joyfully. So like him, he thought—*simchah* at every bend! Still he felt compelled to ask: "Why are you dancing?"

"Look about you. The boat—the world—is reeling! I am overjoyed at the thought that I shall soon arrive in the mansion of my Father."

"I shall join you then," said the Rebbe from Nikolsburg, and he, too, began to dance.

But the storm spent its force, and the ship reached port safely.[2]

There came a point in the journey when Empress Maria Theresa was on one side of the Danube River and the Rebbe and Moshe Leib were on the other side. Word had already got to her that two holy Jews were on their way to see her with a message that would enrich her life. Their message was so important, she was informed, that her very life could hang in the balance if she did not heed their counsel. So she waited for them.

How they would get over the Danube to see her was another matter. It was bitter, freezing weather, and the Danube was full of ice floes in gelid water. At this sight, Moshe Leib, in one of those rare instances in his life, grew morose. "How are we going to cross this river—and live?" he wailed. "Rebbe, I'm scared—even more scared than when I faced my father with his whip." And he suddenly started to shiver all over.

But Reb Shmelke, his face serene and his vision undimmed, said, "Calm down, dear friend. Let me speak, you listen. When a Jew cannot provide an answer, he at least can tell a tale. Once, my brother and I petitioned our teacher, the *Maggid* of Mezeritch, to explain to us the words of the Mishnah: 'A man must bless God for evil in the same way that he blesses Him for the good which befalls.' The *Maggid* told us: 'Go to the House of Study and you'll find there a man—Rabbi Zisha—smoking. He will explain this passage to you.' When we put our question to Rabbi Zisha, he laughed and said, 'I'm surprised that the *Maggid* sent you to me. Go elsewhere, and ask someone who has suffered in his lifetime. As for me, I've never experienced anything but good all my days.' But the truth of the matter was, as well my brother and I knew, that from birth to the present, Rabbi Zisha had endured terrible tragedies and sorrows. So you see, my dear Moshe Leib—"

"Say no more, Rebbe. I, too, understand the meaning of the Mishnah, and the reason the *Maggid* had sent you and your brother to Reb Zisha, and now I know why I chose you as a teacher. It's just a matter now of our finding a vessel to cross the Danube."

"Yes, the empress is waiting."

The river! Both Jews were up to it. Shortly, they purchased a narrow boat that could not hold more than two men. They were forced to leave their scant belongings on the bank of the river. Once in the boat, the two men gingerly stood up in it and, as they guided the boat with long, thick sticks, Rabbi Shmelke started singing the song in the ancient language of the Israelites that had been sung beside the Red Sea, and Moshe Leib sang the bass. The ice floes seemed to part like the waters of the Red Sea. Over and over, the two Jews sang the "Song of the Red Sea,"[3] and the little boat moved forward safely. Along the way the teacher even had time to teach his pupil. "We read in the Talmud[4] that when the Egyptians were drowning in the Red Sea, the angels wished to sing for joy, but the Lord silenced them, saying, 'The works of my hands are perishing. How can you wish to sing?' What this means to me, dear Moshe Leib, is that the angels desired to sing so loudly that the souls of the Egyptians would take their departure through the sweetness of their celestial melodies. And the Lord said: 'They have caused my children to perish; should they not perish of themselves, rather than die from your singing?'"

"Yes," shouted out Moshe Leib, making sure he kept his balance in the boat, "that is what separates the Jew from the Egyptian. Our passage is sweet and filled by music sung by us. We live—we Jews live on!" And the two sang their "Song of the Red Sea" again with all their might.

In Vienna the people—Jews and non-Jews—gathered at the shore and stood there, flabbergasted, in awe. Was this the Danube or the Red Sea? That depended on whom you asked. For the Jews cheering their own on in the river, there was no question. Quickly the news of this extraordinary arrival reached the court. Maria Theresa was overjoyed. A firm believer in signs and stars, she took this to mean that the messenger was bringing her the message she'd been expecting a long time. On the very same day they reached her shore, the empress received the two holy Jews.

When the two holy men appeared before the Austrian empress in her palace, Reb Shmelke lowered his eyes to the ground in order that he might not not have to behold a woman's form.

Feeling insulted, the empress reproved him, saying, "Why do you look at the ground? Why don't you look at me?"

Reb Shmelke replied: "I am looking at the ground because it is from the earth that I was taken."

The ground was broken. The empress smiled warmly. "I am deeply touched by your words," she said. "Speak, holy men, tell me what you've come to say."

In humble and wise words, they stated their case. And in this private conversation with them she bared her secret yearnings.

"I have many enemies in my court. How can I stop their evil plots against you Jews?"

Both rabbis offered advice. Said Reb Shmelke: "It is hard to be a Jew, yet we Jews are a stiff-necked people; for your own greatness, hold out your hand in peace to us." Said Moshe Leib: "Because you have a sincere desire for peace, don't become involved in a full-scale conflict with Prussia." After that the empress granted the request of the two holy men. "You shall know peace and respect in my lifetime."

The Rebbe Reb Shmelke made a final journey, this time without his favorite disciple, now the beloved Rabbi Moshe Leib of Sassov, although Leib was there at his deathbed.

These were the last words of the Rebbe Rabbi Shmuel Shmelke of Nikolsburg: "This is my dying day," he told his bereaved disciples, who surrounded his bed. "You should know that my soul is that of the prophet Samuel. Proof of this is that my name, like the prophet's, is Samuel. The prophet was a Levi, and so am I. The prophet lived to be fifty-two years, and I am today fifty-two years old. Only the prophet was called Samuel, but I have remained Shmelke." With this he bade his weeping disciples leave, leaned back in his chair, and died.[5]

Hearing of Reb Shmelke's death in 1778, the empress of the Holy Roman Empire confided to a court Jew: "He and the other holy man were right in what they told me. 'Bitter is death to the wicked, but sweet is death to the pious, since it brings them eternal rest.'"[6] Two years later she died—peacefully.

31

Tateh

S trange things were happening to Rabbi Yechiel Michel.[1] Even his youngest son, Binyomin Wolf, deeply concerned, rushed from the town of Zbarash to Zlotchov to be at his side. Shortly after, another son, Mordechai of Kremnitz, arrived. Already in the humble home of their *tateh* were Yitzchok of Radvil, Moshe of Zvil, and Yosef (Yossele) of Yampol (died 1812), the other three sons, who arrived the day before. When they were seated at table for supper with their young sister Miriam, their mama confessed, "I don't know what to make of *Tateh*. He's continually falling into trances of ecstasies."

"Yes," pouring water into their drinking glasses, Miriam said, "it's been going on for a long time. He's getting more and more remote from us."

"I don't know what to do, children." Mama wiped her eyes. "I fear *Tateh* may die soon, *chas vesholom*."

It was not like their *tateh* to warm himself at the stove, even on a cold day, or to scratch any part of his body, or to bend down to his food while eating his meager meal.

"Yet," said Miriam, "*Tateh* is doing these very things—things I've never seen him do in my entire life. Right, Mama?"

Mama nodded. She had a pained look in her eyes that scared Binyomin Wolf. Was it the look of a person who was about to die? Was it the look of a person who was watching someone close to her die? Or was he reading too much into her face that had nothing to do with his *tateh*? Binyomin Wolf had to shake his head. He always had a wild imagination. He shook his head, to block his thoughts. When that didn't work, he shouted out inside himself, "*Yeitzer hora*, out, out, get thee hence!"

But all the children knew whence their seed came from.

Their grandfather was Rabbi Yitzchok of Drohobycz (about 1700–1768), who had criticized the amulets of the Baal Shem Tov. Full of hostility, he was certain that the Baal Shem Tov gave people amulets containing slips of paper inscribed with the secret names of God. So, once, he confronted the Baal Shem Tov about that, and the Rebbe opened one of the amulets to show Reb Yitzchok that on the slip there was nothing but his own name and that of his mother, "Israel ben Sarah." Never again did Yitzchok criticize his newfound rebbe.

Yet all manner of uncanny rumors continued to circulate about Yitzchok, that he once did a favor to the "prince of the forest," for instance, or that he sent those of his newborn children who displeased him back to the upper world. (It was said that Reb Yechiel Michel remained alive only because his mother refused to let his father see his face before he had promised to let him live.)

In spite of the fact that his father drew close to the chasidic movement, yet always maintaining his individual ascetic approach, Reb Yechiel Michel himself became a follower of the Baal Shem Tov only after some hesitation. All the children had heard the story numerous times—once from their *tateh*'s lips, many times from their mama. The Besht took their *tateh* on a journey to a certain place. When they had been driving for a while, it became evident that they were not on the right road. "Why, Rebbe," said Rabbi Yechiel Michel, "don't you know the way?"

"It will be revealed to me in due time," answered the Baal Shem Tov.

They took another road, but this one, too, did not place them on the right path.

Frustrated, Rabbi Yechiel Michel blurted out, "Why, Rebbe, I believe we are lost."

The Baal Shem Tov broke out into a warm smile. "It is written," he said, "that *Hashem* 'will fulfill the desire of them that fear Him.' And so He has fulfilled your desire to have a chance to laugh at me."

After that, he joined the master with his whole soul, but that was the last time Reb Yechiel Michel, who refused to give up his ascetic heart and body, ever laughed.

From what Reb Yechiel Michel's children witnessed or heard, growing up, they were determined to be different from him in chasidic outlook. His five sons and one daughter became ardent, smiling, outgoing, and humane followers of the chasidic movement. Yet they were also dedicated to their *tateh*, from whose limbs they had learned the Torah, however strange he acted at times.

That night, they all agreed that each of them would keep a sharp eye on their *tateh* for the coming days and report back to the others any unusual doings. But what was unusual about an ascetic? What was normal about such a holy man?

"I fear something terrible is going to happen," said Binyomin Wolf.

"Shame on you. You're always conjuring up the worst!" said Yossele, in disgust.

"Where is *Tateh* now?" asked Moshe.

Miriam, pouring each of her brothers a cup of tea, said: "Right now he's in his room, pacing back and forth."

"Praying, I assume?" asked Yitzchok. Taking a sip of tea, he burnt his tongue. Immediately he ran to the kitchen to flush his mouth out with cold water. When he came back, he heard his sister speak at length about her *tateh*'s singing.

"You mean he's been singing all day?" Yossele asked.

"Where?" Yitzchok said as he sat down in his chair again.

"There, in his room. May heaven help us protect him!" said Moshe.

"Don't be so dispirited," Miriam said. "*Tateh*'s only been humming. At no time has he been in danger—*Boruch Hashem*—of falling into ecstasy."

"Aiiyy," Mama winced. "That is my biggest fear."

"Yes," said Mordechai, "we've got to watch him closely."

"Will he see us?" Yossele wanted to know.

Mama and Miriam shook their heads.

"Why?" posed Binyomin Wolf, seemingly miffed.

"Because," answered Miriam, "*Tateh* is communing. He wants to be left alone with his Creator."

"I know, I know," said Binyomin Wolf with a scratch of sarcasm in his voice. "The God of Abraham. The God of Isaac. The God of Yaakov. And the God of our father."

"Stop that kind of talk!" Moshe yelled at Binyomin Wolf.

"Yes, it's blasphemous," Yitzchok added.

The rest of the family kept their thoughts to themselves.

In his own way, Binyomin Wolf tried to say something contrite, but he wasn't fooling any of his brothers or sister. They gave him a cold look, so he said nothing further.

Later, Miriam confided to Binyomin Wolf, when they were alone, "Look, I agree with you. About what you said. Sometimes I do feel *Tateh* pays more attention to *Hashem* than he does to us— or at least to me. But please don't ever repeat this to anybody."

The youngest son took the hand of the youngest sibling to comfort her. "I love *Tateh*, just as much as you do, but we've never gotten along. He is," he shrugged, in the cold air on the bench the two were seated on outside the house, "what he is. Till the day he passes on, that is the only *tateh* we'll ever have."

This time Miriam said nothing further. She had all the love and caring from her *tateh* she felt she was ever going to get. Whatever was left in him, she was coming to accept, had to be lavished on *Hashem*. Yes, there was nothing more to say on that subject.

Even as the two spoke they could hear the beautiful strains of their *tateh*'s voice from his room.

"I love to hear *Tateh* sing," said Miriam.

"Yes," her brother agreed, "anyone who can compose a *niggun* and sing it the way he does deserves a special spot wherever he stands. As the Baal Shem Tov himself said about *Tateh*, he 'has access to the treasure-houses of heaven where he acquires the most beautiful tunes.'"

For a long time they listened in the dark to their *tateh*'s song of light. For a long time, Binyomin Wolf, fearing the worst about his *tateh*, wondered whether he might ever again feel close to him. For a long time he thought about his *tefillin*.

He remembered: In his childhood, he was a wild and self-willed boy. In vain his *tateh* had tried to curb his brashness. When Binyomin

Wolf was almost thirteen years old and about to become *bar mitzvahed*, *Tateh* ordered the verses from the Scriptures written for the phylacteries he was to wear from that time on. Then he bade the scribe bring him the two empty boxes together with the verses from the Scriptures. The scribe brought them. Rabbi Michel took the boxes in his hand and looked at them for a long time. He bowed his head over them and his tears flowed into them. Then he dried the boxes and put into them the verses from the Scriptures. From the hour young Binyomin Wolf put on the phylacteries for the first time, he grew tranquil and was filled with love.

But that had been a long time ago. As his *tateh* became more ascetic, distant, and less the spellbinding orator he had been in the past, Binyomin felt uncomfortable embracing him, nor did he ever see him cry again. As the years went by and they lived apart, Binyomin had heard that his *tateh* began expressing all his joys and pains through *niggunim*.

Very few emotions Rabbi Michel put into words. One of the last homilies Binyomin Wolf heard his *tateh* give began like this: "The Gemara states that Torah scholars do not enjoy a moment's rest. Do you know why? Because they never get tired. You get tired only when your task is burdensome to you. But a *tzadik* never gets tired of serving God."

Through extreme poverty, Reb Yechiel Michel, while the Baal Shem Tov was alive, steadfastly remained dedicated to his rebbe, so much so that one of the first times when he became very ill and could not visit the Baal Shem Tov he composed a *niggun*—forever known as the "*Niggun* of Reb Michel MiZlotchov"—that continues to endear him to all *chasidim*. The first part of the *niggun* expresses the deep yearning of the *chasid*'s soul for his rebbe; the second part, the joy experienced when in the presence of the rebbe; the third part, the bond and total devotion to his rebbe.

Thinking back on all this, Binyomin Wolf, in a wave of love for his *tateh*, said softly to his sister beside him, "Oh, can our *Tateh* sing!'"

The next night, in *shul*, Reb Yechiel Michel, although having acknowledged the presence of his children earlier in the day, never said a word to them; nor at the *Shabbos* dinner table, surrounded by his family and *chasidim*, where he used his little energy to sing one *niggun* after another, after which he went into a deep contemplation. It seemed as if he was beginning to communicate more and more through wordless songs. What was he saying? What could a listener grasp? What could heaven sing back?

By *Shabbos* morning, nothing unusual occurred. But then after *Shacharit*, Reb Yechiel Michel was departing even from his usual religious practices. By *Shabbos* afternoon, everyone was abuzz. He fell into another trance of ecstasy. In his room, he began to pace back and forth, his face aglow with inner light, and his children could see that he was clinging to a higher life rather than to an earthly existence and that his soul had only to take one small step to pass into it.

"It's happening again," cried Mama, burying her head in Miriam's lap. "I fear the worst."

"We must do everything we can to save *Tateh*," Miriam told her brothers.

Later, after *Shalosh Se'udos*, the third Sabbath meal, which he had with his sons, the frail *Maggid* was accompanied by them to the *beis hamidrosh*, to sing songs of praise. Awaiting him there were his *chasidim*. Immediately, the Baal Shem Tov's favorite singer, Reb Yechiel Michel, stood up on a table and sang out his heart and soul. As usual, the sound was so beautiful that nobody else joined in the singing; they chose to listen to his made-in-heaven voice.

But as the afternoon wore on, every man kept a watchful eye on him. Really, the brothers didn't need to inform the *chasidim* of the situation. They already knew that their *Maggid* put so much of his whole being into his songs that when he sang his holy songs, he was in danger of leaving this world. Well enough the *chasidim* knew that.

At once they put into effect a plan. Each *chasid* took a turn watching, penetrating the rebbe's every holy move and sigh as he sang his songs in the *shul*. To keep him grounded, the *chasidim* pinched, tapped, socked, patted, knocked, jabbed, or nipped their *Maggid*, to prevent his soul from leaving his body as he sang in ecstasy. In this way, they'd keep him in this world.

But this time, perhaps thick slumber hung upon everyone's eyes, perhaps they felt certain that God's own ear was ever alert to the voice of Reb Yechiel Michel, that nothing would ever disrupt his wondrous harmony of cadences, and, if a delight to the eyes, how more so with one's eyes closed! So everyone closed his eyes at the sound of Reb Yechiel Michel's heavenly voice.

This particular time he was again singing the Besht's favorite *niggun*—the song he composed for him, and it was so beautiful that suddenly he started to transcend his body, the world, the universe; he forgot where he was. But he knew where he wanted to go.

Reb Yechiel Michel sang and sang and sang and . . . suddenly his singing stopped, and the *chasidim*, taken by his song to heaven themselves, had to forcefully open their eyes, to return to earth, just to see something no eye had seen before: Reb Yechiel Michel had disappeared. Everyone in the *shul* was stunned, remaining paralyzed in their seats.

A few moments later, unbeknownst to the *chasidim* in the *shul*, Reb Yechiel Michel returned to his room, singing and pacing up and down. At that time no one was with him.

A few minutes later, Miriam, who was passing by his door, heard him repeat over and over the words: "Willingly did Moses die. Willingly did Moses die."

Greatly troubled, she ran to fetch Binyomin Wolf.

"He's dying?" he asked Miriam, as the two rushed toward the house.

"Yes, I think. What more can I say!"

When Binyomin Wolf entered the room alone, he found his *tateh* lying on the floor on his back, and heard him whisper the last word of the confession "One," with his last breath.

His tears flowing freely as he held the lifeless body of his *tateh*, Binyomin Wolf cried out, "*Shema Yisroel*"—"Hear, O Israel, the Lord is our God, the Lord is one."

Standing up on his feet just as Miriam rushed into the room, the son said in an audible whisper, "*Tateh, Tateh*, we are one, too. Forgive me for my wildness in my youth."

This is how, in 1786, Rabbi Yechiel Michel, the *Maggid* of Zlotchov, the sweetest singer since King David, departed this world.[2] And that is why *chasidim* still call the *Maggid's* five sons, all eminent Torah scholars, the five *chumoshim* (Books of the Torah). In life as in death, they had learned the Torah from every limb of their *tateh's* body, and from his songs.

32

The Jew Hater

A fierce-looking man ran out of the house, his eyes burning with murderous rage at the coach full of Jews. In his hand, he carried a revolver. At his heels, a massive black dog yelped and snapped at the carriage.

One of the passengers approached the angry householder, who drew his gun and began to shoot at the coach. The gun clicked—but no bullets emerged. Again and again he pulled the trigger, but nothing happened.

Just then, a calm, holy face appeared at the window of the carriage. With a fascinated stare, the angry one lowered the gun and pulled the trigger. A bullet spit out and struck the black dog, killing it instantly.

One of the passengers approached the householder. "Sir, we are *chasidim* traveling with the holy Rabbi Levi Yitzchok of Berditchev,"[1] he stammered. "It is the fourth day of our holiday of Sukkos and it is time for our evening prayers. We would like to ask your kind permission to pray in your house."

"The holy rabbi of Berditchev? Why, yes, of course, you have my permission," said the man, as if in a dream. With that, he turned and strode into his house without a backward glance at his beloved dog.

The servants and friends were puzzled. They expected to enjoy the massacre of the Jews—these Jews who seemed not to know or care that no Jew dared step onto this property since the owner's murderous reputation had become known. The disciples of Reb Levi Yitzchok were perplexed, too. Why had their Rebbe asked them to accompany him to this unknown place, leaving Berditchev very early, traveling quickly, and stopping only once along the way to say Psalms? The homeowner himself was also confused. "I know the gun was in perfect order, and yet it would not shoot when I pointed at the carriage. It must be the power of that holy Rabbi," he muttered to his friends.

News of the arrival of Reb Levi Yitzchok and the estate owner's seeming change of heart reached the Jews living nearby. They began gathering at the estate to see Reb Levi Yitzchok and pray with him. Many non-Jews also joined the gathering since Reb Levi Yitzchok's holiness was known by the entire countryside.

Reb Levi Yitzchok led the evening prayers himself. Before saying the opening words, "And He is merciful, He forgives sin, and will not destroy. He turns back His anger many times and does not arouse his wrath," the Rebbe began to sing a moving melody. It was sad and poignant and had a haunting effect on all who listened. It turned everyone's thoughts to his own private world, contemplating past regrets and the evil and folly of a person's actions. Each heart was full of despair and bitter regret. The disciples understood the melody to depict the suffering of the pure and holy soul, forced to leave the beautiful heavens and come to this evil, false world. On Sukkoses past, his *chasidim* had heard the melodic poem, "The Virtues of the Jewish People,"[2] many times, but even they looked at each other in amazement as Reb Levi Yitzchok sang the song this time:

> I shall speak to Thee, Lord of the Universe, of the virtues of the Jewish people: Their first virtue is—"they are inwardly strong as a fortress"; their second virtue is—"they are bright as the sun"; although "they are exiled and forsaken," yet, "they are likened to a palm tree."

Another virtue they have—"they let themselves be slain for Thee"; still another one—"they are as sheep going to be slaughtered for Thee"; although "they are scattered among their tormentors," yet, "they embrace Thee and commune with Thee."

And again a virtue—"they carry Thy yoke"; and another one—"they alone declare Thy Oneness"; although "they are cramped in Exile," yet, "they learn to fear Thee."

Another virtue—"they allow their faces to be slapped for Thee"; it certainly is a wonderful virtue—"to let oneself be slapped in the face for Thee"; although "they are always being beaten," yet, "they carry Thy burden."

And here is another virtue—"they are poor, yet unbowed"; and still another one—"they are the ones who were liberated by Toiviyo [Moses]." What is their name?—"the holy sheep." How are they called?—"the congregation of Jacob." How do they sign their name?—"they sign in Thy name." How do they cry?—"they cry to Thee for help." Help them, O God, for "they lean on Thee."[3]

But just as the notes seemed to fade into the abyss of doom, the Rebbe raised his voice in a triumphant call of hope and salvation: "Oh God, save us. The King will answer us on the day we call." Suddenly everyone was stirred to confidence and hope. But before the Rebbe had sung the last of the sad notes, the host cried out hysterically and fell to the ground in a faint.

Everyone was mystified by the events. The *chasidim* now understood that the purpose of the journey had to do with their host. But what were the redeeming qualities of this Jew hater that he merited the special attention of Reb Levi Yitzchok?

A few hours later, the *chasidim* saw the host emerge, his eyes red and his face tear-stained. In broken Yiddish, the host stammered, "I am a Jew. I, too, am a Jew." In wonder, they listened to his story:

"I was born in Germany to Jewish parents. As a young man I joined the Kaiser's army. The higher I rose in rank, the looser my ties to Judaism became. By the time I was a personal guard of the Kaiser, I had totally disassociated myself from Judaism. Finally, I became a Jew hater and relished every opportunity I had to persecute Jews.

"Now, with you and your Rebbe here, I remember that I am a Jew. I want to be a Jew again. Please, I beg of you, ask your holy Rebbe to teach me how to be a Jew again!"

The next morning, prayers were led with a festive atmosphere. The host joined the Jewish villagers. He borrowed a *tallis* and *tefillin* and asked to be shown how to use them. After prayers, he was closeted with the Rebbe for several hours, their conversation remaining a secret. The Rebbe warned his *chasidim* never to breathe a word about this journey.

A short time later, the former Kaiser's guard sold his estate and disappeared. Around the same time, a stranger came to live and study in Berditchev. He became a close disciple of Reb Levi Yitzchok and the father of one of the finest Jewish families.

33

The Beloved Disciple

Rabbi Yitzchak Twersky (1812–1885), the spiritual head of the Jewish chasidic community in Skvira (once an ancient city, now a growing town in the Ukraine), was the first to wear it, during Chanukah, and soon many of his band of faithful followers throughout Russia, like a regimented army, also began to wear them. I'm talking about the hat I call "*calpac*," you know, the hats soldiers wore in my days. I'll say no more for now about the *calpac*, but I do have a little joke about the Jews who wear such military hats. Question: "How many divisions of soldiers do the Jews have?" Answer: "They're lucky to have hats."

Still, for my father, it was a good living. I watched all those hat sales as his cash register rang them up that winter. One day, on a lark, I began to wear a *calpac*, too. It was made of fur, tall, black, like military officers wear. Of course, my friends laughed at me, calling me "Jew boy," which I was not. In fact, I was what Jews call a *goy*. Why call myself a *goy*? Didn't I have my own religion, my own set of traditions and values? Yes, and I can tell you everything about me, including my nose, was anything but Jewish. Then why call myself a *goy*? Because I prided myself on being the best *goy* I could be. My father always said, "Be the best you can be." So, here I am; allow me to introduce myself; I'm Vassili the Beloved *Goy*. Available for All Holy Days—and Whenever You Need Me. I make a nice living out of it here in Skvira, where half the population are Jews. Including Rabbi Yitzchak Twersky, known affectionately to everybody as Rebbe Itzikl. To even me. Nowadays, I do most of my work for him, you know.

And if it weren't for the *calpac* we probably would have never met. Let me tell you what happened. It makes for an interesting story to pass the time away until Reb Itzikl lights the first Chanukah candle. One night I was sitting on a fence in front of my father's store on the main street, of course cockily wearing my furry *calpac*. It must have been about 8 P.M., although I'm not sure why I'm telling you that; the time's of no importance—indeed it might have been 9 P.M. So take your pick. Either way, there came Reb Itzikl—or as I knew him then—Rabbi Yitzchak Twersky. Twenty feet away from me, the rabbi saluted me. Turning to my right, turning to my left, to see if he were greeting another person, I had no choice except to conclude that the rabbi was waving to me. I'm shy, a bit, so I nodded back, without a salute.

The rabbi stopped in front of me and asked me my employer's name. Seeing that the sign on my father's store was right in back of me, I told it to the rabbi anyway. Then I asked him who his employer was.

The rabbi smiled. "Come tomorrow to my home. I'm called Reb Itzikl and everybody knows where I live at the end of town."

This time I saluted him. "My name's Vassili. I'll be there on the morrow, Reb Itzikl."

The rabbi continued his stroll and I stayed a little longer on the fence and then went home. The next day I visited him, and that's how this *goy* wound up a servant in his house. Why, I've been asking myself, did he single me out for such a role? After all, I wasn't one of his kind. I admit I didn't have an anti-Semitic bone in my body, nor did I have any Jewish friends until the Rebbe. Yet, when I finally found out the truth why he hired me I flinched. In fact, the Rebbe left it to no one but himself to tell me why.

Why? "I appreciate you, my young *golem*, I really do have a need for you in my household. I need a young man who won't be able to understand anything Jewish before his eyes. I need to feel secure around you whenever I perform an act of special piety."

"Reb Itzikl, what's a *golem*?"

"A *golem*? Vassili, that is the first thing Jewish that you don't need to know about."

Okay, I shrugged. So, whether I liked being a *golem*, I became Reb Itzikl's closest servant. It was I who kept an eye on him to make certain he didn't singe his *capote*. That's how close he sat to the candles. During that first Chanukah I was with him, Reb Itzikl could be seen in his *calpac* for hours on end gazing into the lights of the *menorah*. What was he thinking? The other servants said he did his best thinking inches away from the flame. What new visions danced in the candles before him? I didn't pay them any mind. I knew my job and did it well. Let others think what they may. Still, a dull clod like me (yes, you guessed it—I finally learned the meaning of the word "*golem*," and you want to know something? I determined to be the best *golem* around) has to pick up a pointer or two hanging around a rebbe like Reb Itzikl.

For instance, I began to know the Rebbe's favorite song. Naturally, it was the song of Chanukah. And every hour he took a break from staring at the candles and broke into that song. Even I, a *goy*, could appreciate the spirit in which he sang it. And, you know something, he seemed to sing the song each time a bit differently. And you know something? He had a beautiful voice. Compared to whom? To everybody. I never saw eyes that could—or at least it seemed that way—reach heaven without leaving the sockets, hands whose fingers beckoned the angels to tread on them, a face itself that shone like a candle.

On my first Chanukah with the Rebbe, Reb Itzikl suddenly turned away from the *menorah* candles and said, "The miracle of the lights is accomplished again." He then turned toward his son David[1] and said, "We must create another miracle."

"What, Father?" asked David.

"I want to build a special *menorah* for the coming of *Moshiach* [the Messiah]."

Not a dissenting voice I could hear among the Jews assembled around the Rebbe. From what I could gather about their need for their Messiah, they'd go to any length. And why not? As my father might say to them, "Be the best Jews you can be." Fine, if it meant building a new *menorah*, then I, too, thought that was a grand idea.

And how proud I was to be the servant of the Rebbe in the almost
three years it took a father-and-son team of architects to build the
menorah, following the exact details spelled out by Reb Itzikl himself.

Was there a connection, as some said, between the *calpac* and
the Rebbe's decision to build a *menorah*? Again, who knew! I was
too wet around the ears to know; besides, my Christian work ethic
included faithfulness to my employer, even if he were a Jew . . . and
whomever he was working for.

In the year 1886, the *menorah* was begun and I got married to
a fifteen-year-old Christian girl named Mary in a small Christian wedding. Better that I had been hired to build the *menorah*—that took
a great deal of teamwork between the father Boris and his son Ivan—
than try to build a marriage that took a shorter time to finish than
the *menorah*, but I was never much with females. Mary went back
home—actually, she fled my bed one night—to the other side of
town, and I never did see her again.

So I continued, as I must admit I'd been doing during my marriage, spending a lot of time seeing to the Rebbe's needs and keeping an eye out on the construction of what would be and had to be
the Great Wonder of Skvira, if not the world. During the few years
it took to build, I must have seen many thousands, and they were
not all Jews, visiting Reb Itzikl. From the bits and pieces I overheard
and with my interest in learning Yiddish over the ensuing years, much
of their conversations with the Rebbe centered around the coming
of their Messiah and the new *menorah*. These were not small things
in these Jews' eyes.

But there came a time for me when I wondered if I was growing too attached to Reb Itzikl. I think it was because he seemed to
be having a lot of trouble with a group of Jews who were out to
destroy him and his kind. At first, as a *goy*, I felt very uncomfortable
about it all. After all, this chasidic community was a strange world I
found myself in, even though it was by my own choice I stayed there.
Outside, in the world of my father's hat shop, everything was so
predictable: Christians fighting Christians; Moslems killing Moslems;
Turks killing Greeks, and Greeks in turn beating up on Greeks;
Austrians threatening Prussians; and everybody picking on Jews. But
to hear and see Jew persecuting Jew was something to behold.
During that period I gave much thought to returning to my ailing
father's store, which was thriving, to sell hats. And yet no matter

what, I couldn't bring myself to leave the Reb. Now I felt he needed me more than ever. In my presence he could speak about the most delicate subjects; of course, he spoke in Yiddish, which I pretended that I was deaf to. Yet, slowly, in my own way I began to understand a lot—and, who can explain such deep things! My anger was directed mainly at a certain Jew called Alexander Zederbaum.[2]

Why did he pick on Reb Itzikl and all that he stood for? This Zederbaum, in Skvira, St. Petersburg, Odessa, you name it, he had his hand in it, was a well-known figure, publisher of a weekly newspaper printed in Hebrew, but not much liked by the group of Jews surrounding Reb Itzikl, I overheard many times. Even my father, who had a keen sensitivity that I'd seen only in Reb Itzikl, warned me against the Jew, Alexander Zederbaum.

"Stay clear of him. He's up to no good."

"Why do you say that, Father?" I asked him several times before a fire destroyed his store a year later and my father, asleep, perished in the flames.

"Because," my father said, "there's nothing worse than a Jew who turns against another Jew. He publishes a Hebrew newspaper, but even I can see how he tries to hurt certain types of Jews. He belongs to this Jewish movement called *Haskalah*, and watch out for those kind, Vassili. These so-called Jewish enlighteners, I've been told by my Jewish friends, want to be part of our world by sacrificing other Jews, and it won't work, Vassili; they're doomed. We'll never let them be part of our world, try as they might. In fact, many Christians in our town sit back, laughing at the stupid Jews. Doing the dirty work—for us. As for me, I say a plague on both their houses, Chasidism and *Haskalah*!"

"Father," I shook my head in sincerity, "I really don't understand what you're saying."

"Then, ask your employer, the Rebbe, maybe he'll explain it to you; the subject gets the best of me to explain further." He went back to making another *calpac*, this one with brown fur.

I told my father I would do so, but I never did follow up on it. The Rebbe simply had no time. He was kept so busy with being the spiritual head of thousands of Jews and their problems, overseeing the painstaking construction of the *menorah*, and taking the time out to answer tricky questions—put to him by people like Alexander Zederbaum—all designed to prove that faith, or as the Rebbe called it, *emunah*, in God was riddled with holes.

Once the *maskilim* (members of the *Haskalah* movement) got
their foot into the door of Reb Itzikl, it appeared as if they were
going to swamp him with questions, leaving him no time for anything else. Zederbaum seemed to be in the library room of the Rebbe
every day. Hours went by in heated discussion. From my vantage
point, I could hear Zederbaum, perhaps emphasizing the use of his
Russian language as a powerful argument climax, shout, "There you
have it. Your chasidic God is defeated! I have shaken your faith at
last." If he had, why then did he and those other *maskilim* show up
time again and again, crying out their victory over Reb Itzikl? Something was amiss, I must say.

But my boss, Reb Itzikl, he did his homework. Poring over his
books. Poring over them until he almost got sick a number of times.
But I was always there for him, with a hot or cold towel on his forehead as he lay down on a sofa. He never was, I could see, in the pink
of health. Then, too, he kept me up a lot during that period because he had a bad case of insomnia. Well, indeed he would, considering the weight he carried on his shoulders.

One time, it got so bad for Reb Itzikl that he cried out for me
in the middle of the night—as usual. But this time he looked deathly
sick. Fearing the end was near for him, I said I'd go fetch the doctor.

Brushing aside my fears, Reb Itzikl sat up on his bed and said,
"It's not my death I fear. It's the death of *emunah*, of faith my beloved followers hold so dear. Vassili, help me get up. I must go to
the library. I had a dream. It told me I'd find an answer in a book."

Immediately, with my help, Reb Itzikl, weak-kneed, made it to
the library. In the middle of the room, he sat on a swivel chair, as I
stood a few feet away. Moving about on his chair, he turned to his
twenty-four bookcases outlining the perimeter of the large room.
Suddenly he cried out to his Jewish God. Then, without another
moment going by, he got up off his seat. Straight to one of the
bookcases. Straight to the third shelf from the bottom. Straight to
the fourth book from the right. Straight to a book that had gold
letters imprinted on it: RAMBAM. Whatever that meant.

Silently he went back to his seat with the book. Silently he read
a bunch of pages. Then in the dim light of the room I saw him grin,
smile—no, beam with a shine on his face I'd never seen before. As
if he had found something valuable, like a pot of gold. On a piece
of paper he wrote something down. Then, I watched him read on.

When he reached another certain point in the book, he had that same smile—and he cried, "Thank you, *Hashem!*"

Then, he turned to me, as if I were the most important person in the world to him, and confided, "Vassili, I've found what I was looking for."

"What, Reb Itzikl?"

"I've found faith for my people and God for the likes of Mr. Zederbaum. Namely, I came across a very interesting question on *emunah*—faith. How did I do this? With *Hashem*'s help, I read twenty pages and found a question, one that I'm certain Mr. Zederbaum himself will confront me with this very day. Only he does not have the answer. I do, I have the answer. Oh, thank God, thank God! You see, Vassili, I read further and there on page forty was the answer."

Early that morning, Reb Itzikl and I went to the city's *rav*, a large, bespectacled man, who smoked a long pipe and wobbled along in his study with the help of a silver-handled cane. The *rav's* name I learned was Rabbi Naftali Dayan. Reb Itzikl confided to him the whole story (and later he told me what he had said as we walked home, although I could not in the least grasp why this holy man would want such a *golem* like me to know such details; but plainly I was growing up a lot in those days, so I took such things as Reb Itzikl's confiding in me in stride with my newfound bearing). Reb Itzikl was certain that he had been shown the answer to the question for a definite reason. "When the *maskilim* come, Rebbe Itzikl will be ready," he said in a low voice.

As expected, the big-shot philosopher, Alexander Zederbaum, showed up at the Rebbe's door:

"Reb Itzikl," he shouted, almost in glee, as if this big-shot philosopher wanted the whole world to bask in his sweet victory, "I have a question that will prove that your whole chasidic faith in *Hashem*—that it's not worth anything."

Let me tell you: I was happy to be there as a *goy.* This is what all the Christians I knew, including my devout Catholic father, were always waiting for: the defeat of the Jews. Was I, too, going to savor this victory in the ancient way Christians hated Jews? Was Alexander Zederbaum, whatever his intentions, out to kill the chasidic God? Although I had divided loyalty and knew that Gentiles aren't used to Jewish troubles, or even cared to know about them, still, I was

hoping Reb Itzikl had his trick up his sleeve, as he said. I was hoping—but who really knew!

Sure enough, the big-shot philosopher asked the very question
that Reb Itzikl found in the book in his library. And right on the
spot Reb Itzikl answered it.

Hearing the answer, the big-shot philosopher was stunned. He
fell back on a chair. Something physically was happening to him.
His whole body was shriveling up. The smile of the big-shot philosopher was gone. Replaced by a bleeding lip. His hands fell to his
side and they never stopped shaking while he was in Reb Itzikl's
presence. Meekly, the big-shot philosopher sat, collapsed in the chair,
humbled by a simple answer from a book called RAMBAM, if that was
really its name. Who knew!

The big-shot philosopher, but now let me call him again as the
world of Jews knows him—Alexander Zederbaum—he was a very
changed person from the man who strutted into Reb Itzikl's house
that morning. He started crying to Reb Itzikl that he wanted to
repent.

"Gladly," said Reb Itzikl, who drew up a seat right in front of
the Jewish philosopher. "But what made you come to this, Alexis?"

Still weeping, Zederbaum, not even caring that I would hear
his great confession, said, "Rabbi, it was not exactly your answer itself,
but the way you gave it to me. My question, your answer," and here
he threw his hands upward, leaned back and his eyes shot upward,
"O God, my question, your answer, they fit like hand in glove."

"No, dear friend," Reb Itzikl counseled, "not your question and
my answer. His question, His answer."

Alexander Zederbaum wiped away his tears. "Rabbi, how can I
do penance? I've been all wrong. Your *emunah* in Him is unassail-
able."

"Will you put that in print?" the rabbi asked.

The philosopher nodded.

"To repent," Reb Itzikl said, "the first thing you should do is
stop going to theaters."

"What!" said Zederbaum. He sat bolt upright in his chair. "I-I-
I should stop going to the theater! It's such a beautiful, exciting,
deep experience."

"You call that beautiful?" countered the Rebbe, with a look of
strength. "The theater beautiful, exciting, deep? You want to know
what's beautiful, exciting, deep? Come join me this *Shabbos*, at the

Shalosh Se'udos, our third *Shabbos* meal, and hear the *Shabbos* songs we sing. Then, my dear Alexis, you'll know what beautiful, exciting, deep is. Then your Jewish soul will warm up to things that are really beautiful, exciting, and deep!"

Alexander Zederbaum left Reb Itzikl's house a new man. A complete Jew, dare I say that, without implying anything Christian-like or anti-Semitic? For, as far as I was concerned, I considered Reb Itzikl, for all that he was, a complete Jew, a holy man I admired and who earned my respect. A complete Jew? Yes. Because he had God's ear. Would Alexander Zederbaum be such a man, too? That depended on his so-called *emunah* and his actions. Shortly he moved to another city, another newspaper, where he opened his pages to the works of dissenting writers, including, to the delight of Reb Itzikl, the works of a number of chasidic rabbis. Which, in my book, was Zederbaum's way of keeping his word to Reb Itzikl to "put it in writing."

By now, three years had passed. Suddenly the *menorah* dedicated to the Messiah was built. That night, the Jews had a big party, and Reb Itzikl gave the father-and-son team, Boris and Ivan, a special blessing. For what they did in less than three years, they deserved it, and more. But who knew how to measure the true worth of something on this earth! If it were a *calpac* or any other hat, my beloved father, bless his soul in heaven, would surely know how to rate its worth, but this was a *menorah*, something Jews were very attached to. As for me, I didn't understand why I, a *goy*, was so happy for Reb Itzikl and the Jews, but I was. Seeing the *menorah* brought tears to every Jew.

The base of the *menorah*, made of sterling silver, held eight erect golden lions, on whose extended tongues were eight cups, one on each tongue, where the oil for burning fed into. On one side of the base stood a gold-and-silver-layered pitcher in which the oil was kept. From this pitcher ran eight thin pipes, one to each cup. Once the tap was opened, the oil would flow into the cups. An incredible thing to see! When the *menorah* cups filled up, there was a mechanism attached to the base that played the song of Chanukah. On the other side of the base was another pitcher that held the *shammes* candle.

The base rested on a table, also a part of the *menorah*. Everywhere there were etched engravings of olives, figs, leaves, birds in flight. In the middle of the table was something I had never seen before. In an engraving that dominated the table, a very old, bearded man was standing over a young man who was lying, tied on some kind of altar. In the hand of the older man was a knife, poised over the young man's heart. From what I could see, the older man was about to slay the young man. But, praise God, the older man was being restrained by an angel—it was clearly that. Whatever the picture meant to Jews, it occupied an important part of the *menorah* tableau.

You'd think such a wonder would last a thousand years. It didn't. Attached to the *menorah* were four crowns: the crown of Torah, the crown of priesthood, the crown of Malchus (Kingdom), and the crown of *shem tov* (good name). In the ensuing years one of the crowns broke off. Reb Itzikl was resigned not to have it fixed as it seemed impossible to repair. Then one day, a few years later, a Jew appeared out of the blue (and subsequently vanished into the blue) and said he knew how to fix it. Reb Itzikl was overjoyed. He said, "As the Baal Shem Tov has taught us, 'A soul may descend to this world and live a lifetime of seventy or eighty years, for the sole purpose of doing a favor for another, materially or spiritually.' This Jew surely is fulfilling his purpose in life."

So they gave this wandering fixer all the broken parts from the old crown and he reassembled them into a crown that was not altogether perfect, but stood proudly in the eyes of thousands of Jews who came to see the *menorah* at Chanukah-time. To my eyes, it looked like the old one, but I could see in the eyes of Reb Itzikl till the day he passed on that the *menorah* would be perfect again, as he said to me many times, when "*Moshiach* comes."

When *Moshiach* comes? But first came the Civil War and the communists. By then, I became the servant first of Reb Itzikl's son David and then the grandson, Avroham Yehoshua Heshel, also known as the Machnovka Rebbe. To me, he was so much physically and spiritually like Reb Itzikl that I had to stay with him. The communists were coming to Skvira. But I knew my place. All round me was chaos, destruction of all things Jewish and Christian. *Shuls*, churches, religious places, crosses, and Stars of David twisted out of shape. Everything all shut down, boarded up for eternity.

Clearly, the destruction of Reb Itzikl's *menorah* was only a matter of time. Clearly, it was a race to hide the *menorah*. But where? Communists were all over the place. Local ones—some were old friends of my father—tried to appropriate the *menorah*, but each time I intervened. Seeing me, my father's old friends let things alone, but as they left they spat on me and shouted, "Jew lover, go to hell."

Could I blame them? No. But soon my father's enemies came, and I had no pull with them. Wearing the arm bands of communists, they announced through loud speakers they wanted to confiscate the *menorah*.

In the end, the Machnovka Rebbe yielded. The communists descended on the Jews like vultures. They grabbed the *menorah* and tried to destroy it. But, astoundingly, in preparing to melt it down, the only part of the *menorah* they could break off was the new crown. They could not do anything with the rest of the *menorah*. Frustrated, they left to await further word from the Party in Moscow. "We'll be back in a few days," they threatened.

It looked like a hopeless situation. Some of the Jews fled that very night toward Poland, a long way off. That same night, the rest of the Rebbe's followers surrounded him in the *shul*. They cried. They wailed. They prayed and shuffled their feet. Then, at midnight, the Rebbe spoke.

"*Rabosai*, God has intervened again on our behalf. How so? Do you recall that nameless Jew who appeared out of nowhere and re-constructed one of the crowns of my grandfather's *menorah*? My grandfather said of him that this Jew fulfilled his purpose in life. *Rabosai*, my grandfather, of blessed memory, was wrong. This very day the nameless Jew served his purpose in life. By making an infe-rior product then, he gave us a reprieve now of several days. He gave us time to hide the *menorah*, so the communists will never find it. He gave us time to flee Skvira."

"But where can we hide the *menorah*?" asked a man whom I had seen many times but never knew by name.

"I'll leave that up to my beloved servant, Vassili. He knows every inch of the land's layout."

Suddenly questions broke out all around me. They questioned this about me, they questioned that about me. But the man who hurt me the most, whose name I never knew, he came up to me and took hold of my coat. "Do you know who this person is? The enemy. He can never be trusted." Then, he turned toward Rebbe Avroham and said, "Nothing can change that."

Suddenly, I found myself shouting, moving toward the front of the group, and I finally reached the side of the Rebbe. "Yes," I blurted out, "there is one thing that can change that."

In flawless Yiddish, I said, "I am a Jew—by choice!"

The word went forth, and everyone knew what followed, what

had to be done. We dug a huge hole, burying the *menorah* in a remote place where no one would ever think of looking—in a cave under the ground. But before we put the *Moshiach*'s *menorah* in its final resting place, the Rebbe set off the mechanism and we heard for the last time in Skvira Reb Itzikl's favorite song, the song of Chanukah.

As we walked back to the house in the early hours of the morning, the Rebbe said something that again I didn't fully grasp, yet I think I caught the spirit of the feeling. He said, "My grandfather said, 'I made this *menorah* for *Moshiach*. Let him come and he shall disinter it for all Jews to celebrate with.'"

On the following day, the Rebbe and his band of Jews fled Russia for good. Wearing my black *calpac*, I joined them. Singing the song of Chanukah all the way.

As it is said, "Everything follows the head."

34

You Are What You Sing

He was an ordinary man, deeply religious, and he kept to himself on the streets. But, oh, could he sing in *shul*! His fame, if you could call it that, one day mistakenly transplanted itself into another man's dream, on the other side of Poland. This man, who could never carry a tune—much to his regret—had a dream one night, in which his prayer—or that which he thought was his prayer—was answered in the form of a *niggun*, a melody so beautiful, so holy, so haunting that when the man awoke it was as if he had experienced a nightmare.

Rubbing his eyes briskly, he thought about what he had dreamed. A *niggun*? To him? How cruel! In his dream he had tried to sing it, but even then, as in real life, he was inadequate to the task. In his head the *niggun* stuck like a little nightmare unto itself, but it would not come out of his mouth, try as he might.

Awake now, he concluded: No, that dreamt answer did not belong to him. It belonged to someone who understood music as well as he breathed. But who? In a rush, it came to him: It belonged to that *chasid* far away whose musical fame had by now spread beyond the borders of Poland and Czechoslovakia. Yes, to none other than him!

The man was determined to deliver the message. Finding out where he lived, he set off on the journey to meet the singing *chasid*, although he had never set eyes on him before.

During the trip there were days, with their erratic weather behavior, when he thought about turning back, but he kept the *chasid* in mind. The message was too important to keep to himself. In the end, he bore the brunt of a miserable journey, but he survived through the help of a lot of caring Jews along the way.

When he reached the town where the *chasid* lived, the first thing he did, of course, was to visit the town *shul*, the *beis hamidrosh*. Inside, he noticed an old Jew standing, his eyes closed, *tallis* on his shoulders, preparing himself for *davening*. In one hand, he held a *siddur* (prayer book), and even when he opened his eyes, it was obvious he was deep in thought.

The traveler waited, unsure of what to do. Suddenly, the old Jew began to hum a *niggun*, which the traveler had never heard before. Quietly, from the back of the *shul*, the traveler, very much moved, stood attentively and listened to the melody until it was finished.

When the appropriate time came, the traveler went over to his fellow *Yid* and said, "*Sholom Aleichem!* You must be Reb Boruch."

"*Aleichem sholom!*" said Reb Boruch. But, curious, he asked the man, "We've never met. How did you know who I was?"

The traveling *Yid* said, "Well, I'll tell you. From the way you sang the *niggun*, and from the *niggun* you chose to sing, from the tone and inflection, I was able to understand you. Through the *niggun* you expressed who you are. Your self was expressed in the *niggun*. I don't need to ask your name. I know who you are."

From then on, both men prayed—and, yes, sang—together, side by side. There was no need for the traveler to give the singing *chasid* the message of the dream. He already had it.

After all, you are what you sing.

35

Out of the Mouth of a Babe

I n the time of the Baal Shem Tov,[1] who was the first pioneer of
Chasidus,[2] there was a simple Jewish farmer who lived in a very
small, isolated town. He barely knew how to *daven*; his twelve-
year-old son knew even less about such things. But the man
had heard of the charismatic Baal Shem Tov, who was telling every
Jew that he could serve God with joy in spite of the harshest physical travails.

The farmer had to see the Baal Shem Tov for himself. Yom Kippur, the most solemn day of the year, was coming up. This was a
good time, the farmer felt, to see if this new *Chasidus* was something to live his daily life by. So he and his young son journeyed to
the town where the Baal Shem Tov had his *shul*.

Naturally, it was one of the most pious Yom Kippurs ever experienced by the farmer. Prayers, lamentations, the Sabbath of Sab-
baths, repentance, forgiveness—it was all there for the asking. Even,
as it was once said, if one did not have enough strength to pray fully,
it was enough to say (as Rabbi Levi Yitzchok of Berditchev [1740–

1810] found out when he said: "Master of the universe, we do not have the strength to say, 'And the Lord said, I have pardoned.'") "Say Thou, 'I have pardoned.'"[3]

The farmer knew he was finally in the right place. He started to *daven* as best as he could. Seeing his father pray, the boy, too, wanted to do so. But he couldn't. Overcome with excitement at the holiness of the moment, he suddenly began to whistle.

All eyes turned to the boy and his father. Caught by surprise, the father was totally embarrassed by the glaring looks from the others.

"*Shah, shah,* child, do you know where you are! *Shah!* On Yom Kippur you may not whistle."

At that point the Baal Shem Tov turned around and spoke up. The boy's whistling, he told the worshipers, was so pure that the voice of his soul had emanated from his mouth. There was no doubt, believed the Baal Shem Tov, that this boy had no other way to express himself. To the Baal Shem Tov's ears, what the boy whistled was so pure, so thoroughly honest and sincere, that he was responsible for all prayers of the *shul*'s worshipers being hastened to heaven at that moment.

Yes, said the Baal Shem Tov, *Hashem* saw the gratitude, the charity, the love of fellow Jews—*Hashem* saw it all come out of this boy's mouth, this whistling, this movement of his lips. It was the same with King David. Then, in Psalm 118:108, the young David said: "*Nidvos pi retzei no Hashem, umishpotecho lamdeini*" ("Accept with favor, I beseech Thee, O Lord, the dedications of my mouth, and teach me Thine ordinances"). So now, said the Baal Shem Tov, *Hashem* forgave not only the boy and his father, but also every Jew in the *shul*, and who knew how many others were pardoned because of the boy's holy act.

And so it came to be understood by everyone in the Baal Shem Tov's *shul* that all is holy from the mouths of babes to the mouth of God.

36

Fortunate Is the Man

It is said that many pens are broken and seas of ink consumed to describe things that never happened, yet we must take Samuel the lamp maker at his word. Who was this Jew? Clearly a reformed *maskil,* now totally committed to Torah, "the best of wares," as he put it.

Samuel claims he was there—he says so right in his diary[1]—in the village of Lubavitch, when the incident happened. Some of the circumstantial evidence bears him out. We know that he and his family, who recently had moved to the little village, worked so hard on weekdays that he happily put down the tools of his trade on *Shabbos,* opened his window facing the Rebbe Rashab's[2] *shul,* and luxuriated in the strains of *niggunim* sung by the Rebbe and his *chasidim.* We also know that he wrote in his diary uncanny details about the holy men gathered at that *chasidishe farbrengen.* Often he addressed them, in his diary, using their diminutive names.

One, "Yossi," perhaps understandably could be explained if not tolerated; after all the so-called "Yossi" was to become, in the future, the sixth Lubavitcher Rebbe, Rabbi Yosef Yitzchak Schneer-sohn (1880–1950), but at that time, during Chanukah 1890, Yosef was only nine and a half years old.

How, then, for instance, did Samuel the lamp maker know these men intimately in such a short time? One of them—Reb Zalman—lived on a certain place some thirty viorsts from Lubavitch, leading away to Dubrovna—the Cherbiner farm, an estate belonging to a local squire, where wheat was always harvested for *shmurah matzoh*. In his diary, Samuel the lamp maker tells us that Reb Zalman not only held a long-term lease on the farm, but he also was a scholarly *chasid*, noble both in intellect and character. Why was this so important to know? Because Zalman Cherbiner—Zalman from Cherbin—already some seventy years old at the time, having vivid memories of the Tzemach Tzedek,[3] was in a position to tell Samuel the lamp maker all the details of that night; there's no substantially corroborating evidence that Samuel was there, even though he claims he was.

Besides, Reb Zalman was a master storyteller. Succinct, to the point, punctilious in his narrative, he neither added to nor explained a tale. In the modern idiom, he simply let the details of a story hang out, so that one felt that he was in that very environment of those *chasidim* of long ago; with one's own eyes, one could see filing into that room, on one of the nights of Chanukah in the year of 1890, a small group of elder *chasidim*—and a small boy—whom Samuel the lamp maker continues to refer to as Yossi in his diary. The visitors to the Rebbe Rashab and Yossi were chasidic giants, each one of them: Reb Hendel,[4] Reb Aharon, and Reb Yekusiel from Dokshytz, Reb Zalman Cherbiner, and Yossi's teacher, the Rashbatz, a bespectacled, pear-shape-faced man intent on interpreting everything for his young, scholarly student. Then there was at the *farbrengen*, by his own account and, we have to admit, by several others', Samuel the lamp maker.

In another diary entry we find that Samuel did not play a definitive role that night, but sat silently in a corner and drank *lechaims*. Thank God for that, for when Samuel finally decided to take a back seat to the proceedings, that's when we began to get a strong sense of what went on that night.

When they sat down at the *farbrengen* table, little Yosef Yitzchak (the Yossi referred to only by Samuel the lamp maker) immediately poured a cup of tea for Reb Hendel. Already on the table were silver cups, silverware, napkins, and many bottles of wine, *schnapps*, and a variety of cakes.

Reb Zalman spoke first. "Rebbe," he squarely faced the Rebbe Rashab, "your grandfather, the Tzemach Tzedek, may he rest in peace, has lately been on my mind a lot."

"Aiiyaiyai, who can forget him!" said Reb Yekusiel. "If it weren't for him, I might easily have been conscripted for twenty-five years into the army as a young boy. It was a close call, as it was for many other Jewish boys, I'm certain."

"Yes," said Reb Aharon, "right from the beginning of the period of military conscription for Jews, the Tzemach Tzedek was there for us. He rescued thousands of young Jewish conscripts from apostasy and death."

"*Rabosai*," said Reb Hendel, seemingly very pleased at what he heard, "it seems as if all of us, each one in this room, except for young Yosef Yitzchak, were deeply touched, and in the same way, by the Tzemach Tzedek."

Then Reb Hendel motioned to the young boy, Yosef Yitzchak, to come to him. Approaching the *chasid*, clearly his favorite, Yosef Yitzchak was asked to bring him another cup of tea. There was no need to ask how Reb Hendel wanted it prepared; the boy knew; he had done it delightedly many times. Immediately, he went to the kitchen and returned with the tea still boiling. After pouring it into the *chasid*'s cup, the boy exchanged smiles with Reb Hendel. Then Yosef Yitzchak clambered onto a chest of drawers that stood at the side, to witness the profound respect shown by all those present.

"Do you know what the Tzemach Tzedek once told me?" Reb Hendel said, after he gingerly sipped his tea. "He told me at *yechidus*: 'Study of *Zohar* exalts the soul; study of Midrash arouses the heart; *Tehillim* with tears scours the vessel.'"

For some reason, Reb Hendel looked over at Yosef Yitzchak. As the other holy men spoke about Torah and cleaving to *Hashem*, the two, man and boy, looked lovingly each other. There was no doubt in the eyes of both of them that Reb Hendel continued to have a profound effect on the boy.

The Rashbatz stood up and offered a *lechaim* in honor of the Tzemach Tzedek. All raised their glasses, blessed the Rashab, and honored his grandfather. "And may the *Moshiach* come speedily," added Reb Yekusiel. "Amen!" said Yosef Yitzchak.

"Yosef Yitzchak," said the Rebbe in a good-natured way, "come

down from your heights and tell us what you know about the subject of *lechaim*."

'Yes, *Tateh*," the boy said as he left his lofty bureau and landed
again on his feet. "This much I know: The reason for this blessing
is that the first time for drinking wine is mentioned in the Torah,
there were undesirable results. Noach began, etc.[5]; also, the Tree
of Knowledge was a grapevine.[6] Therefore, we extend the blessing
that this wine be for a good life."

Rebs Zalman and Hendel clapped.

"Wait, there's more," said Yosef Yitzchak. "The *Maggid* of
Mezeritch[7] used to say '*lechaim velivrochah.*' Once at a *farbrengen*,
the Alter Rebbe[8] responded '*lechaim velivrochah.*' After the *farbrengen*, *chasidim* discussed those words, which they heard then for the
first time. One *chasid* said: Since 'When wine enters, the secret comes
out,' which in *avodah* signifies that the emotions are revealed, we
need a *berochah* for this; the expression is '*lechaim velivrochah*,' and
'*livrochah*' may be read, '*leiv rakah*,' a sensitive heart. About that,
the Tzemach Tzedek commented: Such an interpretation could be
proposed only by a *chasid* who has *davened* and labored in *avodah*
for thirty years."

And as they were speaking among themselves from one subject
to another subject, they started to speak about the old memories of
days past, when they were still very young and they met each other
in the city of Lubavitch, when they wanted to be very close to the
Tzemach Tzedek at that time.

And with very deep feelings, the *chasid* Reb Zalman stood up
on his feet and he started humming the sublime melody that the
Tzemach Tzedek used to intone the *Musaf* prayers on Rosh Hashanah. At this, the other elders stood up, too, and sang with him. In
awe, Samuel the lamp maker listened, while little Yosef Yitzchak acted
as if he would never forget what he was beholding.

Within moments, when the *chasidim* came to the stirring theme,
so well known among *chasidim*, that is the part that expresses *deveikus*
(cleaving to God), "*Ashrei Ish . . .* ," all the *chasidim* in the room
became heated up; they were now in such a state of ecstasy that their
faces were enflamed and tears streamed down their cheeks.

Even for Samuel the lamp maker, it became manifest that the
voices and the mien of these five hoary people's singing were reliving their past, of those moments of the holy time when they were in
Lubavitch with the Tzemach Tzedek. And there was no doubt or

even a doubt of a doubt that each one of them was able to feel at that moment exactly the same as if he were standing in front of his Rebbe, the Tzemach Tzedek, right then and there: He was seeing him at the moment, he was listening to him at the moment—as the Tzemach Tzedek was *davening*. There before them—everyone in the room saw him—including Samuel the lamp maker who blinked and rubbed his eyes in belief—"I had to believe! I had to believe!" he wrote later in his diary—there was the sight of the Tzemach Tzedek—the Rebbe Rashab's grandfather, young Yosef Yitzchak's great-grandfather. As the singers sang on in ecstasy, the Tzemach Tzedek, wrapped in his *tallis*, dressed in his white garments, with a white *yarmulke* on his head, said, in Hebrew, "Happy is the man who does not forget You." Later, Yosef Yitzchak ran up to his teacher, the Rashbatz, and told him he also heard his great-grandfather intone, "The son of man holds fast to You."

"Now, finally," beamed the teacher, "you know the power of *chasidim* coming together in *farbrengen* and *niggunim* to bring forth our ancestors. Never forget this lesson, my dear, young Yosef Yitzchak, never forget. Hold fast to Lubavitch! In these cottages of this little village once lived the Tzemach Tzedek, here you were born, and here your luminous descendants remain at hand."

Early that morning Samuel the lamp maker awoke in his corner as if from a dream; seeing nobody else was around, he returned to his house. Before he went to bed, he opened the window that looked out on the *shul* of the Rebbe and luxuriated in the strains of *niggunim* once sung by the Rebbe and his *chasidim*. Suddenly, he asked himself: "Where am I?" Then, he closed the window and murmured, "Yes, I will hold fast to Lubavitch! I know the Lord will help—but help me, Lord, until you help."

Even if Samuel the lamp maker had never been there on that night of Chanukah when some of the stars of *Chasidus* came out, fortunate is the man.

III

Path Three

Come, incline your ear to the parable; solve the mysteries of your life to the music of the harp.[1]

Here, through the voice of parable and *niggun*, you will find your own voice as a Jew. As it is said in the following story, "The Voice-Over," "When there is nothing left to recognize of a Jew, a Jew should always sing out, '*Shema Koleiynu*' ('Hear our voice!') . . . There may be nothing else left that you can recognize him by except his voice, but by his voice you'll know him."

In the second story, "The Prince Who Became a Jew," we find one of our major purposes in life: doing good deeds—keeping the connection to God. In *Chasidus*, the Alter Rebbe[2] explains vividly the concept of how the *mitzvos* that we do in action are of the highest quality and most favored by God.

For instance, if a person studies the secrets of putting on *tefillin* or of wearing *tzitzis* or of eating *matzoh*, which contain many secrets within secrets, he prepares to raise not only himself, but every other Jew from the beginning of time. Even Moses, at that very moment after being in *Gan Eiden* for thousands of years, stands ready to be elevated through a *mitzvah* to a higher level in understanding and Torah that he did not understand or know an hour before.

But what if a Jew studies all the secrets of *mitzvos* and yet does not put on *tefillin* or eat *matzoh*? Nothing. *You have to perform the mitzvah.*

The Lubavitcher Rebbe, *shlita*,[3] gives us an example of a story that happened to the Tzemach Tzedek,[4] after whom he was named. Though he had already passed away many, many years ago, the Alter Rebbe was still in contact with the Tzemach Tzedek, his grandson. In fact, they actually were able to converse, not an uncommon event in *Chasidus*.[5] But one day, try as he may, the Tzemach Tzedek lost his connection to the Alter Rebbe and was at a deep loss.

One day he was walking to *shul* and he met the butcher standing on a corner with a bewildered look on his face. "Why do you look so worried?" the Rebbe asked him.

"Rebbe, today is Thursday and I have to go buy a cow at the fair. But I don't have all the money I need to make the purchase. That being so, the town won't have any meat for *Shabbos*."

Patting him on the shoulder, the Tzemach Tzedek said, "Don't let this bother you. Come to me after *davening*. And when I return to my house from *shul* I will give you what you need. You may borrow the money."

The butcher went on his way, happy and pleased. Then, out of his sight, the Tzemach Tzedek took a few steps and suddenly whirled around. "What did I say?" he said loudly. "I told him to wait till I finished *davening*. Why should he wait! Every minute is painful. That will never do!"

So, even before *davening*, the Tzemach Tzedek hastened home, took out the six hundred rubles he intended to lend, and sought out the butcher. When he found him, he gave him the money.

"Rebbe," the surprised butcher asked, "why did you rush? There is still time."

The Rebbe merely said, "Go and buy your cow for *Shabbos*."

The Tzemach Tzedek continued on his way with a satisfied feeling that he did something good, and as he came into *shul* he walked over to the *aron hakodesh* and kissed it, and then he opened up his *tallis* and put it over his head and made the proper blessing. While he was cloaked in the *tallis*, he again, finally, saw the Alter Rebbe.

"How come nothing seemed to work till now?" he asked.

"You did something practical," the Alter Rebbe pointed out. "You went out of your way: you went home directly to get the money for the butcher. You saw that the carrying out of a *mitzvah* is very important."

Along Path Three, there is the answer to a question that you may ask: "How is it possible that a physical act I do here on earth should send vibrations to the upper world; how is it possible that a piece of leather that I tie around my arm seven times or a *mezuzoh* that I put on the doorpost turns into a holiness of the uppermost level?"

In reading the following parables, please keep this in mind: a *mitzvah* should be done happily. A *berochah* should always be said in joy.

Let's say no more. Let's do it. Begin your journey on Path Three and keep the Jewish connection!

37

The Voice-Over

There once was a king who had a son who fell in with bad company. The king tried everything in his power to dissuade his son to return to normal ways, but the son just couldn't resist the bad company.

The pressure finally became so much that the king said, "Son, you must choose between my world, the king and the castle, your home and your people, or your nether world, the underworld friends you hang out with. You cannot inhabit both worlds. Two voices cannot enter one ear."[1]

Dressed in the latest style of ruffian clothing, the prince, having made his decision, left the castle. He went off together with his cronies, but wherever he roamed in his father's kingdom people ridiculed him: "The king's son has gone bad?" "Pity, pity!" "He's a disgrace!"

There came a time when he had had enough and wanted to return to his father, if only for a brief visit. But that seemed out of the question. By now his reputation had been besmirched beyond recognition, as was his scarred face, and every townsman was certain that the former prince was malevolently out to get his father, to destroy his kingdom, certainly to cast endless shame on it. Nobody could figure him out, and after a time nobody cared, but they kept up their guard. When a good citizen spotted the prince on the street, he spat three times on the ground and walked across to the other side.

Still, the prince couldn't rest until he saw his father again. So one night, he approached the palace within 500 feet. But, scared of something in the air, he turned away. The next night he tried again, but came up again empty. On the third night, he attempted it once more, this time bringing along the smartest crony in his gang as support. Still, it came to nothing. No, let us not say that. The two ruffians were spotted by two sentinels. One of them, a tall, stern-looking sentinel, ran toward the prince and his friend, and when the sentinel saw the prince, whom he had known for years when he was a youth, he cried out, "So now you've come to do your dirty work here!" For a moment the two men's eyes were caught up together. The prince, who wanted to say something, suddenly realized his coming there was a big mistake. Even he knew, or came to know, that this once-friendly sentinel considered the prince dead, for without another moment's hesitation, he stuck the bayonet of his rifle in the prince's arm, leaving the fallen prince lying on the ground in a pool of blood. There was nothing to say, thought the prince as he began to faint, he was no longer the prince but an enemy of the people.

By that time the prince's comrade had fled. As there was nothing else to do, the sentinel walked back to the sentry box and joined the other sentinel.

"What did he want?" asked the other sentinel, inquisitively.

The tall, stern-looking sentinel shrugged. "What does any thug want? He wanted to hurt the king."

"Good," said the other, seeing the prince dragging his body away into the night, "justice is done!"

After a time, the sensitive and badly damaged prince couldn't take it. He had lost his stomach for this kind of life. He left his father's kingdom and traveled to a foreign country where people wouldn't know him or ridicule him, and he could live as he saw fit.

Again he fell in with a bad crowd. In short order, he became destitute, friendless, crestfallen, and self-destructive. He hardly spoke to his cronies, and when he did he blamed them for all his troubles. In the end, they deserted him like thieves in the night, which was exactly what they were. Finally, he was alone, dragged down by his colored vapors, often to be found lying face up or face down in the gutter. Walking over him or even kicking him for being in the way, no one took pity on him, for no one knew who he was.

The prince surely lived a free life, but he paid a heavy penalty for his freedom.

One day, many years later, his father the king paid a visit to this particular country as a guest of the reigning king. With great pomp and circumstance, he was received by people of all stations in life. First came the dignitaries of the land, then the lesser notables, then came the businessmen, landowners, and service-industry personnel. By the time the king finally greeted the ordinary citizens, and the destitute, the sick, and the orphans and widows, he had literally seen 15,000 faces—as it is said, "As in water face answers to face, so the mind of man reflects the man."[2] In paying him homage, the citizens took the measure of this great, foreign king who reflected all the hopes and concerns of humanity, including theirs.

Somehow the son, the prince, had heard of the foreign king's visit and decided to pay homage to him. The line was long, but the prince was used to such things by then. He waited patiently till it was his turn to greet the king. There was no way of his knowing that this very king was his own father. At first neither son nor father recognized each other. Over the years, the father had aged much, and the son had deteriorated physically. His face was scarred, he limped, and his eyesight was slowly beginning to fail.

Yet there was his father—he saw—sitting on a throne in front of him. His father!

In an outburst that had to be peculiar to the line of citizens who were instructed not to speak to the visiting king, the son addressed his father. Bowing first, he bade the king, "Do you recognize me?"

"No," said the king.

"Do you recognize me?" he again asked.

Still "no."

Suddenly, the prince began to hum a wordless song, which surely his father the king had heard his wife sing many times. "Now, do you recognize my voice?"

The king looked hard at the prince in rags. There was something about that beggar . . . something . . . beyond the deformed body in front of him, beyond his voice over all the growing protestations of the other citizens on the line, waiting to greet the king.

The prince hummed the tune again.

Suddenly the king got it. The voice-over!

"Oh!" cried the king, with tears beginning to roll down his face. "My son, it's you!"

As it is said, "When there is nothing left to recognize of a *Yid*, a *Yid* should always sing out, '*Shema Koleinu*'—'Hear our voice!' Remember the voice of a *Yid*. There may be nothing else left that you can recognize him by except his voice, but by his voice you'll know him."[3]

38

The Prince Who Became a Jew

They had never talked—the prince and the Jew—but they each had seen the other many times walking or riding about the kingdom. The prince rode, the Jew walked. Now they both walked. Now they had time to talk.

What had changed? Nearly ten years ago the prince had been convicted of a heinous crime, judged guilty, and locked up in prison isolation for many years. Now the prince, with his newfound freedom, was very approachable; nor did he wait for others to address him—he greeted them first. One day he would replace his father as king and he had to be ready, he realized, by knowing his subjects well.

But in the case of this Jew, this day the prince overheard the Jew humming a song. Surprised, the prince approached the Jew, in front of a *shul*, where the Jew sunned himself at the noon hour. The prince had to know the song's origin.

Not wasting any time, the prince asked the Jew where he had learned that song. Greeting the prince properly, the old Jew said,

"It's not I who have learned this tune, for I have known and sung it all my life, but it's you who learned it from me."

The prince smiled quizzically. "We have never talked until now, yet you say I learned it from you?"

"That is correct," claimed the Jew.

Part of the prince's insolence—or was it a proper disbelief?—returned and he said, "And what else have you taught me?"

Standing up, the Jew said, "Come, Prince, let us walk about your kingdom and we'll talk along the way."

Intrigued, the prince agreed.

As they walked, the Jew discoursed: "A *chasidishe* rebbe taught me that the *mitzvos* (good deeds) that we do in action are of the highest quality and most favored by *Hashem*, which is another name for God. We Jews put it this way, dear Prince. If a person were to study the secrets of putting on *tefillin* [you can safely assume the Jew explained the meaning of the Jewish words as he walked on with the prince] or wearing *tzitzis* or eating *matzohs*, which contain many secrets within secrets, even if he has studied this most of his life and yet does not put on *tefillin* or *tzitzis* or doesn't eat the *matzoh*, nothing magical or divine will occur. A Jew has to perform a *mitzvah*."

Impatiently, the prince wanted to know what this had to do with him or the song.

"The story that I shall tell you is about an answer to a question which one may ask: 'How is it possible that this physical act a Jew does here on earth should send vibrations to the upper world; how is it possible that a piece of leather that I tie around my arm seven times or a *mezuzoh* that I put on a door turns into a holiness of the uppermost level?'"

"I don't grasp what you're saying," the prince said.

"You will, dear Prince," said the Jew. "Let me continue. A *mitzvah*, to please God, to please even a parent, or for that matter, anybody else, should be done happily. A blessing should always be said in joy. Even the song you heard me hum I sang happily."

"Aha," said the prince, "now we're getting back to the song."

"Dear Prince, the song has always been with us. One of the secrets contained in this song tells of your secret past."

"My past?" gasped the prince.

"Yes," pronounced the Jew in a solemn tone. "This song reveals everything about you, and I'll tell you why."

In this way the story unfolds.[1]

With all the money at his disposal, a king furnished his palace in the best of taste. Not stopping there, he also spread the wealth to his people. Little wonder then that many new subjects flocked to his kingdom, as it is written, the desire for paradise is paradise itself. All this was done, the king said, so that his son the prince could live in the lap of luxury.

One day, however, the prince fell prey to his evil inclinations and did an unforgivable thing in the eyes of the law; he had to be punished. Since it was publicly known that the prince committed this crime, the king could not cover it up and had to allow the prince to be brought to court, to go through the regular criminal proceedings.

Even as a prince, his son was not exempt from the law, said the king to the magistrate. If his son were convicted of the crime, the king agreed, the magistrate would decide the outcome. The outcome? Guilty. The prince must be incarcerated in a dungeon, in isolation, reflecting the severity of the crime.

Hearing the harsh sentence, the prince began crying. "I can't leave my father. I love my father. I want to be near my father."

The king also began to cry. "I'll lose my son, my one and only son, the one who will inherit my kingdom."

Just before the prince was about to be locked up in an out-of-way prison, the king came up with an idea, which he quickly talked over with the magistrate. Downstairs, at the bottom of his palace, was a room so deep in the ground that it abutted the very foundations of the palace. This room was actually a replica of a dungeon, he said. "It's a dark cell with a mud floor. Why not let the prince sit in that room and serve his time in solitary confinement?" the king argued. "What's the difference where he serves time? He'll have a tiny window on the side of a wall so he can know whether it's day or night. And the door has a little opening where the jailer can slip in his water and hard crust of bread. He'll be given the regular raw deal."

So the magistrate thought it over and agreed. He assigned a jailer to the prince in this room. Every day the jailer came down to the cell and gave him his water and hard crust of bread. Day after day, there were no leniencies whatsoever.

One day the jailer found the prince crying bitterly. "What is different today from any other day?" the jailer asked.

"I just had a vision of my death," sobbed the prince. "I cannot survive this terrible isolation any longer. I must get out of the dungeon. Is there any way?"

"You know the rules," the jailer said. "The king pardons you and then you are freed. In this case, if your father is disposed to do so, he has the right to overrule the judgment and release you."

"But how can I make my father feel good about me? I can't see him; there's no way to make contact with him."

For the next twenty-four hours, the jailer and the prince didn't speak. The following day, though, the jailer appeared as usual, but this time he opened the door of the dungeon and entered the dank room, coming face to face with the prince.

"Look in this dark corner," the jailer pointed. "See this pile of dust?"

"Y-yes," said the prince hesitantly.

"Let's remove the dust."

When they removed the dust, at first the prince noticed the eighty-eight keys of a piano, and then the whole piano.

Suddenly the jailer pressed one of the keys, and the prince noticed as the jailer pushed a key, a string pulled down from the ceiling. And as both prince and jailer found out together, there were exactly eighty-eight strings—one for each note—dangling from the ceiling.

"Where do these strings lead to?" the prince asked.

Explained the jailer: "When the king built this palace he had a top musician put together this special piano. When the pianist plays down here, the beautiful Chinese chimes in the king's own bedroom chamber respond, to the delight of the king, who loves music. For years now, since the great pianist passed away, no one else has succeeded him."

"Why?" asked the prince.

"Because it's a very difficult job. For one thing, what you play here you do not hear. Not every musician can carry a tune in his head, nor play to an unseen audience. Oh, the king has never been hard to please, but he has high musical standards. One song aroused him to great heights, to a great love for his people, and the previous pianist was able to please the king no end with an endless variation of the one song."

The jailer paused for a sorrowful effect. Then he said, "There is a vacuum in the king's life. He's missing the beautiful music of the chimes. Now look, Prince, if you want to, you have all the time in the world; right here, I'll teach you how to play the music. I'll give you the book. Study it. But keep this in mind: Whatever you click on the keyboard, it's only a click, but to the king upstairs it's music. Whether it pleases the king you will have to take your chances."

And so after years and years of studying, the prince finally mastered the keyboard and he told the jailer he was ready.

When the prince went over to the keyboard and started to play, the king in the palace heard this beautiful music and summoned the jailer. "This is heavenly music!" the king exclaimed. "Where is it coming from? Who is playing the piano? This is the music I have always loved."

The jailer smiled and said, "Sire, it's your son. The music is his tears. He is crying; he is asking to come back to the king. He wants to be in your grace. He wants to bring delight and pleasure, contentment to you."

The king rushed down to the dungeon, flung open the gates and said, "My son, my son, come back to your father, you have brought me delight. I will free you from this prison."

The Jew and the prince returned to the street of the *shul.* "This is where we part for now," said the Jew.

"But pray tell me the rest of the story," said the prince.

"Ah," said the Jew, "for a Jew there is only one ending. The main theme of the story is that we're down here in the dungeon, in the so-called physical world, with its limits and its many advantages and disadvantages. Yet here in this dark room we are given a keyboard to play with, and play it we must, for the glory of *Hashem!* A Jew puts a penny in a *tzedakah* box and it makes a click: music to the ears of *Hashem!* A Jew puts on *tzitzis* and as air blows through the strings it sounds like harp music to the ears of *Hashem.* To *Hashem,* all *mitzvos* are delights. We, as human beings, cannot grasp why. So from here we gain a beautiful insight as to why it's so important not only to intend a *mitzvah* but, most important, to carry it out."

Hearing this, the prince replied: "Strange enough what you didn't say, Jew, was that the very song you were humming was the song I thrilled my father with and thereby gained release from my prison."

The Jew laughed a bit. "I knew that, too. In fact, ten years ago when you passed me on your horse I was humming that very song.

You stopped long enough to record the song in your mind. I was going to warn you of your upcoming conviction, I was going to tell you how to avoid the trouble."

"And so, why didn't you, Jew?" asked the prince. "You could have saved me so much trouble and pain."

"Because," said the Jew, "ten years ago you were not ready to hear the answer. And now you are."

From then on the prince every morning played the tune that delighted his father, and the Jew lived happily ever after.

A Final Word: My Swan Song, Kosher, Of Course

In the end, there are these things—people, places and things—
that made the beginning of, nay, this whole book possible.
Many thanks go to Rabbi Nissan Mindel, Ph.D, whose eye-
opening biography of Rabbi Shneur Zalman of Liadi first
brought the word *niggun* to my consciousness and planted the seeds
for this book in me. I also thank Nechamia Kessler of Levi Yitzchok
Library of Crown Heights, Brooklyn; Eleanor Mlotek of Yivo Institute; and Eli Lipsker, noted musicologist and authority on chasidic
music, for supplying the beginning of a mountain of research that
went into this book.

As for the story leads, I am indebted to Rabbi Aaron Beigel,
Sandra and Daniel Botnick, Rabbi Shie Breuer and his sister Adel,
Yehudis Cohen, Rabbi Yosef (Uncle Yossi) Goldstein, Rabbi Yeho-
shua Graber, Rabbi Akiva Greenberg, Rabbi Abraham Horowitz,
Bostoner Rebbe of New York, Mrs. Simon Jacobson, Avrohom
Keller, Yehuda Nathan, Rabbi Alter Yitzchak E. Safrin, Rabbi Lazer
Spira, Rabbi Shmuel Spritzer and Yitzchak Winner; for the music

research, thanks especially to Cantor Sherwood Goffin of Lincoln Square Synagogue; Aaron Goldring of the Aaron Goldring Orchestra; Rabbi Michoel Kershner; Rabbi Pesach Lemberger; Velvel Pasternak; and Cantor Ben Zion Shenker.

Many thanks to Rabbi Yosef Y. Shagalov for his help. He's the author of *Likkut Niggunim*, three volumes (Kehot Publication Society: Brooklyn, NY, 1992–1994), which contain chasidic insights into many Jewish songs, collected from the talks of the Lubavitcher Rebbe, *shlita*, Rabbi Menachem Mendel Schneerson.

I also shake the hand of Country Yossi, who published many of these stories in his magazine, *Country Yossi Family Magazine*, and who granted permission for such stories to be collected in book form.

Thanks also to both Dr. George Lombardi, who helped keep me alive, and Burton Milenbach, Ph.D, who kept me sane and singing a happy song, while writing this book.

Especially, I wish to acknowledge Rabbi Lipa Brenner for the sensitive understanding and discriminating taste he brought to the shaping of this book. He guided me unerringly along the many paths of the book. There was no way this book could have much validity and truth without him.

Of course, my most S.O.P. (Significant Other Person) is my wife, Ada Staiman, a true woman of valor, who day and night got up like a trooper to read my stories, make corrections in my manuscripts and make innumerable suggestions to improve the stories. It was her enthusiasm, vitality, and perceptive understanding that helped bring this book to fruition.

Finally I want to thank a "thing." From the very beginning of this book I noted that I cannot carry a tune across the street. Now, this is no longer true. During the writing of this book, I learned from Rabbi Reuven Blau two *niggunim*: One is "*Mimitzrayim*— From Egypt," and the other isn't. The "thing" is the *niggun* "*Mimitzrayim*—From Egypt*" that I leave you with. Why end with this? Because as *Chasidus* teaches us, "Every day we must leave Egypt to reach the Promised Land." Happy journey!

Mimitzrayim

Appendix A

Outstanding Chasidic Rebbes Mentioned in This Book

Aharon Rokeach of Belz, fourth Belzer Rebbe, 1880–1957.
Aryeh Leib Sarah's, 1730–1791.
Aryeh Leib of Shpola, the Shpoler *Zeide*, 1725–1812.
Avraham Dovid of Buchacz, the Buchaczer Rebbe, 1771–1841.
Avroham Yehoshua Heshel of Apta, the Apta Rebbe, 1755–1825.
Bentzion Halberstam of Bobov, second Bobover Rebbe, 1874–1941.
Chaim Meir of Vizhnitz, fourth Vizhnitzer Rebbe, 1888–1972.
Chaim of Sanz, the Sanzer Rebbe, the *Divrei Chaim*, 1793–1876.
David of Skver, second Skverer Rebbe, died 1920.
Dov Ber of Lubavitch, the Mitteler Rebbe, second Lubavitcher Rebbe, 1774–1827.
Dov Ber of Mezeritch, the Great *Maggid*, 1704–1772.
Eliezer Horowitz, the Djikover Rebbe, 1790–1861.
Elimelech of Lizhensk, the No'am Elimelech, 1717–1786.
Hershele Eichenstein of Ziditchov, the Zitditchover Rebbe, died 1837.
Israel ben Eliezer, the Baal Shem Tov, the Besht, Master of the Good Name, 1698–1760.
Levi Yitzchok of Berditchev, the Berditchever Rebbe, 1740–1810.

Menachem Mendel of Lubavitch, the *Tzemach Tzedek*, third Lubavitcher Rebbe, 1789–1866.

Menachem Mendel Schneerson of Lubavitch, current Lubavitcher Rebbe, *shlita*, born 1902.

Meshullam Zisha of Hanipol, 1718–1800.

Moshe Leib of Sassov, the Sassover Rebbe, 1745–1807.

Nachman of Bratzlav, the Bratzlaver Rebbe, 1772–1811.

Naphtali Tzvi of Ropshitz, the Ropshitzer Rebbe, 1760–1827.

Shalom Rokeach of Belz, first Belzer Rebbe, 1783–1855.

Shaul Yedidyah Eleazer Taub of Modzitz, fourth Modzitzer Rebbe, 1886–1947.

Shlomoh Halberstam, current Bobover Rebbe, born 1909.

Shmuel Shmelke Horowitz of Nikolsburg, about 1726–1778.

Sholom Dovber Schneersohn of Lubavitch, the Rebbe Rashab, fifth Lubavitcher Rebbe, 1860–1920.

Shneur Zalman of Liadi, the Alter Rebbe, 1745–1812.

Tzvi Elimelech of Dinov, the Dinover Rebbe, 1783–1841.

Yechiel Michel of Zlotchov, the Zlotchover *Maggid*, 1721–1786.

Yehoshua Rokeach, second Belzer Rebbe, 1825–1894.

Yisrael Friedman of Rizhin, the Rizhiner Rebbe, 1797–1850.

Yisroel Spira, the Bluzhever Rebbe, 1890–1989.

Yisroel Taub of Modzitz, first Modzitzer Rebbe, 1848–1920.

Yissachar Dov Rokeach, third Belzer Rebbe, 1854–1927.

Yissachar Dov Rokeach, current Belzer Rebbe in Jerusalem, born 1949.

Yitzchak Eizik Taub of Kalev, the Kalever Rebbe, about 1751–1821.

Yitzchak E. Safrin, current Komarno Rebbe, *shlita*, born 1924.

Yitzchak Meir Alter of Ger, the *Chidushei Harym*, the first Gerrer Rebbe, 1799–1866.

Yitzchak Twersky of Skver, first Skverer Rebbe, 1812–1885.

Yosef Yitzchak Schneersohn of Lubavitch, Der Previker Rebbe, sixth Lubavitcher Rebbe, 1880–1950.

For those who want to know extensive details of the genealogy of chasidic rebbes, see Yitzchok Alfasi's book, *HaChasidut*, considered the bible of genealogical books. It is printed in Israel.

Appendix B

Discography of Chasidic Music

Belzer Rebbe *Niggunim*

"*Adir Hu—Belz Niggunim*." Cassette BZ1334. Aderet Record Co.
"*Ashreichem Yisroel*." Cassette BO7. Aderet.
"*Ashreinu*." Cassette BZP105. Aderet.
"The Best of Belz." Cassette BZ1336. Aderet.
"*Borei Olam*." Cassette BZF1. Aderet.
"Chanukah Melodies." Cassette BZP104. Aderet.
"*Chasdei Avos*." S.M.T. Productions.
"*Echsof Noam Shabbos*." Cassette BO4. Aderet.
"*Geshem—Birchas Hamazon*." Cassette BO3. Aderet.
"*Hinei Yomim Bo'Im*." Cassette BO2. Aderet.
"*Hinei Zeh Bo*." Cassette BZ1337. Aderet.
"*Mimkomcho*." Cassette BZ1335. Aderet.
"*Moshchieni*." Cassette BZP109. Aderet.
"*Niggunim*." Cassette BZ1331. Aderet.
"*Shabbos* (vols. 1–2)." Cassette BZP1027. Aderet.
"*Shalosh R'Golim*." Cassette BZ1332. Aderet.

"*Yomim Nora'Im* (vols. 1–2)." Cassette BZP103/6. Aderet.
"*Zeh Hayom.*" Cassette BZ1333. Aderet.

Bobover Rebbe *Niggunim*

"*Al Har Gohova.*" Sung by the Camp Shalva Choir. Vol. 1. *Niggunim* composed by Moshe Goldman. Cassette CS 5743. 1983.

"*Ashira L'Hashem.*" Vol. 5. Sung by the Camp Shalva Choir. *Niggunim* composed by Moshe Goldman. Cassette MG-5750. 1989.

"*Bni.*" Cassette B72. Aderet.

"Camp Shalva Classics." Vol. 4. *Niggunim* composed by Moshe Goldman. Cassette MG4-5749. 1989.

"Cantor Werdyger Sings New Bobover *Niggunim* with Choir." Cassette CW-303. Aderet.

"*Chuzuk.*" Vol. 6. Sung by the Camp Shalva Choir. *Niggunim* composed by Moshe Goldman. Cassette MG-5751. 1991.

"*E'FDiyah H'Sham.*" Sung by choir of Bobov Bnei Brak. Cassette UBI-102. Produced by U.B.I. Bobov.

"*Hareu L'Hashem Kol H'aretz.*" Sung by the Camp Shalva Choir. Vol. 2. *Niggunim* composed by Moshe Goldman. Cassette CS 5744. 1985.

"*Im Eshkochech Yerushalayim.*" Sung by the Camp Shalva Choir. Vol. 3. *Niggunim* composed by Moshe Goldman. Cassette MG3-5748. 1988.

"*Niggunei Bobov.*" *Shabbos* Vol. 1. Sung by Choir of Bobov, Bobover Yeshivah, Brooklyn, New York. Cassette NB 101.

"*Niggunei Bobov.*" *Yom Tov* Vol. 1. Sung by Choir of Bobov, Bobover Yeshivah, Brooklyn, New York. Cassette NB-102.

"*Shiru Loi.*" Sung by Choir of Bobov. Produced by Bobov Yeshivah of Brooklyn.

"*Shiru Tzion—Mazel Tov.*" Sung by Choir of Bobov. Cassette SZ-1. Produced by Stiel.

"*Shiru Tzion—B'Nei.*" Sung by Choir of Bobov. Cassette SZ-2. Produced by Stiel.

"The Spirit of the Bobover Chasidim." Sung by Cantor Aaron Miller. Available on cassette. Produced by Benzion Miller, 1677 44th Street, Brooklyn, NY 11204.

"Time to Dance: Marches, Waltzes & Hakofa Negunim from the Sanzer & Bobover Dynasty." Music by Neginah Orchestra. Cassette ZLB-17.

"Time to Dance: Marches, Waltzes & Hakofa Negunim from the Sanzer & Bobover Dynasty." Music by Neginah Orchestra. Cassette ZLB-72.

"*Tivneh Choimois Yerushalayim.*" Sung by Cantor Benzion Miller and Choir of Bobov. Cassette NB 101. Aderet.

Bostoner Rebbe *Niggunim*

"*Niggunei Boston: Simcho L 'Artzecho.*" Sung by Sherwood Goffin and Dov Levine. Cassette BOS. Aderet.
"Songs of the Bostoner Rebbe." Chorus and Orchestra conducted by Rafael Adler. Cassette B101. Also a Collectors Guild record, 1964.

Breslover Rebbe *Niggunim*

"*Asader Lis'udoso.*" The *Shabbos* morning family songs. Cassette BRM-105. Produced by the Breslov Research Institute.
"*Ashreinu.*" Dance, joyous, and meditative tunes. Cassette BRM-1003. Breslov Research.
"*Azamer BiShvochin.*" Favorite Breslov *Shabbos* melodies, including "*Lecho Dodi,*" joyous dance tunes, "*Eishes Chayil,*" and "*Azamer BiShvochin*" by Rebbe Nachman himself. Cassette BRM-1001. Breslov Research.
"A Breslov Wedding in Jerusalem." Recorded live. Cassette BRM-107. Breslov Research.
"*B'nei Heicholo.*" The *Shalosh Se'udos, Shabbos* afternoon songs of the third meal. Cassette BRM-106. Breslov Research.
"*Kokhavey Boker.*" Dance and meditative songs. Breslov Research.
"*Me'eyn Olom Habo.*" Songs for *Shabbos* evening meal and morning prayer service. Cassette BRM-1002. Breslov Research.
"*Pli'oh.*" Dance and meditative songs. Cassette BRM-104. Breslov Research.

Elimelech of Lizhensk *Niggunim*

"*Niggunei Reb Elimelech.*" Performed by Chaim Banet. Cassette RE1. Aderet.
"*Vehaishiv Lev Ovois.*" Solos by Rebbe Abraham Kornik and Meir Berman. Cassette 1. Lizensker Institutions in Israel.

Gerrer Rebbe *Niggunim*

"Ger Dances, Marches, Waltzes." Cassette AD202. Aderet.
"Gerer Melave Malke Melodies." Sung by David Werdyger. Composed by Yankel Talmud. Cassette CW-106. Aderet.
"*Ger Niggunim* 5748." Double Album. Cassette GER48. Aderet.
"*Ger Niggunim* 5751." Double Album. Cassette GER51. Aderet.
"*Ger Niggunim* 5752." Double Album. Cassette GER52. Aderet.

"Ger Niggunim 5753." Double Album. Cassette GER53. Aderet.
"Songs of the Gerer Chasidim." Sung by David Werdyger. Composed by
Yankel Talmud. Cassette CW-105. Aderet.
"Shabbos with David Werdyger." Cassette CU312. Aderet.

Kalever Rebbe *Niggunim*

"Kalever Niggunim." Sung by Benzion Miller. Cassette Y&Y 1309. Y & Y
Productions.

Lubavitcher Rebbe *Niggunim*

"Chabad D'veikus Niggunim Instrumentals." Cassette Volumes 1–3. Per-
formed by Chaim Binyomin Burston. (718) 493-3822.
"Chabad Niggunim." Cassette Volumes 1–8. Performed by the Lubavitcher
Chassidim. By Nichoach. Released by W.L.C.C.
"Chabad Niggunim." Cassette Volumes 11–16. Performed by the
Lubavitcher Choir. Distributed by Kehot Publication Society.
"Chabad Niggunim." Special Package Edition Vols. 1–8. Performed by
the Lubavitcher Choir. Distributed by W.L.C.C.
"Lubavitch Melodies—Vol. 1." Cassette MYS770/1. Aderet.
"Lubavitch Melodies—Vol. 2." Cassette MYS770/2. Aderet.
"Mi Armia—From the Archives of *Chabad* Chasidic Music." Sung by the
Boys of Lubavitch Schools-London. Cassette SRT 5KC.
"Music of Lubavitch." Cassette HLC770. Aderet.
"Niggunai Hitvaadus." Six volumes. *Niggunim* sung by Rabbi Menachem
Mendel Schneerson, the Lubavitcher Rebbe, *shlita*, during public
chasidic gatherings. Cassettes NH–01 through NH–06. W.L.C.C.
"Niggunai Kvod Kedushas Admur Shlita, M'Niggunai Hitvaadus." Col-
lection of 14 *niggunim* introduced by the Lubavitcher Rebbe, *shlita*,
Rabbi Menachem Mendel Schneerson. Available on cassette. Re-
recorded from *Niggunai Hitvaadus* and distributed by W.L.C.C.
"Sefer Haniggunim." Original stereo cassette recordings of all 347 melo-
dies from *Chabad Lubavitch Book of Songs.* Seventeen hours of music
on sixteen tapes; includes Index. Available from the Levi Yitzchok
Library, Lubavitch Youth Organization, 305 Kingston Avenue, Brook-
lyn, NY 11213.
"Simchas Bais Hashoevah in the Streets of Crown Heights." Cassette Vol. 1
SBH-1, Vol. 2 SBH-2, Vol. 3 SBH-3. Released by W.L.C.C.
"A Voice from Behind the Iron Curtain." Sung by Cantor Berele Zaltzman.
Cassette.
"Berele Zaltzman 2." Sung by Cantor Berele Zaltzman. Cassette.

Melitzer Rebbe *Niggunim*

"*Melitzer Oneg Shabbos.*" Sung by David Werdyger and Mordechai Ben David. Cassette Stereo 308. 1979. Aderet.

Modzitzer Rebbe *Niggunim*

"The Best of Modzitz—Vol. 1." Sung by Ben Zion Shenker. Cassette NR1207. 1987.

"The Best of Modzitz—Vol. 2." Sung by Ben Zion Shenker. Cassette NR1208. 1988.

"Modzitz Classics 1." Sung by Ben Zion Shenker. Cassette NR1211. S.M.T. Productions.

"Modzitz Classics 2." Sung by Ben Zion Shenker. Cassette NR1212. S.M.T. Productions.

"Modzitzer Favorites." Vol. 1. Sung by Ben Zion Shenker. Cassette C-NRS-1203. Neginah Records. 1973.

"*Modzitzer Sholosh R'Golim.*" Sung by Ben Zion Shenker. Cassette NR-1202. Neginah Records. 1975.

"A *Shabbos* in Modzitz." Sung by Ben Zion Shenker. Cassette NM1210. Produced by Mosdos Modzitz. Also: Cassette MODZ. Aderet.

Moshiach *Niggunim*

"*Chaverim.*" Sung by Mendy Werdyger. Cassette AD1465. Aderet.

"Goodbye *Golus.*" Sung by Avraham Fried. Cassette HLC–505. Available on CD. Holyland Records.

"Hold on Just a Little Bit Longer." Sung by Mordechai Ben David. Cassette MBD–409. Aderet.

"Just One *Shabbos.*" Sung by Mordechai Ben David. Cassette BH422. Produced by Suki & Ding. Aderet.

"Live at Town Hall." Sung by Sherwood Goffin. Cassette BMPS–1818. Batya Music Productions. 1984.

"Mordechai Ben David Live." Sung by Mordechai Ben David. Cassette MBD–407. Aderet. 1981.

"*Moshiach* Is Coming Soon." Sung by Mordechai Ben David. Cassette LPW–406. Aderet.

"*Moshiach, Moshiach, Moshiach.*" Sung by Mordechai Ben David. Cassette HLC901. Holyland Music Productions, Inc., through Aderet. 1992.

"No Jew Will Be Left Behind!" Sung by Avraham Fried. The Zeriah Orchestra. Cassette HLC–501. Holyland Records.

"*Shofar Moshiach*—Vol. 1." Sung by Zisha Schmeltzer. Cassette ZS18.
   Aderet.
"*Shofar Moshiach*—Vol. 2." Sung by Zisha Schmeltzer. Cassette ZS54.
   Aderet.
"*Shtar Hatnoim.*" Sung by Avraham Fried. Cassette. Available on CD.
   S.M.T. Productions.
"*Tatenyu.*" Sung by Moshe Ilowitz. Cassette M101. Aderet.
"The Time Is Now." Sung by Avraham Fried, accompanied by the Zimriah
   Orchestra. Cassette HLC–502. Available on CD.
"Time To Dance: Marches, Waltzes & *Hakofa Negunim.*" From the Sanzer
   & Bobover Dynasty. Music by Neginah Orchestra. Cassette ZLB–17.
"Tzlil Vezemer Boys Choir—Vol. 4." Produced by Avrohom Rosenberg.
   Cassette AR104. Aderet.
"We Are Ready!" Sung by Avraham Fried. Cassette HLC506. Aderet.
"We'll Bring *Moshiach* Now!" For Children. Sung by Eli Lipsker and His
   Little Soldiers. Cassette E.L.–113. Available at the International
   Moshiach Center.

Munkatch Rebbe *Niggunim*

"Songs—Munkatch." Vol. 1. Cassette NCM101. Aderet.
"*Vichasdim Birena Yagilu.*" Munkatch *Niggunim.* S.M.T. Productions.

Nadvorna Rebbe *Niggunim*

"*Mizmor Shir.*" S.M.T. Productions.
"*B'Oholei Tzadikkim.*" Cassette NN3. Aderet.

Pittsburgh Rebbe *Niggunim*

"Double Album." Cassette PIT. Aderet.
"*Chaim'ke.*" Cassette PZ03. Aderet.
"*Niggunim—B'Zos Ani.*" Cassette PIT2. Aderet.

Sanzer Rebbe *Niggunim*

"Time to Dance: Marches, Waltzes & *Hakofa Negunim* from the Sanzer
   & Bobover Dynasty." Music by Neginah Orchestra. Cassette ZLB–
   17. 1981.

Skulener Rebbe *Niggunim*

"Cantor David Werdyger Sings Skulaner Chassidic *Niggunim.*" Cassette LPW-307. Aderet.

"Cantor David Werdyger Sings Skulaner Chassidic *Niggunim.*" Cassette CW-304. Aderet.

"*Niggunei Skulen.*" Music and vocals by Yehuda B. Strohli. Cassette DK-5751. Produced by Vaad L'Hotzoas Nigunei Skulen.

"*Niggunei Skulen.*" Music and vocals by Yehudi B. Strohli. Cassette DK-5749. Produced by Vaad L'Hotzoas Nigunei Skulen.

"*Shabbos Skulan Niggunim.*" Cassette DK-5751. Aderet.

Skverer Rebbe *Niggunim*

"*Kol Mevaser.*" *Niggunim* composed and vocals by Josh Breuer and his choir. Music arranged and conducted by Moshe Laufer. Cassette JB50.

Stoliner Rebbe *Niggunim*

"The Double Album Sung By Mordechai Ben David." Cassette HLC 900. Aderet.

"Teva." Sung by Moshe Antelis, Mark Fineberg, and Larry Steppler. Cassette TR1 474. Aderet.

Vizhnitzer Rebbe *Niggunim*

"Chanukah Songs." Cassette VIZ5. Aderet.

"*Niggunei of Beth Wiznitz.*" Produced by the Vizhnitzer Institutions of Israel.

Miscellaneous

"*Anim Zemiros.*" Performed by Chaim Benet. Cassette BAN15. Aderet.

"*Avreichim.*" Performed by Lazer Schwartz. Cassette LMS101. Aderet.

"Best of Chaim Benet." Performed by Chaim Benet. Cassette CB15. Aderet.

"A Chassidic Celebration." Performed by Yoel Sharabi. Cassette DP829. Aderet.

"Chassidic Classics." Performed by Yeron Gershovsky. Cassette AD205. Aderet.

"Classics Part II." Tzlil V'zemer Instrumental. S.M.T. Productions.

"Father and Sons." Performed by MBD and David Werdyger. Cassette AD. Aderet.

"Giora Fiedman—The Incredible Clarinet." Cassette Stereo 13191.

"Golden Chassidic." Performed by Dudu Fisher. Cassette 8090. Aderet.

"*Hallel.*" Composed by Yom Tov Erlich. Cassette JN32. Aderet.

"Hassidic Festival Hits." Performed by Various Artists. Cassette 15270. Aderet.

"Joy of the Festivals." Sung by Ben Zion Shenker. Cassette 711. S.M.T. Productions.

"Joy of the Land." Sung by Ben Zion Shenker. Cassette 876. S.M.T. Productions.

"Joy of the Sabbath." Sung by Ben Zion Shenker. Cassette 661. S.M.T. Productions.

"*Layehudim Hoyco Orah.*" Sung by Ben Zion Shenker. Cassette 1442. S.M.T. Productions.

"*L'Chaim.*" Sung by Cantor Boris Pevsner. Available on Cassette. Produced by Progressive Tape Corp.

"Live at Lincoln Center." Sung by Sherwood Goffin. Cassette BMPS-2200. Batya Music Productions.

"*Machnisei Rachamim.*" Performed by Chaim Benet. Cassette BAN13. Aderet.

"Magic of the Klezmer." Performed by Clarinetist Giora Feidman. D/CD 4005. Produced by Delos International, Inc. 1986.

"*Meheira.*" Performed by Wertzberger. Cassette WER3. Aderet.

"*Mimkomo.*" Sung by Sherwood Goffin. Cassette SAME-3. Batya Music Productions.

"Mordechai Ben David Sings Original Chasidic *Niggunim.*" Cassette CW-402. Aderet.

"*Neshomo.*" Sung by Sherwood Goffin. Cassette SAME-2. Batya Music Productions.

"*Niggunim.*" Performed by Apta Mezboz. Cassette APT. Aderet.

"*Niggunim.*" Performed by Shelley Lang. Cassette SL4916. Aderet.

"*Niggunim* of My People." Performed by Giora Feidman. Cassette 14422. Also available on CD. Aderet.

"Original Chassidic *Niggunim.*" Mordechai Ben David. Cassette MBD402. Aderet.

"Power of Music I." Performed by Michoel Streicher. S.M.T. Productions.

"Raisins and Almonds." Sung by Cantor Boris Pevsner. Available on cassette.

"*Shabbos.*" Performed by Wertzberger. Cassette WER2. Aderet.

"*Shiras Halevi'im.*" Performed by the Hurvitz Brothers. Cassette SHIR-H. Aderet.

"Song of the Rebbes." Performed by Piamenta. Cassette AYP5732. A Piamenta Production. 1991. Also: Cassette P152. Aderet.

"Songs My Father Taught Me." Sung by Gershon Veroba, Martin Davidson, Simon Spiro, and Benzion Miller. On cassette.

"Sounds of Joy." Sung by Ben Zion Shenker. Cassette 808. S.M.T. Productions.

"Suki and Ding—*Zemiros.*" Featuring Avraham Fried, Michoel Streicher, Dov Levine, Tzlil V'zemer, and Piamenta. S.M.T. Productions.

"Uri Shevach Sings with Kol Salonika—Vol. 2." The New Greek Chassidic Sound. Cassette Emes 105. Aderet.

"*V'Harev.*" Performed by Wertzberger. Cassette WER1. Aderet.

"Yiddish." Performed by Zmiros Yisroel. Cassette ZMI. Aderet.

"Yiddish Classics—Vol. 1." Performed by Suki and Ding. Cassette BH28. Aderet.

"Yiddish Classics—Vol. 2." Performed by Suki and Ding. Cassette BH26. Aderet.

"*Yona Motza.*" Performed by Yona Ben Shlomo Carlebach. S.M.T. Productions.

Furthermore

Write to the following record companies and recording artists for their catalogs of chasidic music on records, CDs, and tapes as well as *niggunim* song books:

Aderet Record Co., 1215 39th Street, Brooklyn, NY 11218.

Batya Music Productions, 142 West End Avenue, New York, NY 10023.

Breslov Research Institute, Rabbi Chaim Kramer, POB 5370, Jerusalem, Israel 91053 or Breslov Research Institute, P. O. Box 587, Monsey, NY 10952-0587. (914) 426-4258.

Cantor Benzion Miller, 1677 44th Street, Brooklyn, NY 11204.

Delos International, Inc., 2210 Wilshire Blvd., Suite 664, Santa Monica, CA 90403.

International Moshiach Center (Moshiach Music), 355 Kingston Avenue, Brooklyn, NY 11213. (718) 604-2000. Fax: (718) 363-1221.

Kehot Publication Society, 788 Eastern Parkway, Brooklyn, NY 11213. (718) 774-4000.

Lizensker Institutions in Israel, P.O. Box 5590, Jerusalem, Israel.

S.M.T. Productions Inc., 71-28A Main Street, Flushing, NY 11367. (718) 520-7100. Fax: (718) 520-7145.

Tara Publications, 29 Derby Avenue, Cedarhurst, NY 11516. (516) 295-1061.
Vaad L'Hotzoas Niggunei Skulen, c/o Mr. Shlomo Weiss, 160 Rutledge Street, Brooklyn, NY 11211. (718) 522-0710.
Vizhnitzer Institutions of Israel, Torth Chaim St., #7, Bnei Brak, Israel 51111.
(Lubavitch Music): WICC, 770 Eastern Parkway, Brooklyn, NY 11213. (718) 773-7777.

Notes

PATH ONE

1. For one, Abraham Z. Idelsohn, *Jewish Music: Its Historical Development* (New York: Dover Publications, 1992), 411. For another, Velvel Pasternak, *Songs of the Chassidim*, vol. 2 (New York: Bloch Publishing, 1971), 1.

2. Ibid., 411: In *Shivche Ari* it is related that "once on the eve of a Sabbath the rabbi (I. Luria) went out of the city of Safed, followed by his disciples . . . to receive the Sabbath, and started singing special Sabbath songs in sweet tunes." Compare also *Sefer Charedim*, Venice, 1601, Chap. VII.

3. Pasternak, *Songs of the Chassidim* 2:1.

4. A product of obscure peasant Jewry, his full name was Israel ben Eliezer (also known as the "Besht" and "Master of the Good Name").

CHAPTER 1—THE ROAD THROUGH SAFED LEADS EVERYWHERE

1. These *Tehillim*—Psalms 29 and 95–99—are now a part of our "*Kabbolas Shabbos*" ("Welcoming the Sabbath") service to this day. The

custom began about 400 years ago and was introduced by the kabbalist
Rabbi Moshe Cordovero (1522–1570) of Safed (brother-in-law of Rabbi
Shlomo Halevi Alkabetz, author of "*Lechoh Dodi*").

2. According to Rabbi M. Cordovero, as quoted by Nissan Mindel's
book, *My Prayer*, vol. 2 (Brooklyn, NY: Kehot Publication Society, 1989),
10, and in *Siddur Otzar Hatefilot* 1:590.

3. About 40–135 C.E. Rabbi Akiva ben Joseph. Often called the father of rabbinical Judaism, he was the greatest scholar of his day, a true giant
in the history of Judaism. And if you think you're not where you'd like to
be in embracing *Yiddishkeit*, consider this: Akiva was virtually uneducated
until he was forty years old; after that you couldn't hold the holy man down.
At one point when he established his own school in Bnei Brak, he had 24,000
students!

4. "The seven days of the week may be divided into three parts of
days, each pair adding up to seven (one and six; two and five; three and
four), leaving the seventh day as a single day." Mindel, *My Prayer* 2:28–29.

5. See *Bereishis Rabbah* 11:9; see also Mindel, *My Prayer* 2:28–29.

6. "Rabbi Solomon Alkabetz, a kabbalist of Safed, is reputed for composing the popular hymn '*Lechoh Dodi*' in 1529 (according to others,
1571). The poem is a mosaic of Biblical and rabbinic phrases, and no less
than six of its nine stanzas are devoted to the yearning for Jerusalem. Accepted by all Jewish communities throughout the world, it became a favorite of *chazzanim*, synagogue-composers, and *chasidic* sects. Abraham Z.
Idelsohn, the foremost Jewish musicologist, estimated in the early 1900s
that there were some 2,000 melodies written for the '*Lechoh Dodi*' text.
Certainly this number is far greater now because of the many contempo-
rary settings and oral *chasidic* tunes sung since Idelsohn's time." Macy
Nulman, *Concepts of Jewish Music and Prayer* (Miami: Hallmark Press,
1985), 88.

7. Max I. Dimont, *Jews, God and History* (New York: Penguin Books,
Signet Books, 1962), 186.

8. David Rossoff, *Safed: The Mystical City* (Jerusalem: Sha'ar Books,
1991), 80.

9. Ibid.

10. Chasidic Rebbe, Rabbi Nachman of Bratzlav, 1772–1811.

11. "In the ghetto of Prague between 1594 and 1716, Jews welcomed
the Sabbath with hymns and instrumental music. It was in the synagogues
of Prague where the organ (*ugab*) and string instruments (*nebalim*) were
played. According to rabbinic rule, the musicians had to cease playing their
instruments immediately before the recitation of Psalm 92, *Mizmor shir leyom
haShabbat*, at which point the Friday evening service officially began."
Nulman, *Concepts of Jewish Music and Prayer*, 88.

CHAPTER 2—THE LULLABY

1. Job 38:7.
2. 1717–1786. Chasidic Rebbe, popularly known as the *No'am Elimelech*, after the title of his work.
3. Rabbi Israel ben Eliezer, 1698–1760, founder of *Chasidus.*
4. Elie Wiesel, *Souls on Fire* (Northvale, NJ: Jason Aronson, 1993), 123.
5. 1718–1800. Rabbi Meshullam Zisha of Hanipol.
6. Wiesel, *Souls on Fire*, 122.
7. Rabbi Greenberg: "At that time I was in Israel at the *misnaged yeshivah*, it was not advisable to reveal any *chasidishe* ties. The ties between the groups had been bloodied for a few hundred years."
8. *Hayye, bane, u-mezone*—allusion to a well-known talmudic dictum; *Mo'ed Katan* 28.
9. Talmud, *Sukkah.*

CHAPTER 3—THE MUSIC OF RETURN

1. Rabbi Dov Ber of Lubavitch, the "Mitteler Rebbe." 1774–1827.
2. 1745–1812. Founder of *Chabad* Chasidism. Also known as the Alter Rebbe and the *Baal Hatanya.*
3. Nathan Ausubel, ed., *A Treasury of Jewish Folklore* (New York: Crown Publishers, 1948).

CHAPTER 4—THE SINGING *TZADIK*

1. 1730–1791. An itinerant *tzadik* who wandered through the countryside of Hungary seeking new adherents for *Chasidus.*
2. Avraham Yaakov Finkel, *The Great Chasidic Masters* (Northvale, NJ: Jason Aronson, 1992), 93.
3. Chaim Bloch, Vienna, 1930; see also Finkel, *The Great Chasidic Masters*, 94.
4. 1710–1772. The spiritual successor to the Baal Shem Tov, founder of *Chasidus.*
5. Talmud, *Exodus Rebbah.*
6. Talmud, *Berachos.*
7. One of his favorite songs is "*Szol a Kakas Mar*"—"The rooster is already crowing." The English translation comes from Finkel, *The Great Chasidic Masters*, 94–95.

8. Rabbi Tzvi Rabinowicz, *Chassidic Rebbes* (Southfield, MI: Targum Press, 1989), 123–24.

9. Ibid., 124.

CHAPTER 5—SONG ON FIRE

1. *Bamidbar* 20: *Chukkas.*
2. A term applied to varying manners of carrying out prayers in different Jewish communities.
3. Ben Sira 1:22.

CHAPTER 6—SONG OF THE DEAD: A HAPPY STORY

1. The Vizhnitzer Rebbe Chaim Meir Hager, 1888–1972.
2. The basis of this story was gathered through conversations with Rabbi Lipa Brenner, a Vizhnitzer *chasid* who lives in the Flatbush section of Brooklyn, New York.

CHAPTER 7—BRINGING THE GLAD SONG HOME

1. The basis for this story comes from conversations with Rabbi Lazer Spira, a Belzer *chasid* living today in Borough Park, Brooklyn, New York, the son of Shimon Spira, who was originally known as Shimon Dershowitz, from the towns of Tilicz, Poland, and Bardiov, Czechoslovakia.

2. 1 Samuel 10:22.

3. Rabbi Tzvi Rabinowicz, *Chassidic Rebbes* (Southfield, MI: Targum Press, 1989), 197.

4. Jeremiah 6:14.

5. The old Belzer *chasid* related this to Rabbi Lazer Spira.

6. *Hamachne Hacheredi*, Belz weekly newspaper, August 1992 (Brooklyn, NY, Belz Institutions in Israel Publications).

7. *Yerushalmi, Sukkah.*

8. You can find the full text of "*Kel Mistater*" in *The Complete ArtScroll Siddur*, ed. Rabbi Nosson Scherman and Rabbi Meir Zlotowitz (Brooklyn, NY: Mesorah Publications, 1989), "*Shalosh Seudos*" section, 637–39.

9. Some *goyim* say, when there was nothing left of the Belz *Beis Hamidrosh*, they saw the ghost of the first Belzer Rebbe, Rabbi Shalom Rokeach, walking sadly about the site. Other *goyim*, according to the Belzer Rebbe, Rabbi Aharon Rokeach, reported seeing an old Jew walking around

in the midst of the flames as the Nazis set the *shul* afire. This old Jew, the *Rebbe* declared, was none other than Eliyahu Hanovi, and he could be heard murmuring soothingly, "*Shul, shul,* do not weep. They *davened* in you before and they will *daven* in you again" *The World of Belz*, vol. 1, no. 3 (Summer 1986): 3, Belz Institutions in Israel Publications, Brooklyn, NY.

   10. According to Sol Glick, son of Reb M. M. Glick.

   11. From a pamphlet called *BELZ—A Worldwide Movement of Torah and Chessed* (Brooklyn, NY, Belz Institutions in Israel Publications).

CHAPTER 8—HOW A *NIGGUN* CAME MARCHING HOME

   1. 1793–1876. Rabbi Chaim Halberstam, also known as the Divrei Chaim. His work *Divrei Chaim*, on the four parts of the Jewish Code of Law, the *Shulchan Aruch*, was printed in Lvov in 1875, followed two years later by *Divrei Chaim*, a commentary on the Torah, printed in Munkacz in 1877.

   2. Rabbi Naphtali of Ropshitz, 1760–1827.

   3. The story was told to me by the current Komarno Rebbe, *shlita*, Rabbi Alter Yitzchak E. Safrin, who lives in Borough Park, Brooklyn.

CHAPTER 9—BAM, BAM, BAM

   1. Defining the difference between a *chasid* and a *mitnaged*, Rabbi Pinchas of Koretz (1728–1790) wrote: "For the *mitnaged* what is forbidden is forbidden; but the *chasid* says that what is forbidden is forbidden even at the cost of one's life. . . . The *chasid* is not like the *mitnaged*. The *mitnaged* fears Gehenna, but the *chasid* fears sin. . . . The *mitnaged* fears the *Shulchan Aruch*; the *chasid* fears the Holy One, blessed be He."

   2. Simon Markovich Dubnow, *History of the Jews in Russia and Poland*, 2 vols. (Philadelphia: Jewish Publication Society of America, 1920), 373–74.

   3. 1793–1876. Student of Rabbi Napthali of Ropshitz.

   4. Rabbi Yechezkel Shraga of Shiniava, 1815–1899.

   5. Reb Chaim Meir of Vizhnitz, Shikun Vizhnitz, Bnei Brak, Israel, 1888–1972.

CHAPTER 10—THE RIZHINER CONNECTION

   1. Chaim Bloch, *Gemeinde der Chassidim* (Vienna, 1920), 289; also, Louis I. Newman, *The Hasidic Anthology* (Northvale, NJ: Jason Aronson, 1987), 80.

2. Rabbi Shlomo Yosef Zevin, *A Treasury of Chassidic Tales on the Festivals*, vol. 2 (Brooklyn, NY: Mesorah Publications, 1982), 421.

3. M. Lipson, *Midor Dor* (Tel Aviv, 1929), 250; also, Newman, *The Hasidic Anthology*, 17.

4. Rabbi Chaim Dov Stern, *Ner Yisroel* (Bnei Brak, Israel: A. M. Bergman, 1987).

5. From *Knesset Yisroel*, a Sermon on *Shabbos Teshuvah*.

CHAPTER 11—DAVID WITHOUT THE SLINGSHOT

1. His whole name is David Werdyger, and this story was drawn from conversations with the cantor in Borough Park, Brooklyn, New York.

2. Rabbi A. Y. Bromberg, *Rebbes of Ger: Sfas Emes and Imrei Emes*, trans. Uri Kaploun (Brooklyn, NY: Mesorah Publications, 1987), 163.

3. Although Talmud wrote many of the Gerrer *niggunim*, the Gerrer Rebbes, alas, did not compose any, nor were they endowed with great singing voices. But surely they appreciated *niggunim*. Witness the words of the first Gerrer Rebbe, Rabbi Yitzchak Meir Alter (1799–1866): "Were I blessed with a sweet voice, I could sing you new hymns and songs every day, for with the daily rejuvenation of the world new songs are created." A. B. Birnbaum in his essay, "The Song in the Courts of the *Tzaddikim* in Poland," *Haolam*, 1908; and Abraham Z. Idelsohn, *Jewish Music: Its Historical Development* (New York: Dover Publications, 1992), 415.

4. *The Complete ArtScroll Siddur*, ed. Rabbi Nosson Scherman and Rabbi Meir Zlotowitz (Brooklyn, NY: Mesorah Publications, 1989), 861, footnote.

CHAPTER 12—I AM A *NIGGUN*

1. 1790–1861. It's been said that the Djikover Rebbe ordered, in his testament, that his sermons not be printed. He added an explanation: "If my manuscripts are printed, what will happen? My disciples will eat and drink too much on *Shabbos*, take my book, lie down on a couch, open my book and fall immediately asleep. I do not care to be their companion in slumber." Y. A. Kamelhar, *Dor Deah* (Bilguray, 1933), 327; also Louis I. Newman, *The Hasidic Anthology* (Northvale, NJ: Jason Aronson, 1987), 25.

2. 1698–1760. Founder of *Chasidus*.

3. The Ropshitzer Rebbe, 1760–1827.

4. Another story: Once, on *Shabbos Hagadol*, he returned home exhausted after delivering a long discourse on how important it was to provide poor people with the necessities of Pesach. His wife asked him if he

were successful. "Fifty percent," he said. "The poor are willing to accept, but the rich are not yet willing to give."

5. 1793–1876, also known as the Divrei Chaim.

CHAPTER 13—THE STORY OF THE BOXES

1. Born 1873. Murdered by the Nazis in 1941.

2. Rabbi Shlomoh Halberstam. Current Bobover Rebbe in Brooklyn, New York. Born 1909, survived the Holocaust.

3. Rabbi Tzvi Rabinowicz, *Chassidic Rebbes* (Southfield, MI: Targum Press, 1989), 308.

4. This was adapted from *Kedushas Tziyon*, the Bobover Rebbe's commentary on the Torah. The first part was printed in New York by his son in 1967, and the second part, in 1978.

CHAPTER 14—FOR THE LOVE OF A *NIGGUN*

1. The basis for this story comes from conversations with Ben Zion Shenker, a Modzitzer *chasid* and himself a composer and singer of *niggunim*.

CHAPTER 15—THE MYSTERIES OF A *NIGGUN*

1. This story was produced from conversations with Ben Zion Shenker and Yehuda Nathan, two Modzitzer *chasidim*.

2. Retold by Yehuda Nathan in *The Jewish Observer*, February 1988, 24.

3. Found in the *Ne'ilah* prayer of the Yom Kippur service.

4. Founder of *Chasidus*, 1698–1760.

5. Died in 1892.

6. Fourth generation Modzitzer Rebbe, 1886–1947.

7. Isser Frenkel, *Men of Distinction*, vol. 2 (Tel Aviv: Sinai Publishing, 1967), 92.

CHAPTER 16—JAIL HOUSE ROCK

1. Reb Aryeh Leib from Shpola in the Ukraine (1725–1812), known as the *Shpoler Zeide* (grandfather), was known for his exceptional love for his Jewish brethren (*ahavas Yisroel*), and would travel from village to village to help them materially and spiritually to collect funds for *pidyon shevuyim* (ransom of Jewish captives), and to bring his estranged brethren closer to their

Heavenly Father. The melody of "Hop Cossack" is very similar to the tune traditionally known as the "*Shpoler Zeide's Niggun.*" As a matter of fact, the song is sung at joyous occasions such as Simchas Torah and Pesach.

CHAPTER 17—LEONARD BERNSTEIN UNBOUND

1. "*Niggun Shamil*" was introduced to the Lubavitcher *chasidim* by the Lubavitcher Rebbe, *shlita*, Rabbi Menachem Mendel Schneerson, on Simchas Torah, 5719 (1958), in keeping with the Rebbe's tradition of teaching a new *niggun* each Simchas Torah evening following *hakofos*, during the years 1956–1963.

CHAPTER 18—THE SONGS THAT ALMOST WEREN'T

1. A recent anecdote told to Ben Zion Shenker by his neighbor.
2. 1698–1760, founder of *Chasidus.*
3. 1880–1950, sixth generation of Lubavitcher Rebbe.
4. 1886–1947, fourth generation of Modzitzer Rebbe.
5. Yehuda Nathan, *The Jewish Observer*, February 1988, 26.
6. Ibid.
7. Isser Frenkel, *Men of Distinction*, vol. 2 (Tel Aviv: Sinai Publishing, 1967), 93.
8. Yehuda Nathan, *Jewish Observer*, 24.
9. Ibid., 28.
10. Frenkel, *Men of Distinction*, 93.
11. Ibid.
12. Ibid.
13. Ibid.
14. Reb Shaul got his wish. This Polish refugee, whose heart always belonged to *Eretz Yisroel*, passed away on November 29, 1947, and that same night the United Nations sitting in General Assembly voted for the establishment of Israel. He was subsequently buried on *Har Hatzeisim* in Israel.

CHAPTER 19—A FAIR EXCHANGE

1. Quoted in Bellasis, *Cherubini* (1874) and in *A Dictionary of Musical Quotations*, comp. Ian Crofton and Donald Fraser (New York: Schirmer Books, 1985), 30.
2. Sixth generation Lubavitcher Rebbe, 1880–1950.
3. Fifth generation Lubavitcher Rebbe, 1860–1920.

4. Judges 20:80.
5. Seventh generation Lubavitcher Rebbe, *shlita*, Rabbi Menachem Mendel Schneerson.

CHAPTER 20—EMBERS MIDST THE RUINS

1. This essay was excerpted and adapted from an article by Rabbi Nosson Scherman that appeared originally in the June 1978 issue of *The Jewish Observer* magazine and was anthologized in *A Path through the Ashes*, ed. Rabbi Nosson Scherman (Brooklyn, NY: Mesorah Publications, an ArtScroll Judaiscope book, 1986).
2. 1890–1989. Miraculously survived the Holocaust.
3. 1894–1977.

CHAPTER 21—TRAVELS OF TWO *NIGGUNIM*

1. This story is based on Dovid Eliezer Popack's short article in *N'shei Chabad* newsletter, February/March 1991, 12; on notes supplied by Nechamia Kessler, librarian of the Levi Yitzchok Library in the Crown Heights section of Brooklyn, New York; and on p. 99 of *Hayom Yom* (From Day to Day), an anthology of aphorisms and customs arranged according to the days of the year assembled from the talks and letters of Rabbi Y. Y. Schneersohn of Lubavitch, compiled and arranged by the present Lubavitcher Rebbe, *shlita*, Rabbi Menachem Mendel Schneerson.
2. During the time of the previous Lubavitcher Rebbe, Reb Shmuel Zalmanov was the foremost expert in *Chabad* melodies and entrusted by the Rebbe to transcribe all the traditional melodies of *Chabad*.
3. Also called "The Song of the Ensemble of the Mitteler Rebbe."
4. 1774–1827.

CHAPTER 22—REBBE HOPPIN'

1. Reb Shraga Feivel Mendlowitz, "though ordained in Nitra, Czecho-slovakia—at the age of sixteen—refused to be addressed as Rabbi. 'Mister' or Reb Shraga Feivel Mendlowitz came to the United States as a young man in the early 1920s and, after a few years as a teacher in Scranton, Pennsylvania, became the head of the fledgling Yeshiva Torah Voda'ath in Brooklyn. His dream was to meet the needs of America by combining chasidic warmth with Lithuanian-type analytical scholarship. In addition to building his own institution, he sent his best students to form the nucleus of other institutions,

such as Mesvita Rabbi Chaim Berlin of Brooklyn, Telshe Yeshivah in Cleveland, Ohio, Ner Israel Rabbinical School in Baltimore, and Beth Midrash Gohova in Lakewood, New Jersey. A practical dreamer, he also fostered the creation of out-of-town day schools, founded Torah Umesorah (National Society for Hebrew Day Schools), and encouraged the establishment by his family of what is now Boys Town Jerusalem." Berel Wein, *Triumph Over Survival* (Brooklyn, NY: Shaar Press/Mesorah Publications, 1990), 334.

2. Translated by Gitty Stolik, from *Sefer Haniggunim, Book of Chabad —Chasidic Songs*, ed. Rabbi Shmuel Zalmanoff (Kfar Chabad, Israel: Kehot Publication Society, 1980).

3. Rabbi Chaim of Vizhnitz, 1888–1972.

4. Rabbi Shmuel Eliyahu, born 1905.

CHAPTER 24—THE FRENCH DON'T HAVE A WORD FOR IT

1. From "Musical Rhapsodies," a pamphlet published by the Women's Youth Organization (W.Y.O.), Book of the 29th Annual Convention, 22–26 Iyar 5744 (May 24–28, 1984). Reprinted with permission of the W.Y.O.

2. Raymond Pronier, *Videes*, 13 July 1990.

3. The text of the Rebbe's talk was translated into English as part of a Project of Sichos in English. Reprinted with permission of Sichos in English.

4. 1745–1812. Founder of *Chabad Chasidus*.

5. Macy Nulman, *Concepts of Jewish Music and Prayer* (Miami: Hallmark Press, 1985), 90.

CHAPTER 25—JERUSALEM ON HER MIND

1. Composed by Naomi Shemer.

CHAPTER 26—THE NIGHT A JEW SANG FOR HIS SUPPER IN THE KREMLIN

1. 1864–1935. Chief Rabbi and spiritual leader of Palestine.

2. Rabbi Nachman of Bratzlav, chasidic Rebbe, 1772–1811.

CHAPTER 27—A TWICE-TOLD STORY

1. Called "*Niggun Simcha*," it is listed and printed as *Niggun 207*, in *Sefer Haniggunim*.

PATH TWO

1. Shneour Zalman, Hebrew poet, 1887–1959.

CHAPTER 28—THE PURPOSE OF LIFE

1. Psalm 65:13.
2. R. Alcalay, ed., *Words of the Wise: An Anthology of Proverbs and Practical Axioms* (Jerusalem: Masada Press, 1970), 145.
3. 1717–1786. One of the leading figures of Chasidism. *Chasidim* delight in recounting the adventures of the two roaming brothers, Rebs Elimelech and Zisha. Writes Elie Wiesel in *Souls on Fire* (Summit Books, 1972): "One tradition has it that every place they stayed—even for just a night—became annexed to the Hasidic kingdom. . . . There is a curious legend that tells of the two brothers arriving in a small village near Cracow [Poland] with the intention of staying overnight. But they were restless and felt compelled to leave. As dusk fell, they left. The name of the village: Auschwitz."
4. This concept is the basis of his book, *No'am Elimelech*, which is one of the principal works on *Chasidus.*
5. Rabbi Meshullam Zisha of Hanipol, 1718–1800.
6. Job 38:7.

CHAPTER 29—REB YID

1. This story is based upon the writings of the Ropshitzer Rebbe, Rabbi Naphtali Tzvi Horowitz of Ropshitz, 1760–1827, and many other chasidic sources, including Elie Wiesel, *Somewhere a Master: Further Hasidic Portraits and Legends* (New York: Summit Books, 1981) and Louis I. Newman, *The Hasidic Anthology* (Northvale, NJ: Jason Aronson, 1987). According to chasidic legend, the fate of Napoleon was decided not on the battlefields, but in the courts of the chasidic rabbis. One of these rebbes was Naphtali of Ropshitz, who mobilized *chasidim* against the Corsican.
2. A disciple of the Ropshitzer Rebbe, Rabbi Feyvish would recite "'Lamentations' every midnight as if Jerusalem the city of God had been destroyed that very day" (Martin Buber, *Tales of the Hasidim,* New York: Schocken Books, 1991). He later became a disciple of the Apter Rav, Rabbi Avroham Yehoshua Heshel of Apta, the *Oheiv Yisroel,* 1755–1825.
3. In those days, the pious were accustomed to rise at midnight from their beds, sit down on the floor, without shoes, put ashes on their forehead, and read "Lamentations" on the fall of Zion and prayers for redemption.

4. Rabbi Chaim Halberstam of Sanz—the *Divrei Chaim*—1793–1876.
5. Disciple of both the Ropshitzer and the Belzer Rebbes. Died 1875.
6. A disciple of the Ropshitzer Rebbe.
7. Another disciple of the Ropshitzer. Died in 1872 (or 1873), his motto of life was "Give and take." "Everyone must be both a giver and a receiver. He who is not both is as a barren tree," said Reb Yitzchok Eizik of Ziditchov.
8. Another follower of the Ropshitzer Rebbe.
9. The "Jew" died young (1766–1814).
10. Died in 1847.
11. 1740–1809. This chasidic luminary wrote a compilation of ethical sayings; his Hebrew work *Kedushat Levi*, a commentary on the Torah, is considered a classic of chasidic literature.

CHAPTER 30—THE JOURNEY

1. 1745–1807. Rabbi Moshe Leib of Sassov. Popularly called the Sassover Rebbe.
2. J. A. Frankel, *Menorah ha-Tehorah* (Prezemsyl, 1911), 49, also, Louis I. Newman, *The Hasidic Anthology* (Northvale, NJ: Jason Aronson, 1987), 68.
3. "The oldest song in Jewish history in existence today is the one of national triumph sung by Moses and the children of Israel after their miraculous deliverance at the Sea of Reeds (*Yam Suf*), generally called the Red Sea. The song is identified in Jewish literature as 'The Shirah' (Exodus 15:1–18). . . . Scripture records that Moses led the men, and his sister Miriam led the women in song. . . . Miriam and the women's singing, however, was accompanied by instruments and dance." Macy Nulman, *Concepts of Jewish Music and Prayer* (Miami: Hallmark Press, 1985), 137.
4. *Megillah* 10.
5. Frankel, *Menorah ha-Tehorah*, 48.
6. From the sayings of the Sassover Rebbe.

CHAPTER 31—*TATEH*

1. The Zlotchover *Maggid*, 1721–1786.
2. There is another version: Rabbi Yechiel Michel generally appointed "his son Yossele (Rabbi Yosef of Yampol) to stand guard and prevent him from going so deep in his *deveikus* that he leave the physical world entirely. One *Shabbos*, Yossele was sick with a high fever and thus not in the room

when his father began to sing the *deveikus niggun*. Even though Rabbi Michel had appointed the *chasidim* present to substitute for Yossele, they all became involved in the *niggun*, so that when they finally returned to their earthly consciousness, they realized that Rabbi Michel had passed away while singing. Just then, a scream was heard from the next room. They ran in and found that Yossele, too, had died. The *chasidim* were so overcome with sadness that they began to weep. After a short time, Yossele suddenly bolted upright on his bed. Startled and horrified, the *chasidim* asked him what had happened. Yossele related how he had died and gone up to the other world, where he met his father. Rabbi Michel was saddened to find his young son there. He said that his merit was not great enough to influence a decision to send Yossele back, but perhaps the Baal Shem Tov might be able to effect this. The soul of the holy Baal Shem Tov appeared and said that he had heard that Yossele had a very sweet voice. He asked Yossele to sing a *niggun*. When he sang the *deveikus niggun*, the Holy Court was persuaded to send Yossele back to this world, where he was so needed." As heard from Rabbi Levi Yitschok Bender (1898–1989) and printed in *Asadeir Lis'udoso, The Breslover Songbook*, vol. 2, collected and transcribed by Ben Zion Solomon (Jerusalem: Research Institute, 1992), 36.

CHAPTER 32—THE JEW HATER

1. 1740–1809. Chasidic master, affectionately known as the Berditchever.
2. This is a chasidic interpretation by Rabbi Levi Yitzchok of Berditchev of one of the *"Hoshanos"* written by the famous Reb Elozor Hakolir, or by one of his pupils, in seventh-century Palestine. The poem follows the Hebrew alphabetical order. The Berditchever divides it into stanzas of four lines each. The first two of every four he interprets as virtues of the Jewish people, the third as a misfortune, and the fourth as a virtue again. He used to sing this song on the holidays of Sukkos. From *Folks-Gezangen* as interpreted by Chaim Kotylansky (Los Angeles: Chaim Kotylansky Book Committee and the folks-farlag Alveltlicher Yiddisher Kultur-Farband "Yeuf," 1954).
3. Ibid., 20.

CHAPTER 33—THE BELOVED DISCIPLE

1. Reb David of Skver, died 1920.
2. 1816–1893. A pioneer of Jewish journalism in Russia.

CHAPTER 35—OUT OF THE MOUTH OF A BABE

1. 1698–1760. Also known as the Besht and the Master of the Good Name.
2. This story was related to me by the current Komarno Rebbe, *shlita*, Rabbi Alter Yitzchak E. Safrin, who lives in Borough Park, Brooklyn, New York.
3. S. Y. Agnon, *Days of Awe* (New York: Schocken Books, 1965), 214.

CHAPTER 36—FORTUNATE IS THE MAN

1. This short story is based on parts of *Likkutei Dibburim*, an anthology of talks by Rabbi Yosef Yitzchak Schneersohn, vol. 1, trans. Uri Kaploun (Brooklyn, NY: Kehot Publication Society, 1987); *Hayom Yom*, an anthology of aphorisms and customs, arranged according to the days of the year, assembled by the current Lubavitcher Rebbe, Rabbi Menachem Mendel Schneerson, *shlita*, from the talks and letters of the previous Rebbe, Rabbi Yosef Yitzchak Schneersohn of Lubavitch (Brooklyn, NY: Kehot Publication Society, 1988); and the notes on *niggun* 179 from *Sefer Haniggunim, Book of Chabad–Chasidic Songs*, vol. 2, ed. Rabbi Samuel Zalmanoff (Kfar Chabad, Israel: Kehot Publication Society, 1980).
2. 1860–1920. Fifth Lubavitcher Rebbe, Rabbi Sholom Dovber Schneersohn of Lubavitch.
3. 1789–1866. Third Lubavitcher Rebbe, Rabbi Menachem Mendel Schneersohn.
4. An elder *chasid* when the Sixth Lubavitcher Rebbe, the previous Lubavitcher Rebbe, was a child, he had a profound influence on the rebbe-to-be and was often cited in the previous Lubavitcher Rebbe's *sichot*.
5. Bereishit 9:20.
6. See *Tikunei Zohar, Tikun* 24.
7. 1704–1772. Rabbi Dov Ber. Popularly known as the Great Maggid.
8. 1745–1812. Rabbi Shneur Zalman of Liadi. Founder of *Chabad* Chasidism.

PATH THREE

1. A paraphrase of Psalms 49:5: "I will incline my ear to the parable; I will solve my riddles to the music of the harp."
2. Rabbi Shneur Zalman of Liadi, founder of *Chabad* Chasidism, the first Lubavitcher Rebbe, 1745–1812.
3. Rabbi Menachem Mendel Schneerson of Lubavitch.

4. The third Lubavitcher Rebbe, Rabbi Menachem Mendel Schneersohn of Lubavitch, 1789–1866.

5. This was constantly confirmed by Chabad *rebbeim* and *chasidim*, that many times previous *Chabad* rebbes were in contact with their successors. There's a story told about the Rebbe Rashab (Rabbi Sholom Dovber of Lubavitch, 1860–1920) that, at a *farbrengen*, he gave over seven teachings that he heard from the Baal Shem Tov in *Gan Eiden*. Unbelievable, but true! From the *sefer, Kesser Shemtov*.

CHAPTER 37—THE VOICE-OVER

1. Talmud *Yerushalmi, Megillah.*
2. Ecclesiastes 27:19.
3. Quote from Rabbi Avraham Horowitz, the Bostoner Rebbe of New York, who quoted the Stanislav Rav.

CHAPTER 38—THE PRINCE WHO BECAME A JEW

1. This story comes from the repertoire of Rabbi Yosef Goldstein, otherwise known as Uncle Yossi, a consummate Jewish storyteller.

A FINAL WORD: MY SWAN SONG, KOSHER, OF COURSE

Mimitzrayim is reprinted from *Sefer Haniggunim: Book of Chasidic Songs*, ed. Rabbi Samuel Zalmanoff. Copyright © 1985. Brooklyn, NY: Nichoach Kehot Publications Society. Reprinted by permission of Agudas Chasidei Chabad.

Glossary

Aggadah The sections of rabbinic literature that contain homiletical expositions of the Bible, prayers, stories, maxims, etc., in contradistinction to *halachah.*

Ahavas Yisroel Love of a fellow Jew, as enjoined by the biblical precept "Love your fellowman like yourself" (Leviticus 19:18).

Aliyah "Ascent"—being called upon in synagogue to ascend the dais for the public reading of a portion of the Torah.

Aron Hakodesh The Ark.

Avodah The service of God, whether in sacrifice, prayer or self-effacement.

Avodah Zorah Idol worship.

Baal Shem Tov Literally, "Master of the Good Name." A name given to Rabbi Israel ben Eliezer (1698–1760), founder of the chasidic movement.

Baal-Tefillah A sort of choirmaster and leader of prayer who stands at the pulpit in the synagogue and is responsible for musical compositions.

Baal Teshuvah (pl., *baalei teshuvah*) One who returns to God; a penitent who returns to the Torah way of life after having been astray.

Bas daughter of.

Beis hamidrosh A synagogue and place of study.

Beis Hamikdosh The Holy Temple (First or Second) in Jerusalem.

Beis din   Literally, "house of law"—assembly of three or more learned men acting as a Jewish court of law.

Ben   Son of.

Bench   To say grace after a meal.

Berochah (pl., *berochos*)   Blessing.

Besht   Acronym of the Baal Shem Tov, Master of the Good Name.

Bimah   The dais in the center of the synagogue, where the Torah is read.

Bnei Yisroel   Sons of Israel.

Bochur (pl., *bochurim*)   An unmarried young man.

Boruch Hashem   Thank God.

Bris (pl., *brisim*)   Circumcision.

Bubbe   A term for grandmother.

Calpac   A nineteenth-century military hat.

Cantor   "The officiant who leads the musical service in the synagogue has been known throughout history by twelve different names in three different languages. In English he is called cantor, precentor and reader. In Hebrew he is known as *kerobah, Sheliah Tzibbur, Ba'al Tefilla* and *Chazzan*. In Germany he was called *vorbeter, vorsinger, schulsinger, sangmeister,* and *oberkantor*. Subtitles are *ba'al Shaharit, ba'al Musaf, chazzan-rishon* (*chazan elyon*), *chazzan-sheni* (*unterkantor*) and *mathil*." Macy Nulman, *Concepts of Jewish Music and Prayer* (Miami: Hallmark Press, 1985), 90.

Chabad   A chasidic movement founded by Rabbi Shneur Zalman of Liadi, 1745–1812. The word comprises the initials of *Chochmah, Binah, Daas:* Hebrew for wisdom, understanding, and knowledge.

Chanukah   Literally, "dedication"—an eight-day festival, beginning 25 *Kislev,* commemorating the Maccabees' rededication of the Temple in the second century B.C.E. and marked by the kindling of lights.

Chasid (pl., *chasidim*)   Literally, "a pious man"—a follower.

Chasidic   Related to Chasidism.

Chasidishe   Related to Chasidism.

Chasidism   The movement of spiritual reawakening within Judaism founded by the Baal Shem Tov.

Chasidus   *See* Chasidism.

Chas vesholom   Popularly known as "Heaven forbid" or "God forbid."

Chazon   *See* Cantor.

Cheder   Elementary Hebrew school for religious studies.

Chometz   Leavened bread or substances, altogether prohibited to be enjoyed or even possessed on Pesach.

Chupah   The wedding canopy under which the marriage is solemnized. Also, the ceremony itself.

Daven   Pray.

Deveikus   The ecstatic state of cleaving to the Creator.

Diaspora *See* Golus.

Dibbuk The restless soul of a deceased individual that takes possession of the living body of a man or a woman.

Divrei Torah A formal or informal discussion of Torah subjects.

Ein Sof The Infinite One.

Emunah Faith.

Eretz Yisroel The Land of Israel.

Esrog (pl., *esrogim*) Citron, one of the four spices used during the Festival of Sukkos.

Farbrengen (a) An assemblage addressed by a rebbe; (b) an informal gathering of *chasidim* for mutual edification and brotherly criticism.

Gabbai In the chasidic community, the rebbe's personal aide and attendant.

Gadlus hamochin Exuberant frenzy.

Gadol hador Greatest sage of any generation.

Gan Eiden Garden of Eden.

Gehenna Hell.

Gemara Discussion and rulings forming part of the Babylonian and Palestinian Talmud; the Oral Law.

Geulah Redemption.

Golem Inanimate body. Although there have been numerous man-made *golems* in Jewish history, the *golem* I refer to was alleged to have been created in the time of the Crusades in France by Rabbi Samuel, the father of the famous Judah Hasid. He fashioned a mannequin, but he could not make it talk. Wherever he went, this *golem* accompanied him as his servant and vigilant bodyguard.

Golus Literally, "exile"—the Diaspora.

Haggadah Literally, "telling." The *Haggadah* is the book that tells the story of the Exodus from Egypt.

Hakofos The sevenfold procession made with the Torah scrolls in the synagogue on Simchas Torah and accompanied by singing and dancing.

Halachah Body of Jewish Law.

Hallel "Praise"—Psalms 113–118 recited on *Rosh Chodesh* and certain festivals.

Hashgochah perotis Divine providence.

Haskalah Literally, "enlightenment"—a movement originating in eighteenth-century Germany to acquire culture and customs of the outside world. An adherent was called a *maskil*.

Havdalah Literally, "distinction"—the blessings recited over a cup at the conclusion of a Sabbath or festival to distinguish it from the ordinary weekdays that follow.

Hishtapchus hanefesh The outpouring of the soul and its effort to rise out of the mire of sin, out of the shell of the evil spirit, the *kelipah*, and to reach the second stage, *hishorerus*, spiritual awakening.

Hislahavus Religious enthusiasm, or flaming ecstasy.

Hispashtus hagashmiyus A stage when the soul casts off its garment of flesh and becomes a disembodied spirit.

Kabbalah The body of classical Jewish mystical teachings.

Kabbolas Shabbos Service to welcome the Sabbath.

Kallah Bride.

Kapote Black frockcoat, usually worn in honor of the Sabbath.

Kavonah Inner direction, inwardness in prayer or religious observance.

Kedushah Sanctity.

Kelal Yisroel The entire Jewish Nation.

Kelos hanefesh Expiry of the soul out of spiritual rapture.

Kiddush Blessing over wine expressing the sanctity of *Shabbos* or a festival.

Kiddush Hashem Sanctification of God's Name.

Kinor A little harp.

Koach Strength.

Kohen (pl., *Kohanim*) High Priest.

Kol Nidrei Opening words of the evening service of Yom Kippur.

Korban The sacrifice offered in Temple times on the eve of a festival.

Kotel The Western Wall of the Temple.

Lechaim Literally, "to life"—traditional words of a toast on alcoholic drinks.

Loshon hora Slander.

Lulav Palm branch. One of the four species used during Sukkos.

Maamar In *Chabad* circles it means a formal chasidic discourse first delivered by a rebbe.

Maariv The evening prayer service.

Maggid Usually, a popular, roving preacher, a teller of stories.

Malach Angel; divine messenger.

Mashke Strong alcoholic drinks.

Maskil (pl., *maskilim*) Exponent of the *Haskalah*.

Master of the Good Name Rabbi Israel ben Eliezer, the Baal Shem Tov (1698–1760).

Matzoh The unleavened bread eaten on Passover.

Mechitzah Literally, "partition"—the partition separating the men's and women's sections in a synagogue.

Megillas Esther The biblical scroll of Esther, which relates the story of Purim.

Melamed (a) Teacher at Torah school; (b) private tutor.

Melaveh Malkah A festive meal eaten after *Shabbos* is over.

Menorah Seven- or eight-branched candelabrum.

Mesiras nefesh Self-sacrifice.

Mezuzoh (pl., *mezuzos*) Tiny parchment scroll affixed to a doorpost.
Midrash (pl., *midrashim*) A general term applied to a large and very important section of Jewish literature.
Mikvah Body of water used for ritual immersion.
Milah Ritual circumcision.
Minchah Afternoon prayer service.
Minhag (pl., *minhagim*) A Jewish custom.
Minyan Quorom of ten Jewish men required for divine service.
Mishnah Collection of the discussion and legal interpretations of the Bible by the Rabbis (*Tannaim*) compiled by Rabbi Yehudah Ha-Nasi, about 200 C.E.
Mishnayos Passages from the Mishnah.
Misnaged (pl., *misnagdim*) An early opponent of the chasidic movement.
Mitzvah (pl., *mitzvos*) Literally, "command"—a religious obligation; one of the Torah's 613 commandments.
Mizrachi A religious-Zionist home.
Mohel One who performs circumcision.
Moshiach Messiah.
Moshol A parable.
Motzoei Shabbos The time of the departure of the *Shabbos*.
Musaf Additional prayer recited on *Shabbos*.
Neginah Chasidic and liturgical music.
Ne'ilah Concluding service of Yom Kippur.
Neshomah Jewish soul.
Niftar A deceased person.
Niglah The revealed or exoteric part of the Torah or Jewish tradition, touching specifically upon *halachah*.
Niggun (pl., *niggunim*) A wordless song, generally.
Nistar The concealed or esoteric part of the Torah or Jewish tradition.
Nusach A term applied to varying manners of carrying out prayers in different Jewish communities.
Ohel Edifice over a grave.
Olom habo The World-to-Come.
Olom hazeh This world.
Pesach Passover, seven-day (eight in the Diaspora) festival commemorating the Exodus from Egypt.
Pidyon Contributions given to a rebbe.
Pidyon shevuyim Ransom of Jewish captives.
Pintele Yid Spark of Judaism.
Posuk A sentence.
Purim Literally, "lots"—a one-day festival falling on 14 *Adar* and commemorating the miraculous salvation of the Jews of the Persian Empire in the fourth century B.C.E.
Rabbi A qualified authority in Torah learning.

Rabosai   Yiddish expression of respect, equivalent to "gentlemen."

Rambam   Moses ben Maimon, also known as Maimonides, Spanish physician, theologian, jurist, codifier of the Jewish law, 1135–1204.

Rashi   Acronym for Rabbi Shlomo Yitzchaki (1040–1105), the sage whose commentaries on the Torah and the Talmud are regarded as the classic guides to these texts.

Rav   A rabbi; the halachic authority and spiritual guide of a community.

Rebbe (Reb, pl., *rebbeim*)   Religious leader of a chasidic community.

Rebbitzen   The wife of a rabbi or *rav.*

Reb Yid   An informal term of address to an individual whose name is not known.

Rosh Chodesh   Sanctification of the New Moon.

Rosh Hashanah   The New Year festival.

Rosh yeshivah   *Yeshivah* principal.

Ruach hakodesh   Prophecy.

Sabbath Queen, Shabbos Queen   The Sabbath personified.

Seder   The order of the festive meal at home on the first and second nights of Pesach.

Sefer (pl., *seferim*)   Book.

Sefer Torah   Scroll of the Law.

Se'udah   Meal.

Se'udas hodo'ah   A festive meal to thank God for saving a person's life.

Se'udas mitzvah   Meal held in celebration of a religious obligation.

Se'udah Shelishis   The third meal held at sunset on the *Shabbat.*

Shabbos   The Sabbath.

Shacharis   Morning service.

Shalosh Se'udos   The third meal eaten after the afternoon service on *Shabbat.* Often the setting for chasidic teachings.

Shammes   A beadle. A man responsible for the cares of the synagogue or, the head candle on a *menorah.*

Shavuos   Literally, "weeks"—festival commemorating the giving of the Torah at Sinai; in *Eretz Yisroel*, falling on 6 *Sivan*, and in the Diaspora on 6–7 *Sivan.*

Shechinah   Divine Presence. The spirit of the Omnipresent as manifested on earth; the indwelling presence of God.

Shechitah   The Jewish ritual method of slaughtering animals for food.

Sheliach (pl., *sheluchim*)   An emissary of the Lubavitcher Rebbe, *shlita.*

Shema   The *Shema* is one of the central sections of the *siddur.* It comprises three paragraphs taken from the Torah: *Devarim* 6:4–9, *Devarim* 11:13–21, and *Bamidbar* 15:37–41.

Shemini Atzeres   The last day of Sukkos.

Shemoneh Esrei   The prayer that is central in the three daily services.

Shemurah matzoh   Special *matzoh* that is used solely during Passover, the making of which never involves water.

Shiur   Torah lecture.

Shivah   Seven days of mourning after a person dies.

Shlita   An acronym for the Hebrew words meaning, "May he live a long and good life."

Shochet   Ritual slaughterer.

Shofar   A ram's horn, blown on Rosh Hashanah and at the termination of Yom Kippur.

Shomer Shabbos   Sabbath observant.

Shtibel   Small chasidic house of prayer and study.

Shtraimel   Fur hat usually worn on *Shabbos* and festivals.

Shul   A synagogue.

Shulchan Aruch   Code of Jewish Laws.

Sichah (pl., *sichos*)   A talk. In *Chabad* Chasidism, generally an informal talk delivered by a rebbe on a variety of subjects ranging from expositions of Torah to pronouncements on topical themes.

Siddur (pl., *siddurim*)   Prayer book.

Simchah   Joy or festive occasion.

Simchas Torah   The Festival of Rejoicing with the Torah, celebrated on the 23rd of *Tishrei*.

Spodek   A chasidic hat often worn on weekdays in Ropshitz.

Sukkah   Thatched hut one resides in on the holiday of *Sukkos*.

Sukkos   Feast of the Tabernacles, celebrated from the 15th to the 22nd of *Tishrei*.

Tallis   Prayer shawl with four fringes.

Talmid Chochom   Torah scholar of standing.

Talmud Torah   School for young students, preparatory for the *yeshivah*.

Tefillin   Small black leather cubes containing parchment scrolls inscribed with *Shema Yisroel* and other biblical passages, bound to the arm and forehead and worn by men at weekday morning prayers.

Tehillim   Book of Psalms.

Teshuvah   Repentance.

Tisch (pl., *tischen*)   Festive table at which a chasidic rebbe presides and delivers a discourse.

Tisha B'Av   The ninth day of the month of *Av*; fast day commemorating the destruction of both the First Temple and the Second Temple in Jerusalem.

Toite chasidim   Dead followers.

Traif   Not kosher.

Tzadik (pl., *tzadikim*)   A completely righteous person; a rebbe.

Tzedakah   Charity.

Tzitzis   Fringes on a prayer shawl or on *tallis katan*, a rectangular under-garment worn continuously.

Tzivos Hashem   Literally, "Army of God"—name of the Lubavitch Children's Organization.

Yahrzeit   Anniversary of the passing of a near relative.

Yarmulke   A skullcap worn especially by Orthodox and Conservative Jewish males.

Yechidus   Private interview at which a *chasid* seeks guidance and enlightenment from his rebbe.

Yeitzer hora   Evil impulse.

Yerusholayim   The city of Jerusalem.

Yerushalmi   Jerusalem (or Palestine) Talmud, as distinguished from the more common *Bavli* (Babylonian Talmud).

Yeshivah (pl., *yeshivot*, or *yeshivahs*)   Talmudic academy.

Yiddishkeit   The Torah way of life.

Yiras shomayim   Fear of heaven.

Yom Kippur   Day of Atonement.

Yom Tov (pl., *yom tovim*)   A festival.

Zemiros   *Shabbat* table hymns.

Zohar   Title of basic work of the *Kabbalah*, essentially composed by the second-century *Tanna* Rabbi Shimon bar Yochai.

Index

About the Author

Mordechai Staiman has been a writer and editor for over twenty-five years. His articles have appeared in publications including *The Jewish Press*, *Wellsprings*, the *Algemeiner Journal*, *N'Shei Chabad*, and *L'Chaim*. He lives in the Crown Heights section of Brooklyn, New York, with his wife, Ada.